Resilient Children

Stories of Poverty, Drug Exposure, and Literacy Development

Diane Barone

University of Nevada, Reno
Reno, Nevada, USA

INTERNATIONAL
**Reading
Association**

800 Barksdale Road
PO Box 8139
Newark, Delaware 19714-8139, USA
www.reading.org

nrc

NATIONAL READING CONFERENCE

National Reading Conference
122 South Michigan Avenue
Suite 1100
Chicago, Illinois 60603, USA

Director of Publications   Joan M. Irwin
Assistant Director of Publications   Jeanette K. Moss
Editor-in-Chief, Books   Christian A. Kempers
Senior Editor   Matthew W. Baker
Assistant Editor   Janet S. Parrack
Assistant Editor   Tori Mello
Publications Coordinator   Beth Doughty
Association Editor   David K. Roberts
Production Department Manager   Iona Sauscermen
Art Director   Boni Nash
Electronic Publishing Supervisor   Wendy A. Mazur
Electronic Publishing Specialist   Anette Schütz-Ruff
Electronic Publishing Specialist   Cheryl J. Strum
Electronic Publishing Assistant   Peggy Mason

Project Editors   Matthew W. Baker and Mara P. Gorman

Library of Congress Cataloging in Publication Data
  Barone, Diane M.
  Resilient children: Stories of poverty, drug exposure, and literacy development / Diane Barone.
    p.   cm.—(Literacy studies series)
  Includes bibliographical references and index.
  1. Children and prenatal substance abuse—Education (Primary)—Case studies.   2. Poor children—Education—Case studies.   3. Reading (Primary)—Case studies.   4. Literacy—Case studies.   I. Title.   II. Series.
LC4806.4.B37   1999   98-54836
371.91—dc21
ISBN 0-87207-199-5

Contents

Note From the Series Editors

Resilient Children: Stories of Poverty, Drug Exposure, and Literacy Development is a rich tapestry of the lives of drug-exposed children as they advance toward literacy. Diane Barone's riveting profile of the literacy needs of children who are born of drug-addicted mothers provides a rational and useful knowledge base for all educators. Her sensitive and poignant case studies of resilient children help us to understand the methods and approaches that work best. This first-of-its-kind book will be a treasure for all its readers.

We hope that this excellent volume will serve as a reference tool as educators plan literacy programs for learners of all ages and cultures. This book as well as others in the Literacy Studies Series broadens our understanding of research and provides guidance as we design our instructional practices. The goal of the Series is to advance knowledge in the literacy field and to help make research a more important focus in the literacy community. The volumes in this Series are intended to inform literacy instruction and research by reporting findings from state-of-the-art literacy endeavors. We believe that this text successfully accomplishes this goal.

James Flood
Diane Lapp
Series Editors
San Diego State University
San Diego, California, USA

Review Board

Dr. Nancy C. Padak
Kent State University
Kent, Ohio

Dr. Jeanne R. Paratore
Boston University
Boston, Massachusetts

Dr. Victoria Purcell-Gates
Harvard University
Cambridge, Massachusetts

Dr. Nancy L. Roser
University of Texas at Austin
Austin, Texas

Dr. Diane L. Schallert
University of Texas at Austin
Austin, Texas

Dr. Lyndon W. Searfoss
Arizona State University
Tucson, Arizona

Dr. Peter N. Winograd
University of New Mexico
Albuquerque, New Mexico

Dr. M. Jo Worthy
University of Texas at Austin
Austin, Texas

Foreword

"But this too is true," Tim O'Brien writes in *The Things They Carried*, "stories can save us" (1990, p. 255). And the very truth of this statement shines through in the literacy stories of Sean, Billy, Melina, Curtis, Ray, and Laquisha that unfold on the pages of *Resilient Children: Stories of Poverty, Drug Exposure, and Literacy Development*. Their stories can save us because they are stories of hope and promise about each child's potential for literacy development and acquisition. They teach us that despite the bleakest of beginnings from prenatal drug exposure to crack/cocaine, children can be active seekers and learners of literacy. Rather than giving up on such children, the six stories herein tell how we might keep what seemed spent and reclaim what seemed lost so early in life.

We can have faith in the stories we are told in this book. Diane Barone carefully outlines her 4-year longitudinal research work with 26 children that produced the 6 case studies from which the stories emerge. In sometimes shocking detail, she describes her selection process, the children's early days, their foster care placements, and schooling. She situates these specifics in the broader framework of cocaine addiction, intervention programs, and related research on the effects of prenatal drug exposure on young children's development and learning. She also documents her role as an "insider," informing us as to the diplomacy and sensitivity involved in gaining access to children's foster homes and classrooms. You will grow to admire, as I did, her patience and skill in building trust with these children's families—the fruits of which are evident in the richness of her data. Her 4 years of careful observation yield a promising insight for literacy educators:

the resiliency of prenatally drug-exposed children to recover their "developmentally instigative characteristics" and to use them to their advantage (Bronfenbrenner, 1995, p. 634). In other words, these children, like all children, are active agents in, and on, their environments. They are literacy learners. And thus it follows that we, as literacy teachers, should strive to promote and integrate writing and reading into their home and school environments in the best ways we know.

What is resilience in the face of health risks, poverty, foster care, and miseducation? It can be seen in the literacy histories of Sean, Billy, Melina, Curtis, Ray, and Laquisha. It can be found, for example, in the sturdy self-perception of a Sean, who never doubted himself as a writer and a reader, or the adaptiveness of a Ray, who made the best of poor classroom instruction. In each case study, rich with detail, we can observe how each child's resilient characteristics were knitted into rather stable foster care environments with responsible, loving adults, who encouraged achievement in school. Together these tendencies appear to support processes in the near environment that push literacy development forward. That is the significance of these case studies and the central importance of this research work. This work brings us closer to understanding how literacy can develop, even if its beginnings are terribly poor.

What Diane Barone shares through these six children's stories also speaks to the professional responsibilities and everyday work of teachers. For resilience to thrive in academic work, teachers must make a particular effort to challenge negative attitudes associated with prenatal exposure to crack/cocaine, and help ensure that these children are honored in school. They need to be proactive in serving them, seeking out resources as needed, and confident in these children's abilities to master the complexities of writing and reading. The difficulty is not in saying or embracing these ideas, but in acting on them every day in the press of literacy instruction. In the case studies you are about to read you will meet several teachers who do act on these ideas—responsibly and sensitively every day. Their daily acts may escape notice, but the cumulative effects of their deeds can be seen in the literacy achievements of Billy, who basked in the praise of his kindergarten teacher Mrs. Campbell, or Laquisha, who grew strong through the gentleness of her teacher Becky Schneider.

This book tells stories—real stories—about six young children, prenatal victims of crack/cocaine addiction, who rebound from this initial shock and achieve literacy. Their stories are instructive for educators, not only because they are filled with hope, but also because they indicate how the delicate interplay of person (no matter how small) and environment can make a difference in literacy development. These are stories that can help us, and, if deeply understood, may even save us.

Kathleen A. Roskos
John Carroll University
University Heights, Ohio, USA

References

Bronfenbrenner, U. (1995). Developmental ecology through space and time: A future perspective. In P. Moen, G. Elder, & L. Luscher (Eds.), *Examining lives in context: Perspectives on the ecology of human development* (pp. 619–648). Washington, DC: American Psychological Association.

O'Brien, T. (1990). *The things they carried*. New York: Penguin.

CHAPTER 1

The Beginning of the Study

Have you ever seen a crack baby? A newborn crack baby, 6 hours old screaming its heart out because it's going through withdrawal? You know, over the course of the next year it doesn't learn to crawl or walk or talk on time. It's got deformities: physical deformities, mental deformities. It's got brain damage, lowered IQ, dyslexia. God only knows what else. Maybe it goes to school but it can't learn. And it's violent, so it gets in trouble with the law. It's unable to form any kind of close emotional ties. So it's faced with the prospect of going through this hideous, miserable life completely alone. And there are millions of these babies.

(From the movie *Deep Cover*, 1992)

Why I Chose to Study Children Prenatally Exposed to Crack/Cocaine

The story of the longitudinal research endeavor on which this book is based began at a U.S. national conference on literacy. Early one morning as I was dressing for the day's events, I listened to a national daily news television program. As a feature on this program, the newscaster was discussing the pessimistic future that was predicted for children who had been prenatally exposed to crack/cocaine (either or both crack or the powder form of cocaine). The program included video of newborns who were crying uncontrollably. As the camera moved in for a close view of one newborn, the commentator discussed the sad beginning of life for children prenatally exposed to crack/cocaine. The commentator then expanded on the bleak possibilities of school success for a child who began life by going through drug withdrawal. Although the newscaster's dialogue was not as direct as the opening excerpt of this chapter, it carried the same message. These children were, and would continue to be, in trouble.

Both examples clearly illustrate a distancing from these children. They cease to be represented by personal pronouns, but have become an "it," something less than human. Unfortunately, much of the early press (late 1980s and early 1990s) represented these children in this way. They were identified as crack babies, a biologic underclass, and children of the damned in most reports (Millroy, 1989; Nachan, 1990).

The news program achieved its desired effect on me. I was glued to the screen. Concerns for a presentation I was about to give moved to the back of my mind. I wondered if the dire predictions would turn out to be true. What would teachers do if such out-of-control children entered school? How would teachers cope? My concerns were grounded in my recent experiences as a classroom teacher. How would I have coped with such children and still met the learning expectations of the other children in my classroom? I was just beginning my own career as a university professor and I wondered how I would prepare my university students for their future classrooms. Clearly, I believed the views and biases about these children shared in the media. My questions indicated that I thought they would be difficult to teach and pose considerable problems for teachers.

The Initial Research

With the image of the newborn from the television program ingrained in my mind (years later, I still have that image etched clearly in my memory), a research agenda was born. It started with a simple question: How did children who were prenatally exposed to crack/cocaine develop in literacy? My focus was on literacy development because my recent doctoral degree provided the academic background for this developmental view on literacy. However, I had to learn a great deal in addition to my academic and practical knowledge of literacy development. I began with research on the drug, posing questions such as, What is crack/cocaine? What are the results of the ingestion of crack/cocaine to the person taking it? and What happens to the fetus of a pregnant woman who takes crack/cocaine? Elaborating on this simple start, I considered the results to a woman and her fetus from ingesting alcohol, cigarettes, and other drugs. I found myself investigating medical journals and becoming familiar with the scientific language surrounding drugs and their effects on the body.

As I read in this area, I found that a pediatrician in the Chicago, Illinois, area, Ira Chasnoff, was involved in a major study of children who were prenatally exposed to crack/cocaine (Chasnoff, 1988b, 1991). He had identified 300 children who were prenatally exposed to drugs in addition to a control group. He expected to follow these children longitudinally to discover any possible physical or cognitive difficulties they might have. Early in my study, I went to Chicago for a 3-day intensive investigation of the details of Chasnoff's study. I talked to him and his staff and learned about the testing that they were conducting with each child in his study. All of the tests were formal, standardized tests of language, physical, and cognitive development. I also was able to visit his treatment center for pregnant mothers and women who had just delivered a child, which included a preschool center. At this time, the director of the preschool center was focused on two goals for the preschool: The first was involving parents in the school, so that they would learn to interact with their child; the second was limiting the stimulation that these children would receive in the preschool. She was working from the prediction that these children would be impetuous and would respond poorly to a stimulating environment.

Finding Children to Observe

My reading and observation in Chicago provided the background for my own initial identification of a group of children so that I could begin my observations. Surprisingly, this initial group of children was easy to locate. I met the Director of Special Education for a large California school district at a university function. I talked to him, as I had been talking to anyone willing to listen, about my interest in children who had been prenatally exposed to crack/cocaine. He knew of one preschool in the district with children enrolled who were identified with prenatal drug exposure, and he gave me permission to informally observe these children. One week later, I was on my way for my first observations. When I was trying to locate the group of children for my formal study, I often would reflect on the ease with which these first children were identified and how readily access was granted for my observations.

I spent at least 1 day per week, and often 2 days, observing in this special-education preschool classroom. On most days there were about 15 children in the classroom. There were one teacher and several aides in attendance. The teacher directed the instruction and the aides helped various children as necessary. Sometimes the aides helped with behavior and at other times they facilitated the project with which a child was involved. Although there was no formal literacy instruction in the classroom, the teacher read a story or two to the children on a daily basis. As I observed the three children who were identified as prenatally exposed to crack/cocaine in this setting, I began to create the organization and design for my formal study. I quickly realized that I needed to have informal literacy assessments so that I could adequately represent the wide range of literacy development that I was observing. Grade-level and formal assessments would not provide the detail required to fully describe the literacy development of such young children. I also realized that just observing in school was not enough. I needed to know these children in their home environments. I was missing important background on these children that did not seem to be available to the teacher. I also did not know what learning the children brought from home and how it influenced the ways they responded in school.

Beginning the Formal Study

After the initial 6 months of preparation, I was ready to get started with the formal study. Although I was ready, it would take 4 more months to really get started. Since the pilot observations, I had moved to a new university. Naively, I thought I could pick up where I had left off. Before I arrived at the new university, I started the human subject protocol (This is a procedure required at universities for research studies. A review team scrutinizes the research so that no harm is incurred by the participants.). I surmised that with this process underway, it would be easy to identify the children and get started.

Criteria for Selecting the Children

Securing the children for this study was an interesting and complicated process. For the selection of children, I established three criteria. First, I needed to know through a urine toxicology at birth that each child was in fact prenatally exposed to crack/cocaine. I had discovered in informal conversations that many teachers believed children were prenatally exposed to crack/cocaine simply because they misbehaved in school. Therefore, relying on teacher identification alone could lead me to following numerous children who, although they may have been exposed to crack/cocaine, also may just have been behaving in inappropriate ways. In addition to the positive urine toxicology test, I was looking for children who were about 3 or 4 years old. I felt that this age would be a good starting place to observe the children over time. I expected that 3- and 4-year-olds would be able to talk about the books we would be reading and they also would feel comfortable writing and drawing. The third criterion was that the children were living in stable foster or adoptive home situations. The expectation was that the child would remain in the home through the course of the study. The stable home situation was critical because I wanted to observe these children's literacy development in the best possible situation. I felt that I would not get an accurate picture of the literacy development of children prenatally exposed to crack/cocaine by observing children who were living with their natural mother, who might still have been involved with the drug culture, or by observing children who were being moved from one foster home to another. Children in these situations might have difficulty becoming literate, not necessarily because of their prenatal drug exposure, but because of their current home circumstances.

Finding the Children

I started my search by contacting the local school district. They empathized with my concern but they could not think of any way to help with the identification process. *Yes*, they knew they had children who were prenatally exposed to crack/cocaine enrolled in their district, as they had teachers complaining about these children, but *no*, I could not have access to confidential records. After talking to several more people in the district I was able to secure permission to observe the children in their classrooms once I had identified them and secured permission from their parents. I am sure that the director of research who granted this permission never expected to hear from me again.

I spent the next several weeks calling every local agency that had anything to do with drugs or drug therapy. Most of the people at these agencies were very kind and supported the idea of my research. The difficulty always arose when I needed to identify children for the study. No one seemed to be able to determine a way to do this. And then on one fortuitous day, I called the Nevada State Welfare Department. I decided that because this agency worked with foster children, it might be willing to facilitate my study. Serendipitously, my first call to this agency was answered by a woman who was very sympathetic to my request. She had a nephew who was prenatally exposed to crack/cocaine, and she was worried about him and his future. She decided to put me through to the director who dealt with child placement. He listened to my research proposal and was supportive. He was faced with the dilemma of knowing if children who were prenatally exposed to crack/cocaine should be placed in adoptive situations. With the newspaper and television reports, he and potential adoptive parents were worried about placing children permanently with a family. He saw my study as a way to help answer his questions and provide guidance about adoption placements.

When I met with the director a few days later, he had already identified a caseworker to help me launch my study by surveying the files and identifying potential children for the study. She was able to locate 16 children who were in the age range requested and whose parents would most likely agree to being part of the study. I was reluctant to start the study with only 16 children because it was expected to last from 4 to 6 years, and I was afraid that several of the children would not remain participants until the study's close. The caseworker returned to the files and identified 10 more children who were younger or older than the original 16. Following this initial identification, we set up appointments to visit each foster or adoptive parent and child in their home. The caseworker accompanied me on these first visits and her presence allowed the parents and children to feel more comfortable with me.

During these visits, the parents were introduced to the organization of the study and its duration. All of the parents agreed to participate in the study, although some were a bit uncomfortable about my visits to their home. I tried to assure them that I would be coming to work with their child, but I could tell that it would take several visits before we all would be truly comfortable during my visits.

The Children

I met the children first by scanning the list prepared for me by the caseworker. I was happy that there was a large number of boys and girls. From this list, I also could tell that although most of the children lived in one part of the city, the rest were located throughout the large urban area of Las Vegas, Nevada. I saw this as a positive then and I still do today. While I was in the middle of the study, however, I found it exhausting to visit the children each month either at home or at school. I would have to schedule 2-hour appointments for each hour of observation to include travel time. With 26 children in the study, I spent much of my time driving or observing children during the 4 years of research.

In this book, I will share five case studies of children from this research: Sean, Billy, Melina, Curtis, and Ray. Sean was added during the second year of the study. I had been observing his foster brother and his mother suggested that Sean also be included in the study as he had been prenatally exposed to crack/cocaine. I also will describe a sixth case study, Laquisha, who was chosen because she is unlike the children who were in the primary study. I discovered Laquisha when she was a fifth grader. She had moved from her mother's home to other homes and among numerous schools throughout her elementary school career. Her story provides a contrast to the first five and allows us to consider a child who was prenatally exposed to crack/cocaine and was living in less than ideal circumstances.

The chapters that follow provide much detailed information about these children, but before looking at them closely, the following list will provide an overview of the children at the beginning of the study. This list includes background information for each child. I felt it would be important to know if the child had been a full-term or premature infant, had any health issues, or was or had been involved with any school interventions. I discovered this information in my initial interview with the parents. Table 1 on pages 8 and 9 displays the information that I gathered about each child when I first met him or her.

In scanning the table, it is clear that most of the children were full-term infants (17), most were boys (18), most were African American (15), and most were in foster homes (20). Many of the children had allergies or asthma (11), two had epilepsy, one had cerebral palsy, and one had AIDS. I found it interesting that so many of the children, particularly the 5-year-olds, were receiving special-education support. In most schools, young children rarely qualify for this support. Most of the children receiving this support qualified based on language de-

Table 1
Overview of the Children in the Study

Name	Birth status	Gender	Race	Home	Health	Intervention/Preschool
1- and 2-year-olds						
Chantilly	full term	F	AA	foster	none	none
Twilea	full term	F	BR	foster	allergies	infant-stimulation program
Becky	full term	F	AA	foster	asthma	preschool
Demetri	premature	M	BR	foster	cerebral palsy	none
Patrick	premature	M	C	adopted	none	infant-stimulation program
Sean	full term	M	C	adopted	none	none
3- and 4-year-olds						
Jamal	full term	M	AA	foster	none	none
Jose	premature	M	BR	adopted	fetal-alcohol effects	special-education preschool
Anna	premature	F	AA	foster	asthma	none
Billy	premature	M	AA	foster	asthma	preschool
Jennifer	premature	F	C	adopted	none	preschool
Mark	full term	M	AA	adopted	AIDS, allergies	preschool
Dante	full term	M	BR	foster	allergies	preschool

(continued)

(AA—African American, BR—Biracial, C—Caucasian)

Table 1
Overview of the Children in the Study (continued)

Name	Birth status	Gender	Race	Home	Health	Intervention/Preschool
Chris	premature	M	AA	foster	allergies	none
Mario	full term	M	AA	foster	none	preschool
Ray	full term	M	AA	foster	none	preschool
Curtis	full term	M	BR	foster	none	preschool
Donette	premature	F	AA	foster	asthma, epilepsy	special-education preschool
Melisha	premature	F	AA	foster	epilepsy, Sotos syndrome	special-education preschool
Josh	full term	M	C	adopted	none	special-education preschool
Melina	full term	F	AA	foster	none	preschool
Charles	full term	M	BR	foster	asthma	special-education preschool
5-year-olds						
Lakisha	full term	F	AA	foster	allergies	special-education preschool
Danny	full term	M	BR	foster	asthma	special-education preschool
Dontay	premature	M	AA	foster	none	special-education preschool
Kevin	full term	M	C	adopted	none	special-education preschool
7-year-old						
Loren	full term	M	AA	foster	none	special education

(AA—African American, BR—Biracial, C—Caucasian)

lays. It is also important to know that poor, minority children are over-represented in this study. This is *not* because these children are more frequently prenatally exposed to crack/cocaine than other groups of children (Chasnoff, Landress, & Barrett, 1990; Mayes, Granger, Bornstein, & Zuckerman, 1992). However, these children are more readily identified as being prenatally exposed and are more often in the state welfare system.

The Focus of the Study

As I began the study, my focus was clearly on the literacy development of children prenatally exposed to crack/cocaine. However, as the study developed I found that the prenatal exposure to crack/cocaine moved to the bottom of my list of concerns. The children whom I had chosen to observe did not stand out as being different from the other children in their classrooms. Often, teachers would suggest that I observe someone else who was presenting more of a challenge to them. As I visited the homes and schools of these children, I found that the lesson I was learning was about how poor, minority children are supported or hindered in their education. I learned that children, despite horrendous situations, can be successful in school. I learned what it means to be resilient.

Although most of the children lived in high-poverty situations, a few would be considered middle class. As a result of these socioeconomic differences and the busing policies of the school district, I was able to visit a multitude of schools representing all socioeconomic levels. I found sharp contrasts between the classrooms of the children in schools for middle-class and poor children. I also discovered that children of color who attended middle-class schools could be the victims of discrimination. I found that what I thought were universally endorsed practices for children's literacy development were used infrequently in primary classrooms. I found that parents supported their child's learning but often were distanced from their child's teachers. I found that teachers were often unaware of the home circumstances of the children they taught. The remainder of this chapter will detail each of these discoveries.

Similarities and Contrasts Between Middle-Class and High-Poverty Classrooms

Before addressing the contrasts, I will share the similarities in classrooms for all of the children. In Nevada, all primary (first- and second-grade) classrooms have reduced class size. The typical teacher-student ratio is 1 teacher and 16 children. This is not true for kindergarten however, where a teacher can expect 35 children in the morning and a different 35 children in the afternoon without the benefit of a teacher aide. Kindergarten is not mandatory, so many children appear in first grade for their first year of public schooling, many without any preschool experience. Most of the children in the study, however, began public school in a large kindergarten class and then moved to smaller first- and second-grade classrooms. By third grade the children typically were in classes with 30 other children. Because of the large number of new students to this school district, many of the schools were experiencing overcrowding and were on year-round, multitrack schedules.

Besides class size, another similarity between middle-class and poorer schools was that most of the teachers believed in very traditional literacy instruction. This was true even though the district and the local university provided classes in more holistic, literature-based strategies. I observed that the majority of teachers used ability grouping for reading instruction and these groups rarely, if ever, changed. They predominantly used the basal and accompanying workbooks, and involved children in little or no writing. During the second year of the study, I created a list of characteristics that usually are thought of in relation to literacy-rich classrooms (see Figure 1 on page 12). This list provided a way for me to compare what I was seeing in classrooms with my beliefs about exemplary literacy instruction. Even though I did not expect to observe all these characteristics in one classroom, I had anticipated that in most primary classrooms teachers would read to students and students would write on a daily basis. Unfortunately, I rarely saw classrooms where teachers read to children on a routine basis or where children saw writing, not copying, as a routine activity. This was true in classrooms in all the schools that I observed throughout the 4 years of the study. During most years, I was in more than 20 classrooms in as many different schools.

Figure 1
Characteristics of a Literacy-Rich Classroom

1. Classroom library is available to children
2. Daily silent, sustained reading
3. Student work is displayed
4. Daily reading to students by teacher
5. Student choice of reading materials
6. Student choice of writing topics
7. Journal writing
8. Daily writing
9. Literature discussion groups
10. Written response to literature
11. Children involved in literature projects
12. Integrated reading and writing
13. Thematically organized instruction
14. Children organized in flexible groupings
15. Children working cooperatively
16. Children talking to each other as they work

From Barone, D. (1994). The importance of classroom context: Literacy development of children prenatally exposed to crack/cocaine—Year two. *Research in the Teaching of English, 28,* 286–312. Used with permission.

Schools for Middle-Class Children

Several of the children attended schools that predominantly contained middle-class children. Most of these schools were new or well maintained. They often had sidewalks leading to the school that were lined with trees and flowers. When entering the school, there were welcoming signs everywhere. The secretary would always smile and chat as I checked in and prepared to visit a classroom. On my way to the classroom, I saw children's work and many attractive displays. These schools all had computer, music, art, and physical education rooms. Once I arrived in the classroom, there was always a library and the necessary supplies to support learning activities.

Although not all the children in the classrooms I observed were well behaved, the teacher's primary focus was on instruction. The teachers talked about having students meet the grade-level expectations that were reported in the curriculum frameworks developed by the school district. They indicated that most children would meet these expectations. Although they seemed confident that children would meet grade-level expectations, they also were very preoccupied with the state-mandated achievement tests. These teachers wanted their test scores to be in the highest group in the district; this was important because these scores would be published in the local newspaper.

After observing for 4 years, I noted that only one teacher in such a school provided a literacy-rich environment, one that centered on children's books, meaning-making, and authentic writing experiences. Although I might have expected that teachers of high-poverty children more frequently provided structured, skill-based classrooms, I found that teachers in schools with predominantly middle-class children also focused on skills and more structured literacy curriculums. Rarely were children allowed to read a book they chose, to freely talk or write about their reading, or to write a story on their own topic.

Schools for High-Poverty Children

The majority of children in the study attended schools that contained predominantly high-poverty children. Unlike the schools described earlier, there rarely were tree-lined walkways that led to these schools. They usually had fences around their perimeters, and often these fences had barbed wire on them. When I first visited these schools, they often were in disrepair. Carpets were dirty, ceilings were marked with missing pieces, and the chalkboards were abused. During the course of the study, a school bond issue was passed by the voters that provided for the renovation of most of these schools. After renovation, the classrooms were much more attractive and modern and the outside of the schools were more inviting, although the barbed wire remained.

When I entered these schools, there were signs that told parents that they must report to the office before visiting a classroom. In the school office, I often found the staff busy with children and parents, with little extra time for a visitor. I always left the office with a visitor badge because no one was allowed on the campus without identification. These schools all had computer, music, art, and physical education rooms, although they often served for other purposes, such as a cafeteria. Few of these schools had interior halls, so there was very little children's work in evidence. Even in the classrooms, most of the displays did not include children's work. In the classroom, I infrequently found class libraries or paper available for writing or drawing.

When I talked to teachers in these schools with high-poverty children, they were most concerned with discipline. I found extensive discipline systems in most classes with extrinsic rewards for children who behaved. Although the teachers were aware of grade-level expectations, they seemed resigned to their children not doing well. In most conversations, the parents were seen as the cause of the students' lack of success. These teachers were very concerned about the district's standardized achievement tests, but they did not expect their students to do well on them and they did not think they could do much about this.

The teachers in these schools, for the most part, taught to the whole class. There were whole-class phonics, spelling, and reading lessons. After each lesson, the children would do copy exercises or workbook pages. I found very few opportunities for children to talk to one another or to collaborate on their work. It appeared that most of the teachers were reluctant to allow such interaction for fear of discipline problems.

Discrimination Issues

The school district where I conducted the study had an unusual plan for desegregation that had been in place since the 1970s. All children attended their neighborhood school during kindergarten. Then from first grade to fifth grade, children in the predominantly African American area of the city were bused out of their neighborhood to middle-class schools throughout the city. When children were in sixth grade, they were all bused to the predominantly African American area of the city to sixth-grade centers. From seventh grade on, students went to neighborhood middle schools or high schools. The majority of students in my study went to kindergarten near home. These classrooms were filled with children of color and often had teachers with similar cultural and racial backgrounds. Then the children were bused for 5 years to schools that were far from home, often 15 to 20 miles. In most of these classrooms, children of color were in the minority and there were few, if any, teachers of color. Following these years, the children returned to neighborhood schools in the sixth grade.

I discovered two interesting results of this desegregation plan. First, when the children left kindergarten, they went to a very different school context. The teachers in the new school were not much like their parents or their previous teachers and neither were the students. Teachers frequently complained that the parents of these children rarely participated in school functions. The teachers seemed to be unaware that many of the parents did not have a car at their disposal and the school was far away, making it difficult or impossible to be involved in any routine way. In fact, very few of the teachers had ever visited the neighborhood where these children lived and were unaware of the home conditions and distances traveled by these children. Although this lack of knowledge might not be considered overt discrimination, the teachers often had lower expectations for these children based on what they saw as disinterest and lack of support on the part of the parents. This situation has been documented in other researchers' work and is shared vividly in Jan Nespor's book *Tangled Up in School: Politics, Space, Bodies, and Signs in the Educational Process* (1997).

Second, there was overt discrimination present in at least one classroom where I observed. Several of the children in my study were placed in this particular first-grade setting. Each year, for 3 years of observation, the teacher placed all of her children of color in the lowest reading group. After listening to these children read, it was clear that they were not all at the same level of development. Some children could read independently, while others were still not familiar with the alphabet. The differences in development did not seem to matter, however, and they were placed together for the entire year.

Additionally, during the year that I was observing one of the same teacher's students named Mario, I was surprised by some of her blatantly discriminatory statements. While praising the work of Mario for most of the year, one day she told me that "he had a chip on his shoulder because he is black." I was surprised and shocked by such a comment and did not pursue her reasons for such a statement. In other observations, she made similar comments about the other black children in her class. Allen, Michalove, and Shockley (1993) discussed institutional racism and teachers' attitudes, reporting that black males in lower elementary grades interacted less often with the teacher, used cooperative learning more often, and were more likely to be described negatively by their teachers. Although this teacher was the only teacher to be so direct about her feelings, I began to wonder if other teachers had similar thoughts about the minority children bused into their classrooms.

Parents' Support of Children's Learning

Although many of the teachers did not believe that the parents of their poorer children supported their children's learning, this was clearly not the case. As has been shown in other studies (Chall & Snow, 1982; Delgado-Gaitan, 1987; Goldenberg, 1984; Morrow, 1995; Nespor, 1997; Taylor & Dorsey-Gaines, 1988), the parents do help their children as best they can. Most of the parents told me that it was their job to make sure that their child behaved in school and that the school should teach their child to read. They had clear distinctions about the roles required of them and of school, and although they therefore did not engage their children in numerous reading and writing experiences before school, they did help them with homework once they were in school. I saw families in which the parents worked more than one job find relatives or friends to help their child so that he or she would do well in school. What proved difficult for some of these parents was their own reading and writing levels. In some cases, they found it impossible to help their child with some assignments because they did not have the skills. And in other situations where parents had the skills, they did not have the materials, such as magazines or books, necessary to help their child.

In addition to direct support of their children's learning, many of the parents expressed frustration at not being able to visit school as they had when their child was in kindergarten. They were just as upset with this situation as the teachers. In fact, one of the parents in my study was so upset by this situation that she lobbied the school district to build a new elementary school in her neighborhood and to turn the sixth-grade centers into full elementary schools. Through these additions and changes, parents were able to choose to continue to send their children to school out of the neighborhood or to keep them in their neighborhood school. This one parent's persistence resulted in a new elementary school and the restructuring and renovation of the sixth-grade centers. By the third year of my study, the majority of parents in this African American area were keeping their children in neighborhood schools. They were even instrumental in adding an Afrocentric focus to the curriculum.

Teachers Are Unaware of Home Circumstances

Finally, many of the teachers in this study did not have any knowledge of the home circumstances of the children they were teaching. They did not understand how they might better provide for a child by knowing about his or her home environment. There are at least two specific instances in which this would have helped them educate a child.

During the second year of my study, a verdict was decided in a racially sensitive trial in which the defendants were acquitted. After this verdict, there was looting and rioting in the African American community. The schools in this area closed, although the schools throughout the district did not. The children who were bused did not attend school even though their classes were in session. When they returned, there was no discussion of the chaos in which they had been living. The teachers did not mention the current situation in the classroom at all. The children were expected to leave the events and emotions they experienced at the door and catch up with their classmates once they entered the classroom.

The second circumstance that was not understood by the teachers was that many of the children from the African American area were not allowed to play outside, at least not in their front yards, because of the danger of their being hurt. They were most often confined to the inside of their home. They also had to endure a long bus ride to school. When these children arrived at school, they were bursting with energy and had difficulty being confined to a desk and being asked to stay quiet. Certainly there were other reasons why some of these children found it hard to stay seated, but most were able to remain calm after they had a chance to run a bit. Unfortunately, this problem caused several children to be labeled as hyperactive. There were also many comments from teachers as to what kind of households they came from when their behavior was so bad.

If the teachers had been aware of at least these two situations, they might have better understood the behaviors of their students. If they had learned more about their students, they would have been able to

17

provide curriculums that supported the children's home cultures as they learned about others.

What We Can Learn From Children Prenatally Exposed to Crack/Cocaine

As you read through this book, you will identify my shift in focus from the children's prenatal drug exposure to the children themselves. The children's stories, I believe, will displace the myths that are often told about them.

What to Expect in Reading This Book

The first three chapters of this book provide introductions to the children and the study that allowed me to meet them. In Chapter 1 a backdrop that describes the purpose of the study and how the study began is provided. It also shares the evolution of the study and how the initial identification of the children as being prenatally exposed to crack/cocaine moved quickly to the background of interest as the children became known as individuals beyond their label. Chapter 2 provides details about children in general who have been prenatally exposed to crack or cocaine. The foundation for this chapter comes from medical research. Chapter 3 shares the details of the organization of the study, introduces the children, and provides the general results of the longitudinal study.

I then focus on several of the children within the study and one child from a separate inquiry. Chapters 4–9 allow the reader to come to know each child as a literacy learner both at home and at school. All of these children lived in high-poverty situations, all were prenatally exposed to crack/cocaine, and all could be considered resilient. Despite these realities, they were all successful learners. Most of the cases follow a child for 4 years. The last case, Laquisha, is a bit different. She was the focus of a 1-year inquiry.

Chapter 4 provides a description of Sean, who loved reading and saw himself as a reader when he was 2 years old. Chapter 5 is focused on Billy, a child whose classroom rarely allowed him to become involved with books. Chapter 6 centers on Melina, who found learning interesting only when she could work with a friend. Learning needed to be socially constructed for her or she was not excited to be a participant. Chapter 7 describes Curtis, a child who could read and write fluently before entering first grade. Chapter 8 is focused on Ray, a child who saw reading as an escape. Unfortunately for Ray, his classrooms did not always allow him time to read, and in one classroom he was punished for reading. Chapter 9 shares the story of Laquisha, a child who lived in a variety of homes and went to many schools, yet she became a successful reader and writer.

The final chapter, Chapter 10, brings the book full circle. The discussion in this chapter centers on why these children's stories should be considered important.

As you read and reflect about these children's life experiences, I am sure that they will become important to your thinking and feeling about other children who may have been prenatally exposed to drugs. My hope is that their stories stay in the forefront of your thoughts. I anticipate that Sean, Billy, Melina, Curtis, Ray, and Laquisha will be etched vividly in your memory.

CHAPTER 2

What We Have Learned About Children Prenatally Exposed to Crack/Cocaine

Lisa:	I think I know where the mother gets the bones, the blood, and the water to put in the baby.
Deana:	What's the water for?
Lisa:	For crying.
Deana:	I think everything just grows inside of you.
Lisa:	Before it grows. She gets bones from dead dinosaurs and blood from a dead person and water from a glass of water.
Deana:	People can't collect bones. God does it. He gets the bones from cave men.

(Paley, V. [1981]. *Walley's Stories: Conversations in Kindergarten* [pp. 74–75]. Cambridge, MA: Harvard University Press.)

Prenatal Drug Exposure: Myth and Reality

The children in Paley's kindergarten class were discussing how babies grow and develop inside of their mothers. Their descriptions of this process demonstrate how myth has been mixed with fact. They know that bones, blood, and water are important to the developing child but they have very interesting ideas about how these items get inside the mother. Deana finally says that it must be God who does this. Future discussion and research will help these children sort out the puzzle of a child's in utero development, just as research is helping to sort out what is reality and what is fantasy in the ideas about development of children who have been prenatally exposed to crack/cocaine. This chapter will provide evidence to counter the prevailing myths about these children.

These myths have been slow to go away. Part of the reason for this intractability is the vivid media coverage of these children. Television and newspaper accounts have sensationalized them; often only the worst-case scenarios have been shared as if they were the norm (Griffith, 1995). These accounts often were narrow and did not mention the other life circumstances of the children. For example, while the children were prenatally exposed to crack/cocaine, they also were living in high-poverty situations with parents who were still using drugs. Additionally, in the first studies on these children, few commentators or journals published or shared results that countered the early reports of calamitous outcomes for these children (Gonzalez & Campbell, 1994; Greider, 1995; Hutchings, 1993; Lester & Tronick, 1994). Frank and Zuckerman (1993) eloquently discussed the first studies of these children and allow us to see the difficulties that resulted:

> The early reports of adverse effects of prenatal exposure to cocaine including neurobehavioral dysfunction, a remarkably high rate of SIDS [Sudden Infant Death Syndrome], and birth defects were initial observations that constitute the legitimate first step in the scientific process. However, these unreplicated findings were uncritically accepted by scientists and lay media alike, not as preliminary, and possible unrepresentative case reports, but as "proven" facts. It is not easy to disseminate scientific data contrary to prevailing popular belief. Our own experience, confirmed by others, has been that the popular media is disinterested in negative reports or in statements by researchers indicating uncertainty regarding the impact of prenatal cocaine exposure. (p. 299)

It is understandable, given the way these findings have been reported, that teachers are holding on to their beliefs that children who were prenatally exposed to crack/cocaine will be out of control in the classroom or that when they see children enter their rooms who are having difficulty conforming to the established behavioral expectations, they are quick to assume that they have been prenatally exposed to crack/cocaine or other drugs. The media and the public in general have considered prenatal drug exposure as a simple problem with one cause. That is, that the effects to children are a result *only* of drug exposure.

The myths about crack/cocaine's influence center on three basic assumptions: first, that all children who have been prenatally exposed to it are affected severely; second, that little can be done for these children; and third, that all the medical, behavioral, and learning problems exhibited by these children are caused directly by their exposure to cocaine (Griffith, 1995).

Background Information About Cocaine

Cocaine is sold in a variety of forms, the most common of which is crack cocaine. This drug consists of a fine, crystalline powder that is potent, extremely addictive, and inexpensive (Lewis, 1991; Villarreal, McKinney, & Quackenbush, 1991). Cocaine is a stimulant that acts directly on the central nervous system, resulting in an increase in blood pressure and body temperature. In addition, the user usually becomes more alert and active (Weiss & Mirin, 1987). However, this condition is short lasting; the crack cocaine high continues for approximately 6 to 10 minutes (Rist, 1990; Schneider & Chasnoff, 1987).

An important fact to note about cocaine is the way that authorities respond to its use. There are biases evident in the punishments doled out depending on one's cultural background. For instance, African Americans and Latinos are more frequently sentenced to jail for drug use (Bartolome & Macedo, 1997) than are Anglos. An interesting example of this bias is shown with the treatment of crack/cocaine use. Cocaine is considered a "white" drug and penalties for its possession are less severe than for crack, which is more readily found in high-poverty, urban neighborhoods (Bartolome & Macedo, 1997).

The question that many researchers are trying to answer is exactly how many children are prenatally exposed to crack/cocaine. The estimates vary but the estimate most frequently cited is about 11% to 18% of newborns each year, or 500,000 to 700,000 children, have been exposed to crack/cocaine (DeSylvia & Klug, 1992). These percentages can be much larger in metropolitan areas. For example, in San Francisco, California, rates have been as high as 45% (Osterloh & Lee, 1989). Although it may seem that discovering how many children have been prenatally exposed to crack/cocaine should not be difficult, it is a very complex problem. Most hospitals do not require urine tests on all newborns, and in those situations in which a hospital chooses to screen a newborn, positive toxicology reports will occur only if the mother has used cocaine in the previous 48 hours (Miller, 1989). Another reason for the difficulty in pinpointing an exact number is that most pregnant, drug-abusing women use more than one drug; they smoke, consume alcohol, and use other drugs (Freier, Griffith, & Chasnoff, 1991; Richardson & Day, 1994). In fact, in most studies researchers have not narrowed in on crack/cocaine use but have broadened the parameters to include polydrug use (use of a variety of drugs, cigarettes, and alcohol). A final complication is that pregnant women who are middle class and using drugs are required to submit their newborns to toxicology tests infrequently (Chasnoff, Landress, & Barrett, 1990), and their children are not reported.

Current Myths About Prenatal Crack/ Cocaine Exposure

Prenatal Crack/Cocaine Exposure Is More Damaging to a Child Than Prenatal Exposure to Other Drugs

This myth most likely developed as a result of news reports. The early stories always identified these children as "crack kids" (Frank & Zuckerman, 1993, p. 298). Contrary to the facts presented in many video clips that have been shown on television, there is no documentation of a withdrawal syndrome in prenatally crack/cocaine exposed children. The jitteriness that has been observed in many of these infants is not associated with cocaine exposure (Eyler & Behnke, 1995). Perhaps the label and video clips have resulted in the perception that these children were severely damaged, more so than children who were prenatally exposed to other drugs.

Children prenatally exposed to crack/cocaine *may* present a full continuum of effects from their mother's use of drugs (Chasnoff, 1991; Cohen & Taharally, 1992; Villarreal, McKinney, & Quackenbush, 1991). Some children exhibit no effects and other children have serious physical difficulties. The most consistent documented effects to these infants are lower birth weight and smaller head circumference (Bennett, 1992; Berlin, 1991; Brodkin & Zuckerman, 1992).

In fact, although prenatal crack/cocaine exposure has received extensive coverage by the media, alcohol and cigarettes have been determined to have an equal or greater detrimental impact on newborns (Brodkin & Zuckerman, 1992; Goodman, 1992; Richardson, Day, & McGaughey, 1993). Alcohol, even when women use it moderately, can result in infants who display impulsive behaviors and poor attention spans (Burgess & Striessguth, 1990). As with prenatal crack/cocaine exposure, low birth weight and small head circumferences in newborns are the results of alcohol and cigarette use by their mothers (Coles, Platzman, Smith, James, & Falek, 1992).

The area that researchers are now exploring centers on the effects on a newborn of his or her mother's use of more than one drug during pregnancy. Researchers are looking at the possibility of a synergistic interaction among these drugs that would produce more serious effects in a newborn (Bateman, Ng, Hansen, & Heagarty, 1993; Miller, 1989).

In addition to the mother's use of more than one drug, in most cases other events also make it difficult to determine the reason for problems in newborns. First, most drug-using pregnant women do not seek prenatal care. Only about 30% to 40% of them seek this support (Schutter & Brinker, 1992) because they are often afraid that their doctor will report them to the authorities. In many states, pregnant, drug-using women can have their child taken away from them because of their drug use (Villarreal, McKinney, & Quackenbush, 1991). Women who do not receive prenatal care are most often single, young, poor, black, poorly educated, and have inadequate nutrition and housing (Gittler & McPherson, 1990). Bandstra and Burkett (1991) found that when these women do receive prenatal care, their children show no significant physical differences when compared with the children of nonabusing women.

Second, as a result of limited or no prenatal care, many of these children are born prematurely. With prematurity comes a host of possible complications for a newborn. Premature children can display language delays, fine motor coordination delays, and delays in perceptual development (Gregorchik, 1992). Additionally, they can experience difficulties with socioemotional relationships, learning, and focusing attention (Bennett, 1992).

Third, beyond considering the possible insults that the mother might cause in the fetus and the ease or difficulty of the birth process, there are the effects of early home experiences. Approximately 50% to

75% of children prenatally exposed to crack/cocaine return home with their mother or relative (Williams & Howard, 1993). If a newborn returns to the home of a mother still involved with drugs, he or she will suffer from passive exposure either from inhalation of smoke or through breast milk (Chasnoff, Lewis, & Squires, 1987). Along with the presence of drugs, these homes tend to be disorganized, suffer from family violence, and often are isolated socially (Johnson, 1993). Beeghly and Tronick (1994) feel "that the long-term developmental outcome of infants prenatally exposed to cocaine or other toxic substances—as is true for all infants—is primarily determined by the quality of the affective-communicative mutually regulated system established by the cocaine-exposed infant and its caregiver" (p. 159).

In the early studies of prenatal crack/cocaine exposure, the described results to a newborn were presented as a permanent condition. More recent studies have determined that even effects displayed at birth are not necessarily permanent. Mayes (1992) describes the brain's plasticity and how adequate caregiving may compensate for early neurodevelopmental dysfunctions. Zuckerman and Bresnahan (1991) focus on the smaller head circumference issue and describe how this effect decreases as the child matures. Infants who receive adequate nutrition and care rebound from these early insults.

When considering the research in this area, it is clear that the effects to a child from his or her mother's drug use are wide ranging. These effects have for the most part been documented in studies that include poor, drug-using women and their children. It is easy to conclude that if studies included more diversity with respect to mothers and children (including middle-class women, for example), the effects to children would expand correspondingly. Further research also will need to discover the effects of heavy and recreational drug use, the issues of polydrug use, the timing of use (for example, does it matter in which trimester the mother uses?), and the effects of early interventions and long-term follow-up on infants.

The Majority of Children Prenatally Exposed to Crack/Cocaine Are Poor and African American

This myth has been created because urine toxicology tests are more routine in hospitals that generally serve high-poverty families. Because the mothers rarely have private physicians, the hospital can order these tests easily. When hospitals have participated in studies in which all newborns are screened, members of all social classes have been documented to have children prenatally exposed to crack/cocaine (Villarreal, McKinney, & Quackenbush, 1991). In addition to the identification of drug exposure, African American, Hispanic, and Native American parents are reported to child-abuse authorities more often and are investigated for possible child abuse (Chasnoff, Landress, & Barrett, 1990; Rist, 1990; Tyler, 1992).

Unfortunately, crack/cocaine are equal-opportunity drugs: People in cities, in rural areas, and at all socioeconomic levels use them (Mayes et al., 1992; Tyler, 1992). As a result, no simple description of a child who was prenatally exposed to crack/cocaine exists, and there is no typical profile for a woman who uses these drugs. In a Kappan Special Report focused on the use of drugs, Schipper stated that those who work in this area, typically doctors, nurses, and social workers, are just beginning to realize the widespread use of crack/cocaine among middle-class women (Sautter, 1992). Although middle-class women will be identified as drug users less frequently, it is important to remember that there is substantial drug use by this group. This information often moves to the background of our awareness as these women and their children never or very infrequently make the news or are participants in studies of drug use.

Substantial Intervention Will Be Required to Support These Children as Learners

This myth arises directly out of the first myth that described the effects to children of their mother's crack/cocaine use. If one believes that these children are all damaged severely, then it would follow logically that they all would require extraordinary academic interventions. However, because medical research has never documented a prototypical crack baby (Chasnoff, 1992), it does not make sense to assume that all children who were prenatally exposed to these drugs would need intervention at all, let alone substantial interventions. Certainly, some of these children will require intervention to succeed in school but just as certain is the fact that some children will require no intervention.

An interesting discovery made during most of the studies focused on these children is that they score in the normal range on individual intelligence tests (Cohen & Taharally, 1992; Rodning, Beckwith, & Howard, 1989). Additionally, Griffith (1992) discovered that the results on the Bayley Scales of Infant Development show little difference among cocaine/polydrug children from 3 to 24 months and nonexposed groups. There were also no differences for these groups of children on the Stanford-Binet test administered when they were 3 years old.

Although the results of these tests appear to be positive, it is important to remember that in addition to these children's prenatal drug exposure, many of them are living in poverty. As a result, there are numerous risks to their achievement of school success. It is necessary to include environmental *and* biological issues when considering the need for intervention for these children. Environmental factors contribute, either alone or in combination with a child's prenatal exposure. Work done by Heath (1983), Allington (1983), Hiebert (1991), and Delpit (1988), among others, documents the difficulty that poor, minority children have in achieving success in school. These issues must not be set aside when considering the school careers of most children identified with prenatal drug exposure.

The homes that many of these children live in are chaotic and inconsistent. A mother who is using drugs usually will not have adequate nutrition for herself or provide for a child's food needs. There also is often abuse and neglect present in these homes (Coles et al., 1992; Freier, Griffith, & Chasnoff, 1991). Often the result of these problems is that children are taken out of these situations and placed in foster care. It would be naive to assume, however, that just because these children are out of their mother's home, they will be provided with a nurturing environment. Although this can be the result, often the new home still leaves the children vulnerable to the negative effects of poverty, repeated exposure to violence, and multiple care-providing environments (Bennett, 1992; Richardson et al., 1993). Aylward (1990) suggests that "environmental risks have synergistic effects on infants who are biologically vulnerable" (p. 5). He observed that with an increased number of risks experienced by a child, there is a reduction in a child's intelligence. In 24% of children who experienced four or more risk factors (which might include maternal mental health, mother-child interaction, education, and occupation), intelligence scores were generally in the lower range (50 to 84). For children who experienced one or no risks, all intelligence scores were in the normal range (80 to 120).

For some children, particularly those exposed to numerous risks, intervention might be necessary, and many of these interventions are already in place. For example, educational programs such as Head Start, public and private preschools, special education, Title I (formerly Chapter 1), or speech therapy may be the best intervention. In the study that I conducted, many of the children routinely went to Head Start and some were placed in Chapter 1 settings in kindergarten. Several of the children qualified for special-education programs due to language delays.

In Chasnoff's study in which most of the children live with their natural mothers in a high-poverty, urban setting, about 40% of the children showed developmental difficulties in the areas of attention, self-regulation, behavior, and language. Chasnoff (1992) said that although these children are experiencing difficulties, they are all making progress. He noted that for these children living in very detrimental circumstances, Head Start programs and speech therapy have proven successful. It is important to know when considering these results that all the mothers have relapsed to drug use at least once since delivering their child and 60% are still using (Greider, 1995). Therefore, when considering that not all the children are experiencing as much success as we might wish, the fact that 60% are successful while experiencing many risk factors is impressive and demonstrates their resilience.

Although the myth is perpetuated that schools will have to develop large, costly intervention programs for these children, the research studies to date do not document this need. This is not to say that some of these children will not require extensive intervention, but the majority, even those living in less-than-ideal situations, will need support through well-established intervention programs or through no intervention at all.

Children Prenatally Exposed to Crack/Cocaine Need Stimuli-Reduced Classrooms to Learn

This myth is grounded in the previous myths that all prenatally exposed children are similar and affected severely as a result of the prenatal drug exposure. If one believes that all children prenatally exposed to crack/cocaine will be out of control, then it would be logical that they would require classrooms designed for children with attention deficit disorder. Some writers who hold this view (Odom-Winn & Dunagan, 1991; Waller, 1993) have recommended classrooms that do not have mobiles, bright bulletin boards, or center activities. Teachers are even encouraged to set up rooms that have isolated areas for children so that they can focus on learning.

These types of learning environments may be appropriate for a few of the children prenatally exposed to crack/cocaine but certainly not for the majority. Children who have no or a moderate number of identifiable effects need the kind of classrooms that are encouraged for all children. However, classrooms with predictable routines are preferable. In these classrooms, children understand the sequencing of events and the expectations (both academic and social), so that they can focus on learning (Calkins, 1986; Griffith, 1992; Jackson, 1990). Beyond the notion of clear expectations and routines for these classrooms would be a rich supply of literacy. In these classrooms, children can visit a well-stocked classroom library, they have time for and choice of independent reading and writing, and the teachers engage students in authentic reading and writing tasks.

In my study of 26 children (Barone, 1993), I discovered that the children were able to adjust to all the environments that were established by their teachers. In classrooms where the children, even as young as 2 years old, were expected to stay in their seats and be quiet for extensive periods of time, they were able to conform. In classrooms that allowed for more freedom of movement and talking, the children adjusted. In classrooms that were most often out of control, the children prenatally exposed to crack/cocaine were as out of control as the other students in the class. In classrooms where there was an abundance of freedom in the choice of literacy tasks and in movement and where children were expected to be independent learners, these children were able to meet the expectations. In few instances were the children ever out of sync with the teacher's and classroom expectations.

Moving Beyond Myths: Prenatally Exposed Children Can Succeed

The results of my study are not unusual. In other programs, particularly those established to work with prenatally exposed and nonexposed children, similar results have been described. In Project Daisy (Sautter, 1992), for example, prenatally exposed and nonexposed children are integrated into preschool classrooms. The teachers believe in active learning that includes learning centers, decision making, and holistic reading and writing activities. Children usually stay in their preschool classroom for several years, with a portion of new students entering each year. Through this structure, the teachers are able to create long-term relationships with their students and families. After 2 years of operation, the founders of this program predict optimistic futures for the children. They believe that none of these children will need special-education support as they move into and through elementary school. They feel that the early intervention provided in this program is responsible for the predicted success of these children.

Although it may not be as easy to think about a multitude of possibilities for these children, it is realistic. Because there is no such thing as a crack baby, there is no one academic placement that is appropriate for all of these children.

The Role of Foster Care

An important issue to consider with respect to these children is their foster-care placement. A negative aspect of these placements is that many of these children will remain in foster care until they are 18, and will not return to the homes of their parents. If they are in a stable foster-care situation, this placement might be positive and result in a secure environment for the child's development. However, if the child is moved from home to home throughout his or her childhood and never has the opportunity to bond with an adult, then this placement might be detrimental. However, if a child is placed in a permanent, stable home, he or she can grow up in a secure environment free of the drug culture. Children growing up in such an environment have been described by their foster parents as being advanced in their expression of feelings and affection. They also were described as having a strong attachment to their foster parents (Yolton & Bolig, 1995).

The Importance of Expectation

A second issue that is important is the idea of the self-fulfilling prophecy. If teachers and parents expect these children to be out of control, these expectations can lead to reality. Howard and O'Donnell (1995) talk about this issue directly:

> The stereotype that paints all drug-exposed infants as destined for disastrous outcomes can be a self-fulfilling prophecy. Not only may the professionals involved with the family give up before they start to provide assistance for whatever the individual child's needs might be, but also the parents may have their hopes and dreams for their child distorted by these negative expectations compounded by their guilt for having brought these difficulties on them. The harmful effects of negative expectations are especially important to avoid in a population such as this one in which 47% of the infants were born prematurely and 13% were small for gestational age, both of which are factors that tend to make the infant less likely to elicit positive responses from their parents in the newborn period. (p. 664)

Replacing Stories of Failure With Success Stories

A third issue to consider is that although some headlines are talking about the successes that many of these children have had and how they have beaten the odds, the earlier headlines are still fixed in many peoples' minds. No one is talking about the damage of the earlier headlines, and as a result the myths linger (Greider, 1995). It is proving difficult to move beyond the stigma attached to a crack baby. By holding on to this myth, many believe that punishment is being brought to the parents for their drug use by having a child doomed to failure. And with this punishment comes the issue of how much time and love teachers and social workers should give to such children (Greider, 1995).

Medical research does *not* document a new category of learning difficulty labeled "crack baby." These children are simply children. Some will require additional academic support for behavioral or learning problems and others will not. The problems that these children may bring to a school setting are nothing new. Creative teachers have handled them for years and have done so successfully. The issue with all teachers is finding the time to be able to work with the individual needs of all students, including students who may have been prenatally exposed to crack/cocaine.

CHAPTER 3

Discovering Resilience: The Structure and Results of the Study

It's the first day of my life—my remembered life. I'm 3 years old, sitting on the floor with Mama. Cutting out a picture for my scrapbook, a picture of a loaf of bread. Cutting it out and pasting it in my book with the flour-and-wheat paste I had helped to make....

My school life began 2 years later. Mama walked my cousin Vilma and me down P Street, through the open doors of John F. Cook School, and into Mrs. Staley's kindergarten class. Vilma and I were both scared. I was scared quiet; she was scared loud.

(Greenfield, E., & Little, L. [1979]. *Childtimes* [pp. 129–130]. New York: Crowell.)

The home and school memories described by Greenfield and Little were the kinds of memories and current images that I hoped to capture as I began this study. I wanted to uncover the reading and writing adventures in each home and in classrooms. I was looking to see how home and school environments helped or hindered children as they developed in literacy. I was curious about the match or mismatch between home and school literacy instruction. Thus, the study was organized so that observations began in the home, just as literacy development would, and then moved into school environments.

This chapter focuses on the organization of the study and addresses the specific literacy activities that were selected for purposeful observation. The second part of the chapter focuses on the results from all the children as they were synthesized to provide for cross-case comparisons. These descriptions provide an overview of the children's experiences and share more general discoveries. They do not provide rich details about the individual children; the stories of individual children appearing in the following chapters provide this closer view.

Organization of the Study

Length and Structure of the Study

Extensive observation over time was required to answer my question about these children's literacy development and this resulted in the selection of a longitudinal multicase study design (Yin, 1994). This design allowed for the exploration of literacy development without any deliberate manipulation of the home or school environments (Merriam, 1998; Yin, 1994). Once the children were identified, I visited them in their home and school classrooms. In each home, I engaged the child in reading, drawing, writing, and talking. To support these activities, I brought books, paper, and pencils and crayons. If the child had these materials in his or her home, we used the child's own books, paper, and writing implements. If they were not available, we used the materials that I brought. In school classrooms, I observed the teaching and learning that was occurring and only occasionally worked with the children.

Use of Multiple Participants

I purposely chose multiple cases for this study. Because of the bias and opinion already reported in the media, I was worried that if I observed only one child over time, I might add to the biased ideas about these children. If the child I chose to study had great difficulty behaving or learning to read and write, then my description would add to the already existing perception of such children. If the child did not exhibit any difficulty with behavior or learning to read and write, then critics would say that this was, in fact, only one child and therefore not worth much attention. In multiple case studies, the results are more compelling than single cases and contribute to literal replication (that is, prediction of similar results) (Miles & Huberman, 1994; Yin, 1994). Additionally, case study research is most appropriate "when the investigator has little control over events, and when

33

the focus is on a contemporary phenomenon within some real-life context" (Yin, 1994, p. 1). The case studies shared in this study are meant to be descriptive. The goal of the cases is to allow us to come to know individual children behind the label of prenatal drug exposure.

Credibility of the Study

Credibility for this study was secured in two ways. First, as was mentioned earlier, the study was conducted longitudinally. Through extended time with the children, teachers, and families, I was able to gain an understanding of the children's development as seen through a variety of perspectives. The parents, teachers, and children developed a comfortable relationship with me; this allowed for the development of an authentic picture of the children's literacy learning (Eisenhart & Howe, 1992). The parents and teachers often called me to relate the news of a significant literacy event in a child's life. In addition, they would frequently save work that they thought was important to include in this study. Second, data were gathered systematically throughout the study from a variety of sources and situations. After each observation, the observational notes or artifacts were assessed to determine each child's literacy development. A chart was kept for each child which highlighted his or her literacy development as the study progressed. Each addition to the chart exhibited a code that referred to an observation or artifact. For example, if a child represented words using initial consonants, a code next to this entry on the chart referred back to the field notes and to the child's actual spelling sample. This code included the date and whether the observation was at home or school.

The criticism of multiple cases is that by observing more than one individual, the richness of detail is lost (Wolcott, 1994). Wolcott compared multiple case study with an attempt to replicate quantitative comparative measures, and he argued that much is lost in such studies because the focus is on comparison, rather than a detailed description of one. In this study, I chose to include a large group of 26 children. Although critics might say that this was too large a group to follow, I would counter this argument by saying that being with these children, even if there were a large number of them, for *4 years* and spending time with each of them allowed me to learn about them as individuals. However, I also would concede that I do not know any child as well as I would if he or she were the only child I followed over this length of time. As with most studies, trade-offs are made. In this study, I chose to include many children so that a more representative picture of the literacy development of this special group of children would result.

My Role as a Researcher

My Background

As would be expected, my professional background influenced what I considered data, how I collected data, and how the data were interpreted. I began my elementary teaching career working with children in a children's hospital. None of the children were expected to live much longer than a year and they were residents in the hospital. It was my job to work with the youngest children each day in a preschool or kindergarten setting. I found this experience both exciting and frightening. None of the children were able to walk and all were confined to bed. In order to work with the children and move beyond their physical difficulties, all medical needs were provided outside the classroom. I never asked about the physical condition of a child and as a result, I was able to focus on each child and his or her instruction. This early teaching environment sensitized me to the physical conditions that can affect children's development and showed me that even children with these problems will respond to instruction. My teaching experiences following this first endeavor were all with young children from preschool through third grade who were generally from high-poverty, urban situations. These placements were in public school classrooms.

My last elementary teaching position was as a demonstration teacher for a public school district where I taught a multiaged classroom of children from first to third grade. The children remained in this room for 3 years, with a new group of first graders entering each year. This teaching experience, in particular, provided the necessary background for informally observing children over time, documenting their literacy development, and providing instruction matched to their development.

Working as an "Insider"

In addition to the selection of a multiple case study design, I decided that in order to understand each child's literacy development I needed to observe in each home and in each school. As a result of my frequent visits to the children's homes and their classrooms, I could not, nor did I want to, take on the role of noninvolved researcher. I instead chose to try to become an insider, someone who was passionately involved with this study, the children, and their families. In doing this, my hope was that parents and teachers would share the realities of their child's or student's literacy development. I did not want them to tell me only what they thought was safe to tell someone from the outside.

This role of an insider was not easy to attain. When I first started visiting homes without my escort from the Nevada State Welfare Department, I found that the parents would not respond to my knocks on their door. I always called to set an appointment, but when I arrived it appeared that no one was there. Sometimes, while I was standing at the door, I could hear talking or the television but no one would respond to my knocking. In some homes, it took four or five visits before I was let in. Once I was allowed entry, I was told that I could work with a child in the living room. Clearly, this room was a place for outsiders. In most of the houses, the living room looked more like a museum. There was beautiful furniture with plastic covers. There were numerous framed photographs, vases, and other art objects in it. It was certainly not a place where young children could play without breaking something. When in this room, I always moved to the floor with the child. Usually the parent was surprised by this and encouraged me to sit on the sofa. I kindly refused and we would work on the floor, as it was the only location where it was safe to spread out our materials. Often, the parent would come by to check on how we were doing and then we could engage in conversation. After three or four visits during which I was definitely treated as an outside guest, this formality would dissipate and I would be invited into the kitchen or bedroom where the real activity of the house occurred.

The transition from formal guest to friend began because a younger or older child (often a sibling of the child I was studying) would come to share in my activities and this child would bring a drawing or book to show his or her parent. The children would encourage me to come along and I often did. Once I had moved from the formal part of the house to a more informal area, I often would hear excuses such as "I just was going to start cleaning" or "These kids are always messing up the place." These phrases were familiar as I had used them many times when I had unexpected guests. I responded with a laugh and details of similar experiences. On many occasions I joined in to help straighten things by picking up toys or washing a few dishes. Soon after these initial forays, I was assimilated easily into the home and the door was answered immediately the next time I came to visit.

My visits became more complicated after this shift from outsider to insider, and required about 2 hours for each visit rather than 1. For example, I often would find several children waiting for me when I arrived, all of whom wanted to see my books and draw and write. It was almost like a small classroom where I would engage five or six children while keeping my eyes on the child I had come to observe. In another home, I was asked to join the family on the king-sized bed to help an older brother read his college catalog. He was the first child in this family going to college and no one could understand the text in the catalog; they asked questions such as "What is a credit hour?" and "What is upper division status?" In another home, I spent most of a morning helping the family chase chickens after they had broken out of the coop. After this adventure, I found myself staying for lunch. Becoming an insider took time and a willingness to engage in what was important to the family when I came to visit. Additionally, it meant that if a family called me and requested that I come over, I cleared my schedule so that I could respond to this need.

Later in the study, this role was sometimes uncomfortable and posed ethical dilemmas. For example, one family did not particularly like their child's teacher. They wanted me to talk to this teacher or the principal and get the child moved to another classroom. In this case, I talked to the parents and found out exactly what was bothering them about the teacher. They did not like her strategy for dealing with behavior problems as she would isolate a child at a desk for a week for one infraction. In this case, I suggested that the parents visit with the teacher and talk to her about their concerns, because they had told me that they had not consulted her about this issue. Fortunately, the teacher and the parents were able to discuss this issue productively and the teacher modified her response to inappropriate behavior.

In a second instance, the situation was more complex. A parent had her child in a religious preschool and she decided that she should have her child evaluated by the school district because she was worried about his language development. As a result of this evaluation, the school psychologist wanted to take the child out of the religious preschool and place him in a public school setting. The mother called me and was very upset because she wanted her child to be raised in this religion and she saw the preschool as critically important to this development. She was worried that if she did not agree with the school district she might lose her foster child, who was also her grandchild. She asked the school psychologist to contact me. This situation posed a real dilemma for me. Although I knew how important the preschool setting was for this family, I also knew that the instruction provided was not exceptional; in fact, it was most often inappropriate for young children. However, I knew that the public school setting was not what the family wanted and I questioned whether a teacher or this student would be able to be successful when the family would be so upset about the placement. I told the psychologist about the importance of the preschool to this family and recommended that when making a final decision he should consider what was important to them. He listened to this information and allowed the child to remain in this school through preschool. During the kindergarten year, the child attended public school. The result was a compromise for everyone, but the family respected the school district for listening to them about what was important for their family. This attitude proved beneficial for the child and school district as the child moved through elementary school.

Observation Schedule

Each child was observed initially in his or her home. As was mentioned earlier, a case worker from the Nevada State Welfare Department scheduled the initial appointments and accompanied me to each home. During this meeting, I explained the study and secured written permissions. I then talked to the parent or parents about their child's early physical growth and literacy development. Following this discussion, I spent time with the child in informal reading and writing activities.

After this meeting, I observed each child either at home or in school once a month for 1 or 2 hours. The monthly observations continued throughout the study. For the children enrolled in school, I visited their homes only once each year during summer vacation; all other visits were at school. For children not enrolled in school, all of my monthly visits were at home. During home visits, I engaged each child in talking, book reading, drawing, and writing. I brought materials to the homes because I discovered that books and paper were available inconsistently. While the children were involved with these activities, I engaged the parents or parent in an informal discussion about their child's literacy development. Because the parents and I shared a similar goal we all benefited from these discussions. I learned about their child's literacy development through their eyes and they asked me about how the larger group of children was doing. The parents were worried and concerned about the learning possibilities for their child because they had been influenced by alarming media reports.

Although I interacted directly with children when I observed them in their homes, I acted as a participant observer when in their classrooms (Jorgensen, 1989). I found an unobtrusive location in the classroom and recorded the interactions taking place. If the teacher or a child requested my participation, I quickly responded and then returned to my note taking.

The Children

All of the children in this study lived with adoptive parents or foster parents. None of the children lived with their natural parents, although some visited their parents occasionally. Interestingly, 23 of the children's foster mothers did not work outside their home. They were full-time homemakers and foster-care providers.

During the 4 years of the study, only 6 children left the study. Three of these children were adopted out of state and were therefore impossible to follow. Three other children left their original foster-care homes and were moved among many homes over a short period of time. Because of this lack of stability, I discontinued the children from the study. During the second year of the study, one additional child, Sean, was added because he was the foster brother of a child already in the study and had been observed informally during the entire first year.

The Children's Teachers

The foster parents or adoptive parents all agreed to let me observe their child at home and at school for the duration of the study.

They also were willing to provide an update on any literacy developments that they noticed with regard to their child. The public school district allowed me to observe the children as they entered public school at any of the schools they might attend. In order to protect the children from any biased behavior on the part of a teacher due to his or her perceptions about children prenatally exposed to crack/cocaine, the teachers were told only that I was observing foster or adoptive children's literacy development. Although I was not being honest and forthright with the teachers, I decided that I would take no risk that might hurt a child's chances to be successful in school. Although I worried about this decision at the beginning of the study, at the conclusion of the study I was thankful that I had proceeded in this way.

Occasionally, I would hear teachers talking about a child who was causing them difficulty. In several of these instances, the teacher was convinced that the child must have been prenatally exposed to drugs, which was the cause of the child's inappropriate behavior. Although I believe that most teachers would have tried not to let the label influence their thoughts about a particular child, tacitly their perceptions might have been changed as a result of this knowledge.

The Children's Focused Literacy Behaviors

During my systematic monthly observations of children, I recorded developmental literacy concepts that were documented easily and that represented a variety of reading and writing activities. These concepts provided a means to compare the children in the study. These included drawing and name writing (Harste, Woodward, & Burke, 1984), concepts of print (Clay, 1985), storybook reading (Sulzby, 1985), concept of word in print (Morris, 1983), and orthographic knowledge (Henderson, 1990). These developmental literacy concepts provided a rich array of data, which represented a broad-based view of literacy acquisition.

Drawing and writing. At each home session, I began by asking the child to draw a self-portrait and to sign this drawing as the artist. These samples collected over time allowed me to determine a child's ability to distinguish drawing from writing, the evolution of a child's name-writing ability, and the child's artistic development. While the child was drawing, we engaged in informal discussion about his or her current interests, upcoming family events, or school activities. The drawing activity often served as a comfortable way to begin our time together.

Concepts of print. As I observed in school or interacted with a child at home, I engaged the child in discussion about the structure of books. Based on Marie Clay's work (1985), I asked a child to locate the front and back of a book, the top and bottom of a page, the illustrations and the text, and a word. I recorded exactly what the child was able to do (for example, I recorded when a child pointed to the top and bottom of a page). I wrote descriptions of these behaviors, but I did not quantify them in any way.

Storybook reading. At each visit to a child's home, I asked the child to read a story to me. As the child read, I wrote down the text produced orally by the child. Although a tape recorder would have facilitated my recording of the reading, I elected not to bring a recorder into the homes I visited because it seemed intrusive. Following the session, I classified the child's reading in accord with the categories identified by Sulzby (1985). These categories included (a) attending to illustrations, not forming a story; (b) attending to illustrations, forming a story; (c) attending to illustrations, forming a story using storytelling and book language; (d) attending to illustrations, forming a story using book language; and (e) attending to print, reading a story (refusal, aspectual—reads parts and discusses parts of text, holistic—independent reading). Once the child could read independently, I no longer used these categories but began to look at comprehension and fluency.

Concept of word in print. As children moved into independent reading, I noted their ability to match speech to print or the concept of word in print (Morris, 1983). As children read, I asked them to point to the words. I used the ability to synchronize reading and pointing as a benchmark in a child's movement toward independent reading. Children were classified as having (a) no concept of word when they could not point to words in text in relation to the words they were reading; (b) as almost grasping concept of word when they could match single-syllable words to their pointing (they might experience difficulty with multisyllabic words or pages with a significant amount of text, however); and (c) as grasping concept of word when they were able to synchronize reading and pointing to each word read.

Orthographic knowledge. At many of the home sessions, I asked the child to spell words from a developmental list that represented the typical orthographic development of children (Henderson, 1990).

The words in this list began with single-syllable short-vowel words such as *bed* and moved to more complex words such as *pleasure* (Bear & Barone, 1989; Bear, Invernizzi, Templeton, & Johnston, 1996). Children were asked to spell a group of five words at a time; if they were able to spell three of five words correctly, they were then asked to spell the next five words. The four groups of words were as follows:

- *bed, ship, drive, bump, when*;
- *train, closet, chase, float, beaches*;
- *preparing, popping, cattle, caught, inspection*; and
- *puncture, cellar, pleasure, squirrel, fortunate*.

In addition to this spelling inventory, I collected samples of journal writing, story writing, and expository writing both at home and at school. These samples were initially analyzed only for orthographic representation or how accurately a child was able to represent a word. Later I also considered the child's ability to write cogently about a topic and the structure of the written piece.

The children's spelling and writing samples placed them into one of the following categories that represented their orthographic knowledge: (a) prephonemic, which implied that the child had not yet developed sound-symbol correspondence (for example, *bed* as *8Z*); (b) semi-phonemic, which meant that the child represented the correct initial consonant and perhaps a final consonant (for example, *bed* as *B* or *BD*); (c) letter name, which was when the child began to represent vowels (for example, *bed* as *BAD*); (d) within-word pattern, which was when a child differentiated between short and long vowels (for example, *bed* as *BED* and *drive* as *DRIEV*); (e) syllable juncture, which was when a child represented most single-syllable words correctly but would experience difficulty with prefixes and suffixes (for example, *popping* as *POPING*); and (f) derivational constancy, which was when a child would be expected to spell most words correctly, but may have had difficulty holding roots constant when sound changed (for example, *pleasure* as *PLESURE*) (Bear & Barone, 1989; Henderson, 1990).

At each observation session, I recorded the majority of the interactions that were occurring. When I observed and interacted with a child at home, I acquired samples representing all of the literacy concepts I had targeted. Because classrooms are complex, I was not always able to observe literacy activities. All of my observations were scheduled for times when the teacher had indicated that students would be involved in reading or writing activities, but because of interruptions or changes in plans, this was not always the case. When I had observed a child on two consecutive occasions and had not observed reading or writing activities, I asked the teacher if I could work with a small group of students for about 30 minutes. I worked with a small group so that no child was singled out. I served as an instructor only with the permission of the teacher and in classes where the literacy concepts that I was hoping to observe occurred infrequently. Subsequently, even though I observed each child once a month, I rarely observed all of the literacy concepts at one session. Therefore, only at the end of each year did I finalize a chart for each child that summarized the most prevalent patterns of literacy development observed throughout a year.

Data Analysis

As I observed these children over time, I wanted to describe their literacy development using broad parameters, not grade-level achievements. This choice was particularly important in this study as the children were enrolled in schools that varied from middle-class settings to low socioeconomic settings. In each school the grade-level expectations varied considerably even though all the schools were in the same public school district. For instance, a child in a middle-class setting was expected to read independently any picture book by the end of first grade. At a low socioeconomic setting, the expectations for first grade centered more on behavior than literacy outcomes. To facilitate this descriptive process, three broad literacy categories were developed.

Categories of Literacy Development

My categories reflected three phases of overall literacy development. They closely resembled the first three stages of reading acquisition described by Chall (1983), which are prereading (birth to age 6), decoding (age 6 to 7), and fluency (age 7 to 8). The categories used for broad classification also were influenced by the work of Weaver (1988). In Weaver's phases of reading development, orthographic knowledge is related to particular reading strategies. In the *schema-emphasis* phase, children exhibit prephonemic spelling patterns and

43

reading-like behaviors (for example, turning pages and reading or storytelling based on illustrations). During the *semantic-syntactic* phase, children exhibit semiphonemic or letter-name spelling patterns and begin to read some words in context. In the *graphophonemic* phase, children represent words using letter-name or within-word patterns and read in a staccato or word-by-word fashion.

Getting the idea of reading and writing. The first category included children who were getting the idea of reading and writing. These children usually were enrolled in preschool or kindergarten. They pretended to read using storytelling focused on illustrations. They were beginning to understand how books were constructed in that they recognized the front and back of books and knew how to turn pages. They recognized the difference between illustrations and words, although they rarely pointed out individual words. Their writing consisted of scribbles or random letters or numerals usually written with a linear orientation (Holdaway, 1979; Morrow, 1983; Taylor, 1983; Teale, 1984).

Beginning readers and writers. The second category included children who were considered beginning readers and writers. These children were usually in kindergarten or first grade. Their reading was often word by word as they discovered concept of word in print. When they read, they pronounced each word carefully without expression. It was as if they were reading to the rhythm of a metronome. They fully understood a book's structure and the role of illustrations and text. In writing, they included the appropriate initial and final consonants with some confusion about the vowel (Carver, 1992; Clarke, 1988). For example, they might write *FESH* for *fish*. When writing on their own topic, they most often wrote narratives or created lists (Calkins, 1986).

Fluent readers and writers. The third category included children who were becoming fluent readers and writers. These children were most often in second to fifth grade. In both reading and writing, they were developing confidence and fluency in their choices of text and written compositions (Calkins, 1986; Carver, 1992; Henderson, 1990). They were able to write most single-syllable words without difficulty. For example, they could represent most short- and long-vowel patterns. They often experienced difficulty with how to add a suffix to a word, spelling *driving* as *DRIVEING* for instance. In reading and writing, they moved among genres depending on their purpose or interest. This last category was quite broad and perhaps ambiguous, but because most of the children did not mature to this category until the final year of the study, it was not further defined.

Creating Literacy Profiles

I constantly searched the data I collected to create a literacy profile for each child. After each observation, I would reduce the running text recorded at the observation to about a one-page report of the literacy behaviors that were observed. When I next observed in the classroom or home, I would bring these summaries and validate the accuracy of my recording of the child's present literacy abilities with the teacher's or parents' observations. At this time, the parents or the teacher usually updated me on new literacy events that they had observed, or they extended my reports of the literacy concepts I had noted. Through this dialogue, I was able to triangulate my data (I had many informants providing data for each child) and enrich my observations by the added insights of these key participants.

Periodically, I made comparisons among all the children in the study to note similarities and differences in literacy development. These comparisons were done by scrutinizing each child's literacy chart, products, and my observations and discussion notes. These comparisons were based on the age of the children and provided a framework from which to observe and discuss the individual children within the study.

Results: How Did the Children's Literacy Develop?

The study began with 26 children and ended after 4 years with 21 children (see Barone, 1993a, 1993b, 1994, for details of the first and second years of the study). During this time the children were enrolled in as few as 15 schools to as many as 20 schools. With the exception of one child whose parents chose to homeschool him, the children all entered public schools during their kindergarten year.

Throughout the study, the majority of the children were described as being within the broad literacy categories that were established. In the Appendix, yearly summaries of each child's literacy growth, grouped by the age of the child at the beginning of the study, are provided. The following sections include summaries of the literacy growth of each age group.

One- and Two-Year-Olds

There were 6 children who began the study at the ages of 1 or 2. Chantilly, the only 1-year-old at the beginning of the study, moved away at the end of the second year. During the entire study, I considered these children to be in the category of children who were getting the idea of reading and writing. However, they did understand more about reading and writing over the 4 years. They began the study scribbling for both writing and drawing. By the third and final years of the study, they were able to create a self-portrait. During the second year of the study, most of the children could write the first letter of their first name and by the third year, they could write their first name. By the second year of the study, they began to be aware of a book's organization. They turned a book in the right direction for reading, they turned pages, and they recognized the top and bottom of a page. When I first interacted with these children using books, they were content to provide labels for the illustrations on each page. By the second year of the study, they were forming an oral story based on the illustrations. And by the last year of the study, they were able to memorize predictable texts such as *Hattie and the Fox* (Fox, 1986). These children moved from scribbling and random letters and numerals to including the appropriate beginning consonant when they tried to write words.

Three-Year-Olds

There were 6 children who were 3 years old at the beginning of the study. These children demonstrated remarkable development from the beginning to the end of the study. During the first year, these children were in the first category of getting the idea of reading and writing. They all progressed to the second category, beginning readers and writers, and one child, Jennifer, moved to the most sophisticated category of fluent reading and writing.

Most of the children began scribbling during the first year and were unable to represent their first names. By the second year, they were drawing self-portraits and writing their first names. By the third year, they wrote their last names. They knew which way to hold a book and how to turn pages when the study began. By the second year, they fully understood how a book was organized. At 3 years old, these children could not match speech to print, but by the third year they had developed a full concept of word in print. At first when they were asked to read, they created a story using storytelling and reading or book language. During the second year, they were easily able to memorize predictable text. By the last year, they could read independently in a word-by-word manner. At age 3 they represented words by using any letters or numerals. During the second and third year, they used the appropriate first consonant. By the last year, they were representing all of the phonemes in single-syllable words, although they were confusing the vowels.

Four-Year-Olds

There were 10 children who were 4 years old at the beginning of the study. Four of these children moved away as the study progressed. These children made similar progress as the 3-year-olds. They began as children who were getting the idea of reading and writing. Unlike the 3-year-olds, the majority of these children became fluent readers and writers by the end of the study. They began the study being able to draw self-portraits and write their first names. They understood the structure of books somewhat; by the second year, they fully understood the organization of a book. During the first year, they were unaware of the speech-print match but they developed this knowledge fully by the third year of the study. When asked to read a book, they started by retelling the story using some book language. During the second year, they could read memorized, predictable text. By the third year, the children were divided between reading in a word-by-word manner or fluently. During the last year, the majority were fluent readers and writers. Like the 3-year-olds, these children began representing words with random letters and numerals. During year two, they discovered the alphabetic principle. In year three, they experimented with representing vowels. At the conclusion of the study, they were able to represent short vowels accurately and were experimenting with long-vowel patterns.

Five-Year-Olds

There were four 5-year-olds in the study. They began as beginning readers and writers and moved to being fluent readers and writers. At the beginning they were able to create self-portraits and to write their first and last names. They knew about the organization of books and they understood concept of word in print. They were able to memorize predictable text and they used initial consonants to represent words. By the second year, they were able to read independently and in a word-by-word manner. They were experimenting with representing vowels. This development continued through the third year. During the last year, they were independent or fluent readers. They were confusing long-vowel patterns or trying to figure out how to add suffixes to single-syllable words.

One 7-Year-Old

Loren began the study being able to draw a self-portrait and to write his first and last name. He understood the details of a book's structure and he had full concept of word. He was an independent reader who read in a word-by-word manner. He represented short vowels accurately and was experimenting with long-vowel patterns. By the second year, he became a fluent reader and writer. He was able to write most single-syllable words correctly and was learning how to add suffixes to words.

Children Who Experienced Difficulty

Five children experienced difficulty achieving age-appropriate literacy development at various times over the course of the study. Three children who experienced difficulty had an emotional or physical occurrence or physical or sexual abuse that helped to explain their slower rate of growth. Melisha, a 5-year-old, was diagnosed with Sotos Syndrome in addition to epilepsy. This syndrome results in rapid growth and moderate to severe mental deficiency among other characteristics (Jones, 1988). In addition, she experienced physical or sexual abuse while she was in respite care because of her foster mother's surgery. Josh, a 5-year-old, was moved to a new school as a result of a school busing dispute. He was placed in a classroom for children with emotional difficulties, and had a hard time adjusting to his new school and frequently had difficulties because of behavior problems. Because of his behavior and his parents' concerns, Josh moved to three other schools during the year. Dontay, a 6-year-old, was moved to a program for emotionally disturbed youngsters after he was attacked by another child on the school bus. He had difficulty with schoolwork after this incident. Jamal, a 5-year-old, had problems adjusting to a kindergarten class and qualified for special-education support. When he was tested for this placement, his intelligence as measured by an individual intelligence test placed him in the above-average range. However, he was not able to handle the limited movement allowed in his classroom and became frustrated with many of the academic expectations of his teacher. For example, he did not yet know how to write his name independently and his teacher became very upset when he would whine about this inability. She expected that all children entering kindergarten would be able to write their first name correctly. Heath (1991) might suggest that he was having difficulty moving from his home culture to school culture. He was not familiar with the language and routines expected in school.

One other child, Lakisha, a 6-year-old, failed to develop in literacy due to a lack of literacy instruction. Her special-education teacher provided instruction in phonics, but never provided time for reading anything beyond worksheets. Unfortunately, the worksheets focused on singular skills infrequently understood by Lakisha (for example, marking the words that had long vowels when she was just beginning to understand short vowels). As a result Lakisha was still not very proficient at reading or writing in second grade. By third grade, through the efforts of a new teacher, Lakisha became a reader and writer and tested out of special-education support. At the end of the study, Lakisha was the only child not to have achieved age-appropriate literacy development.

Special-Education Support

Many of the children received special-education support before and during elementary school. The qualification for this support was most often cited as language delay. During the first year, eight children received special-education services (four in preschool, five in first grade, and one in second grade). The number of special-education placements during the second year was reduced by four children who were dismissed from these services. At the conclusion of the study, seven children still received special-education support; however, three of these children were no longer eligible for these services during the next academic year. Additionally, four children qualified for gifted and talented programs.

Resiliency

I described this surprising age-appropriate literacy development as the result of the children being supported by stable home situations (the children remained in the same home throughout the study), early intervention (speech or special education) for many of the children, and the resiliency of the children. These characteristics were selected by doing repetitive searches through the data and were informed by the work of others (Aylward, 1990; Griffith, 1995; Mayes, 1992).

Resiliency was not something that I thought about as I began this study. I came to the idea of resiliency as I poured over the observation transcripts. These children, unlike children prenatally exposed to drugs and still living in homes where their natural mother is using drugs, had a stable, predictable home environment that contributed to their resiliency. Aylward (1990) supports the importance of a home free of environmental risks (for example, poor mother-child interaction or health care) and biological risks (for example, poor diet or passive drug exposure) in enhancing a child's resiliency. He wrote that environmental deficits and stresses impair cognitive and psychological development. Mayes (1992) and Chasnoff (1988a) concur that the home environment is an important contributor to the outcome of these children, more so than the prenatal drug exposure. Griffith (1995) wrote that when "major risk factors are reduced or eliminated and when early screening, diagnosis, and intervention are provided…the majority of drug-exposed children seem to have the resilience to recover from the effects of prenatal drug exposure" (p. 91).

Although the issue of resiliency may seem an unusual one to discuss in a study of this nature, there are numerous studies that document the relation between this characteristic and school success even in the research that does not focus on children prenatally exposed to crack/cocaine (Allen, Michalove, & Shockley, 1993; Griffith, 1995; Werner, 1992; Wolin & Wolin, 1993). Allen et al. (1993) have written a book about successful experiences of children in urban schools. They identify the factors of improved environmental circumstances, good relationships with teachers, and positive school experiences as supporting the development of children's resilience. The majority of children in this study certainly benefited from these factors. Additionally, they had the support of their parents as they entered school.

Concluding Thoughts

The systematic monthly observations over 4 years documented the success these students can have in their literacy development. Occasionally, a child experienced difficulty in school, but over time, with the support of parents and teachers, the child moved beyond it. The success of these students was also surprising because in addition to prenatal drug exposure, most of them came from minority backgrounds and lived in poor circumstances. The research has documented the educational difficulties of children coming from such backgrounds (Hiebert & Taylor, 1994; Nespor, 1997). The stable home circumstances where a mother and often a father were present and the children were sure of continuity in the home, although most might be considered impoverished, supported the children's emotional as well as academic growth.

When this study began, I had no idea if the children I observed would be successful in literacy learning or if they would experience great difficulty. After observing and interacting with these children over 4 years, I am optimistic about their futures. Once these children moved beyond their prenatal drug exposure and were supported by consistent caregivers, they appeared to be more like non–drug-exposed children than different. The research issue became how children experiencing high poverty and from minority backgrounds succeeded in school. This issue is explored in the case studies that follow.

CHAPTER 4

Sean: A Child Who Sees Himself as a Reader

> When Ob and me met you, honey, you was such a shy thing. Them big ol' eyes of yours looking like a puppy begging for love.
>
> I knew right off I wanted you....I said, "Ob, we've got to take that child home with us."
>
> (Rylant, C. [1992]. *Missing May* [p. 84]. New York: Dell.)

The excitement shown when Ob and May decided to adopt their niece, Summer, is similar to the expressions of joy shared by Sean's parents. They were thrilled about having Sean live with them. Every time I met with Sean and his parents, they smiled about how fortunate they were to have Sean and he always smiled back. Sean came into their home as a foster child when he was 6 months old, and soon after their initial meeting, Sean's parents began the adoptive process. When Sean officially became theirs, there was a huge celebration with family and friends to commemorate this event. Although Sean's parents were thrilled with this event, Sean's pleasure showed when he introduced Becky and Ron as *his* mom and dad. Figure 2 shows Sean's self-portrait.

Getting to Know Sean

> Paradise...started from the minute we pulled up in Ob's old Valiant, to turn their rusty, falling-down place into a house just meant for a child. (Rylant, 1992, p. 5)

Figure 2
Sean's Self-Portrait

I became acquainted with Sean a full year before he was formal-ly included in the study. His foster brother, Demetri, was an initial member of my study. At the beginning of the study, Demetri was not enrolled in a preschool, so I met him at his home each month. During these visits, Sean was always a participant and often spent more time with me than Demetri. Sean loved seeing the books that I brought and there was no way to keep him from them. At first, his mother,

Becky, would try to involve him in a project in another part of the apartment, but Sean always figured out a way to become uninvolved with that project and join in my work with Demetri.

At first Becky was worried that my working with both boys, when I was really interested in Demetri, would ruin my research. Once she became comfortable with the idea of my working with both boys and realized that my research would not be ruined, Demetri and Sean became a team in our work together. When I visited this home, I always was engaged with both boys, and I often worked with another child or children who were placed in this home. Why it took me a full year to include Sean formally is a question without an answer. At the end of the first year, Becky shared Sean's background and we agreed that he would be an interesting addition to the study.

During the first year, Sean would spend more time with the books and paper that I brought than his older brother. At age 2, Sean loved to be read to and he enjoyed looking through books. He would draw on paper but only with encouragement. Books were his love, and he would only draw and write with much prompting.

During my visits throughout the first year, Becky provided background on Sean. She knew that he had "been abandoned in the hospital by his mother." This situation is common with children who have been prenatally exposed to drugs because the mother is afraid that the authorities will arrest her for neglect because of her drug use. These children have been labeled as "boarder babies" (Villarreal, McKinney, & Quackenbush, 1991). In addition, Sean was 6 weeks premature and weighed only 4 pounds 5 ounces; he tested positive for crack/cocaine exposure shortly after birth. After he left the hospital he was placed in a welfare group home and then with foster parents. At 6 months, he moved in with Becky and Ron who had special training to care for children prenatally exposed to drugs or alcohol. During my time observing Sean, there were numerous infants placed with this family. Most of these children stayed only a short time, but two children stayed longer. Demetri was with the family for 4 years and Courtney, a younger sister, was also adopted by this family.

Sean's parents wanted to adopt Sean from the moment he entered their home. They had tried to adopt Demetri, but the courts refused as he is black and they are Caucasian. Becky and Ron were very upset by this decision, especially when the courts took Demetri out of their home and placed him with a single foster mother who was black. They felt that they were punished for trying to adopt Demetri, and so was Demetri, who was now in a home where he spent most of his time in day care. They had been careful about having Demetri interact with adults and children of a variety of racial backgrounds and they were hurt and puzzled by the court's decision. They felt that they had a better chance of adopting Sean because he is Caucasian; this was the case and the adoption, although a lengthy process, did go through. When Courtney, who is also Caucasian, came to their home, they started adoption procedures for her immediately and were again successful. What I found amazing about this family is that even after they had their own children, they continued to care for foster children. In fact, they became leaders in the foster-parent group and provided instruction to other parents contemplating caring for children who were prenatally exposed to drugs or alcohol.

In addition to their work with children with problematic backgrounds, Ron worked part time in an elementary school as a custodian. Beyond this work, he was a minister with a group of people who spent many weekends on motorcycles going to various places and preaching. Becky and the children often joined Ron on these excursions. As a family, they were very committed to this work. Becky did not work out of the home but spent her time taking care of foster children. At home, she often prepared meals for religious meetings and in-home prayer and Bible-study groups.

During my time interacting with this family, they moved three times. Their first home was an apartment that they found to be too crowded. The apartment had only two bedrooms and a small living room. At this time Becky was looking after four children and the space, even with few toys, was jammed. From the apartment, they moved into a trailer. The trailer was in need of repair, but it proved to be a larger space for the children. They had a large area for eating and a large living space. There was also a yard around the trailer, although it was dirt and the children could not play outside unless the dirt was dry. Becky and Ron recarpeted the floors and painted the inside so that it was an attractive place to live. After 1 year in this location, the family moved out of state to another trailer home. Ron was able to find work in this location and the family was closer to his parents who could provide support. This trailer also was in need of work, so again they painted and carpeted. This home was located in a part of the country known for extreme heat, 110 to 115 degrees in the summer, and there was no air conditioning available. However, although I found the inside of the trailer uncomfortable, the family never complained to me.

It always appeared that Becky handled these moves easily. I was invited to visit within a week after the move, and even after being in a new place for such a short time, and with several young children demanding attention, the place seemed as though they had lived there for a long time. Becky had a knack of making her new home feel comfortable right from the beginning. Although many families might be anxious about such moves, I never felt that this was the case with Becky's family. They always seemed calm. The only exception to this calm was when Demetri left their home. This event did cause the family pain, which was evident when they talked about it through tears.

The importance of religion was evident within this home. The cross-stitch work and a Bible were always visible. I never visited when the radio was not playing a religious show, usually a show with music and speaking. The importance of literacy paralleled this focus on religion. Becky and Ron had stacks of books and bookcases full of books in each room. Among these books were adult books, children's books, magazines, the Bible, and an encyclopedia. During most of my time visiting this family, there was no television in the home. Becky and Ron felt that children should not waste their time watching television and wanted their children to be involved with reading and playing, activities that they felt were important. Later, they did purchase a television during the time of the Gulf War because they wanted to know what was happening. The television was never in the living room; however; it was in the parents' bedroom. In the year that I visited when they had the television, it was never on and the children never talked about watching it.

During the 4 years that I visited this family, Becky always sat on a chair and either took care of a baby or did needlework while I was there. As I worked with the children, she often engaged in conversation about them. As she watched Sean draw or balk at drawing, she told me that "he likes to do things well before he will do them. He did not babble much as a baby. When he started to talk it was clear speech." Although it was obvious to me that Sean did not want to do things he did not do well, I had a hard time figuring out how he learned to talk, for example, without babbling. Becky did not really have an answer to my queries about such things as "Does he practice on his own? Did you hear him talking when you were not in the room?" She said that "if he did, I didn't know about it." As our visits continued, she summarized her thoughts about Sean as a person. "He is an easy child. He is quiet and serious. He is stubborn. He wants things his own way." From this description, it was clear that Sean was a complex person even at age 2. As I came to know him, I often saw an easygoing child who was pleased with the process of reading, a serious child who asked important questions based on his reading, and a stubborn child who refused to do anything he was not comfortable with. Many times, I saw all of these facets of Sean in a single visit.

Sean's Literacy at Age 2

> Wonder what May would think of us, sitting on the sofa...passing back and forth covers from paperback books, the front panels of cereal boxes (those with the faces), and *Life* magazine cut to shreds. (Rylant, 1992, p. 18)

The first time that I met Sean, I knew he loved books. Even when he was 1 year old, he listened to me read for a full hour. When I entered the house, he looked through my books, and then one at a time, he brought them to me, sat in my lap, and listened as I read. This love of books was confirmed by Becky. She said, "He loves books and he will listen to a long story." She also told me that each night as part of the bedtime ritual, Sean would be read a story. After this, the lights were turned off and it was expected that he would go to sleep. Becky often checked on the children to see if they were sleeping. On many nights, she found Sean with the lights back on looking at a book. She would take the book, turn the lights off, and hope that he would go to sleep. On some nights this did happen. On others she might go back three times and still find the lights on and Sean reading. She suspected that he had books hidden throughout his bedroom so that he could read late into the night.

Although I brought many books on each visit, I always brought back the books that we had explored on previous occasions. During the first year I knew him, Sean fell in love with *The Napping House* (Wood, 1984). On our first reading, Sean gasped with delight at the first sight of the pictures on each page. When we finished it, he immediately turned to the beginning and wanted it read again. Sean asked me to read it four more times during this visit. During one reading, he focused on the grandma. During the next reading, he centered on when it was raining and when it was not. During the third reading, he noticed the flea and tried to find it on each page. Then on the fourth time through, he just looked at the illustrations as I read.

Sean also enjoyed *Brown Bear, Brown Bear, What Do You See?* (Martin, 1967), *Hattie and the Fox* (Fox, 1986), and *Chicka Chicka Boom Boom* (Martin & Archaumbault, 1989), among other books during this year. However, we usually spent most of our time with *The Napping House*, and Sean's love for this book persisted even when I was not there. He had his grandmother take him to the library to check it out. Becky said that he either read it or had someone read it to him at least 7 to 8 times a day for 2 weeks. She loved listening to him reading the book to himself. She said that it "sounded as if he were really reading." Throughout the year, he would often hide my copy of this book just before I was leaving. In the process of cleaning up, it would be placed under a cushion on the sofa or behind a chair. When we found it, he often cried about my taking it. I had to promise to bring it back. And when I returned, he looked for this book first.

As the year progressed, Sean stopped being just a listener as I read. He often asked questions like "What's that?" or "What is happening here?" He also began to show an interest in alphabet books. When reading *Chicka Chicka Boom Boom*, he became excited on the *s* page. "That's mine," he said. He knew that his name began with this letter. Although he had an understanding of the first letter in his name, he was not able to represent his name conventionally. This was not surprising as he was only 2 years old.

On most of my visits, Sean refused to draw. Sometimes he scribbled but this was not an activity that he entered into joyfully. He often shoved the paper and pencils or crayons under a table as if putting them where they were not visible would end my requests for him to draw. However, at the end of our year together he decided that it would be alright to draw. He drew a self-portrait only after I made a smiley face (see Figure 3). His drawing was an imitation of mine. After he did this drawing, I asked him to sign it; the tight scribble at the bottom is his name. After he wrote this he said, "That's my name." He knew the relation between this scribble and his name. This drawing also demonstrated that he knew the difference between drawing and writing, a difference not distinguished by most children until they are 3 years old (Harste, Woodward, & Burke, 1984).

Figure 3
Sean's Drawing and Signature

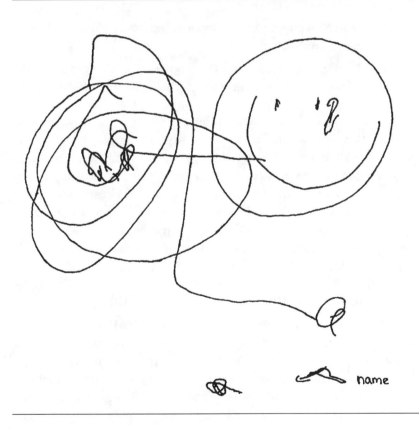

Understandings of Sean's Literacy at Age 2

Based on our interactions throughout this year, Sean knew

- the difference between drawing and writing;
- that the letter at the beginning of his name was an *s* (he also recognized the letter *s* in text);
- that books have fronts and backs;
- how to turn pages from front to back, one page at a time;
- that pages have tops and bottoms;
- that a book has a beginning and an end;
- that when retelling a story, it is continued from page to page;
- how to use storytelling language and book language when retelling a story (he used the exact words from books when he had memorized a text);
- that marks on paper represent words (he used tight scribbling to represent words); and
- that books were pleasurable (he enjoyed interacting with books for at least an hour and on many occasions longer than this).

It is evident looking at Sean's literacy strengths at age 2 that the issue of his crack/cocaine exposure really did not play a part in his literacy development. Although this exposure initially allowed me to include Sean in the study it never was in the forefront of my attention. The only time I thought about it was in thinking about what a contrast Sean was to the children who had been described as being typical of prenatally exposed children. If it had been possible, it would have been a great pleasure to take a video of Sean and send it to a television station to show the promise of children like him.

Formal Testing While Sean Was 2 Years Old

Becky brought all of the children she cared for to a special clinic for assessment and she had formal testing done with Sean before and during this year. She wanted to know everything about the children she watched. If they needed a special program to facilitate their development, she made sure that they participated in one. Her commitment often resulted in very hectic days. For example, Demetri needed physical therapy for his cerebral palsy and Becky had to take him to this therapy at least two times each week. This meant that all the children had to be packed up to go to his therapy sessions. However, unlike other parents who were part of my study, Becky had a car, so she was not further inconvenienced by having to take the children on a bus ride to these sessions.

Sean was tested on the Bayley Assessment Test at 6 months and at 15 months. He tested in the normal range on both of these assessments. When he turned 2, Becky had a thorough psychological and physical assessment completed. The results indicated that "he was developmentally ahead on all measures. He scored off the charts on the language assessment." When Becky showed me the test results, she had a large smile on her face. She knew that he was a bright boy and now she had proof.

Sean's Literacy at Age 3

Sean and his brothers were living in a new trailer now and each time I visited, Sean was waving through the window. Becky said that he waited at the window all morning until I arrived. On my first visit to this new home, he was worried that I would not be able to find him in the new location. His smile as I arrived let me know that he was happy that I did find him.

He opened the door and immediately looked through the books that I brought. He was pleased to see *The Napping House*. Before we settled into our reading and drawing routine, Sean told me about Demetri. He moved to a new home during the last week and Sean was upset about it. Becky said that Sean was very close to her this week and very prone to tears. She was worried that he was afraid that he may have to go to another home too. She kept telling him that he would stay with her but she did not think that he really believed her. She said that the whole situation was awful. She had talked to Demetri's new mother and they were planning to meet in the park. She thought that it would help both boys if they could see each other occasionally. Becky also was anticipating a new child coming into her home and she thought that this would help fill this emptiness. The new child arrived at the end of September. Courtney was an infant and the house took on a different feeling when she arrived. Sean loved showing her off and she enjoyed the attention. She became the third child that this family tried to adopt.

The other big news for this family during this year was that Sean was formally adopted in January. Sean and his family had a big party to celebrate this event. On each occasion after this event, he always told me his new last name and that Becky and Ron were his mom and dad.

Sean continued to love books and was always eager to read. However, during this year, for the first time, Sean refused to read to me. Occasionally, he joined in with text as I read, but he would not retell a story. He said no to my requests and was firm in his response. His behavior reminded me of the Cluster B children described by Bussis, Chittenden, Amarel, and Klausner (1985). In Bussis et al., children are described as having preferences when they are beginning readers: Cluster A children maintain momentum when they read and will guess at words to keep going; Cluster B children are concerned with accuracy and often will stop and wait for assistance before moving forward because they want each word to be read accurately. "It never seemed to occur to these children that they could omit anything in their early reading attempts" (p. 185). Sean's attempts at reading and writing were similar to the style of Cluster B children. Becky said that "he wants things his way." It seems that "his way" was an accurate way. Even at age 3, he knew that the words on the page supported the meaning in a story and he wanted the words read accurately. When he did not remember all the words, he refused to retell a story. This same pattern was evident when he drew or wrote. He wanted his pictures and words to be accurate renditions. When this was not possible he refused or avoided the tasks of writing or drawing. Sean's expectations for accuracy resulted in frustration when he drew or read and the picture or text was not as he expected.

Sean's interests in books expanded during this year. He loved nonfiction. On one serendipitous occasion, I brought *The Very Hungry Caterpillar* (Carle, 1981). He had found a caterpillar in his yard the previous day. We spent our whole hour looking at the caterpillar and reading the book. Whenever he did not understand a word such as *larvae*, he asked me to explain it. He wanted to know all the facts about caterpillars and he wanted them to be accurate. To support this interest, Becky had enrolled Sean in a book club that included books about science. Sean showed me the club's brochure on several visits. We looked through each picture and he would tell me what the book was about and why he wanted it. When the books started coming, we spent much of our time together investigating them. The first books were about bugs and the planets. We looked at each page in great detail and he often requested that I read and reread certain parts. Becky said that he spent hours with the books. Later in the year, she signed him up for another book club. In this club, he received all the books written by Beatrix Potter.

In addition to Sean's insistence on having each illustration described in detail, he was considering stories on an inferential level. On several occasions, I shared the book *Fizz and Splutter* (Melser, 1982). I chose this book because I felt that it would let me know when a child began to recognize letters and when he or she understood that the pictures on a page began with a certain letter. In the book, a wizard would shake a magic wand and things would appear that began with a letter, for example *book* and *bee* for the letter *b*.

Sean was more interested in the story than in the letters. He asked, "What is that man doing?" When a man was shown with fireworks, Sean said, "He should be arrested for making a fire." Then he talked about how "the man might burn his eyes and nose." He showed a similar response when I was reading *Mary Had a Little Lamb* (Hale, 1990). He started by asking where Mary was going. Then he wanted to know "why isn't Mary on the page when you said her name?" Then following this thinking, pertaining to illustrations not matching text, he wanted to know why the teacher was not on the page that mentioned him. After this, he wanted to know why the lamb was crying. He was no longer happy just listening to a story or nonfiction being read, he wanted to understand it. He also demanded an explanation as to why text did not match its corresponding illustration.

Sean developed an interest in letters throughout the year. He built on his knowledge of *s*, and added other letters to his list such as *c* and *r*. He had developed a sophisticated level of metalinguistic awareness as shown by his ability to identify letters and words by their abstract labels. He also enjoyed spelling his name. He did this orally with ease, although he could not write it yet. Figure 4 on page 64 shows his interest in letters and words. In this figure, his imitation of my *s* is shown along with his writing of the names of all the people in his family.

Figure 4
Sean's Writing of the Names of His Family

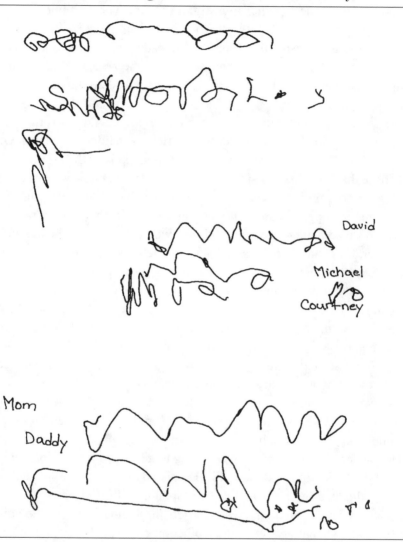

Sean also recognized that there are words on a page in a book. He questioned me about why there were no words in many of the books I shared. Although he did not overtly express these thoughts, he seemed puzzled about how a book could be a book if it did not have words.

As Becky observed, "Sean memorized all the books that he owned during the year." He even memorized the books that I brought each month. Once he seemed confident in his ability to remember text, he again attempted to read to me. In June, after Sean complained that "we hadn't read this book in a month," he read *The Napping House* for the first time. This book is structured around a cumulative tale. Creatures keep coming to sleep in grandmother's bed. When the flea arrives, all the animals and the grandmother wake up. His reading went as follows:

The Napping House
Everyone is sleeping in the house.
Uh, oh, the flea
The rainbow
Everyone is asleep. The fence is open so the dog can get out.
Everyone is asleep. The flea is not asleep.
He [the boy] got out of the chair and went to the top of the granny.
He is sleeping on top. She likes it. The dog is next.
The kitty wakes up.
The cat is in the bed.
The mouse wakes up. The flea is on the mouse.
The kitty cat wakes up. There is light in the bedroom. Everyone is waking up. The kitty cat is up.
She is not awake yet.
Now she is awake.
Now she breaks the bed.
She's playing.
They came outside. She should keep that door shut so the dog can't get out.

Sean's reading of this book showed great risk. He did not repeat the exact words of the book, and his reading sounded very much like a summary of the book. He also let us know about the background of many illustrations when he read about the rainbow and light coming into the bedroom. Finally, he shared his own opinion of what was happening by saying that "she should keep the door shut so the dog can't get out." This reading was unusual for Sean. The only other reading that he did throughout this year were exact renditions of text that he had memorized.

Understandings of Sean's Literacy at Age 3

Sean's literacy learning had expanded to include the following strengths:

- He was able to represent himself in a self portrait that was more than a scribble;
- He could spell his name, although he could not write it yet;
- He fully understood the organization of a book. He knew where the words were in a book and he could point out some individual words such as *caterpillar*;
- He only used book language when he read or retold a book. He preferred to read only those books he had memorized;
- He used scribbles to represent the words he was writing;
- He understood the metalinguistic labels of *letter* and *word*;
- He enjoyed nonfiction material; and
- He extended his enjoyment of reading through membership in two book clubs.

As might have been predicted from Sean's literacy development when he was 2, he continued with his precocious development. Sean truly understood the construction of a book and the meaning of the words *letter* and *word*. This knowledge is sophisticated and is not seen often in children before kindergarten (Clay, 1991). However, Sean continued with his safe pattern. He preferred to read when he had words memorized and he continued to balk at drawing and writing.

Finally, when looking at Sean's literacy development, it was clear that he was moving beyond the classification of emergent reader and writer. Typically, emergent readers and writers are described as not being able to memorize a short poem, focusing mainly on illustrations when engaged in reading, and often losing their place when tracking print. Sean was able to do the first of these three tasks easily, and he had begun to be able to track print in books where there was only one sentence on a page. Children who are considered emergent readers and writers also mix scribbles, letters, and numerals when writing. They do not yet understand the correspondence among letters and their sounds, but can recognize environmental print when it is in its context. Sean was more easily classified as emergent when considering these descriptors, which fit well with his literacy understandings in this area (Bear & Barone, 1998). Considering the whole of Sean's literacy understandings indicates that he was on the cusp of becoming a beginning reader and writer who would be able to read text on his own and understand the correspondences among letters and their sounds.

Sean's Literacy at Age 4

I began to see Sean in another new home when he was 4. His family moved to a neighboring state for Ron's work. The trip to Sean's house took at least an hour, and during this year I alternated between visiting Sean at home and Sean visiting me at the university. Becky had need to come into the city at least once a month and we tried to coordinate these trips with my visits with Sean. When Sean came to the university, Becky ran errands during our time together. As a result most of our visits were longer than an hour. My visits to Sean's home also extended beyond the hour length. I usually arrived in the late morning and I would stay and have lunch with the family before I left.

His new home also was a trailer, which was larger than the previous one. Sean and his sister, Courtney, now had a playroom. In this room, there were toys, books, and a chalkboard. Becky had decided that she would homeschool her children and she was expecting that this room would become their classroom. Her decision to homeschool was not achieved easily. She was worried about the possible negative influences on her children of having them enrolled in public school, with a concern about behavior in particular. She did not want her children coming home and being disrespectful. Her other concern was that Sean was so far ahead in his literacy knowledge and she did not want him to be bored or limited in what might be expected of him in school. As a result, during this year, Becky started to investigate what would be required by the state for her to homeschool her children.

This was a quiet year for this family as far as their responsibilities for taking care of foster children. Because they had moved to a new state, they had to go through the process of becoming qualified to care for children all over again. This process was lengthy, and during the majority of this year, Sean and Courtney were the only children in the home.

Sean continued with his literacy interests during this year. He continued to enjoy nonfiction and his questions about text expanded. On one occasion, we explored *The Grouchy Ladybug* (Carle, 1971). He spent extended periods of time scrutinizing each illustration. He disagreed with the ladybug and he thought that the creatures were big enough to fight. When he visited me at the university, we always met in the young children's room of the literacy clinic. This room was full of Big Books and small books for children. There were many non-fiction Big Books and many predictable stories for beginning readers. When Sean first came to this room, he selected the Big Books that were written about dinosaurs and the weather. He knew a lot about dinosaurs and said that he had seen a video about them at his grandmother's home. As we looked through this book, he compared one dinosaur to the giant Goliath. He said that "they were both big and fierce." When reading these books, Sean spent a lot of time on each page. He read the text and then we engaged in discussion about it and the illustrations. For example, when reading a book about bugs, we spent about a half hour on a page with a cockroach. He wanted to know the name, then he wanted to know what it might eat. When I said that maybe it eats little bugs, he commented that he wasn't "sure about that but birds eat little bugs." Although Sean occasionally chose fictional stories for me to read, these were only selected after we had spent most of our time exploring nonfiction books.

Sean's knowledge of letters and their sounds grew during this year. He was able to recognize all the letters of the alphabet. He knew the beginning letters and sounds for the names of all the people in his family. During this year, Becky created a chart with all the alphabet letters on it. She practiced saying the letters and their corresponding sounds with Sean. He was also willing to write the letters in his name. In Figure 5, Sean wrote his name and drew the members of his family. Although the letters are not written from left to right, it was clear that he made an *s*, then he skipped a space and made an *e*, then the *a*, and finally he went back and made an *n* after his *s*. The pictures represent the four people in Sean's family. The father is the biggest, and then the mother. Sean and Courtney are the smallest. His people are a variation of the traditional tadpole people seen in the drawings of young children.

Sean's knowledge of the alphabet was shown in his writing. During this year, he moved from using tight scribbles to using letters. At first the letters were random, but as the year progressed he started to represent initial consonants that matched the correct initial sound in a word. In Figure 6 on page 70, Sean dictated the letters that he

Figure 5
Sean's Signature and Family Drawing

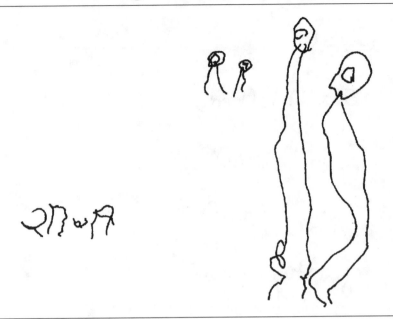

thought spelled the words that I asked him to write for me. He was unwilling to write so I took dictation of his oral spellings. This sample
shows his new knowledge of using letters to spell words; it does not
demonstrate his ability to match sound and symbol.

During this year, as a result of his visits to the university, Sean
learned about reading books and composing on a computer because
during all of Sean's visits we spent time reading CD-ROM versions of
stories. It took only a few minutes for Sean to figure out how to move
the mouse and get various parts of an illustration to become animat-
ed and talk. He also learned that if he clicked on a word, the word
was read by the computer. As he gained experience with the computer, I asked him to find specific words. At first, he randomly clicked
on words until the word I requested was read. As the year progressed,
he abandoned his guessing strategy and started to use a strategy where
he remembered where the word was in text. If it was in the beginning, he scanned the words at the beginning of a page until he found

Figure 6
Sean's Dictated Spelling Words

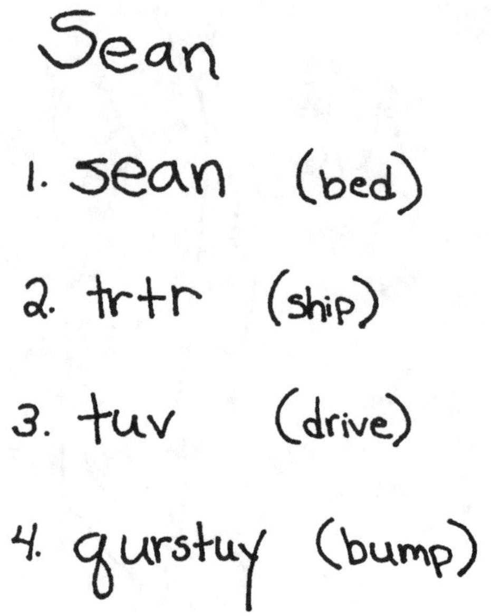

Sean

1. sean   (bed)

2. trtr   (ship)

3. tuv   (drive)

4. qurstuy (bump)

the word I requested. If it was at the end of text, he moved to the end and used his scanning strategy. This strategy demonstrated that he was beginning to understand what a word is in text. When he was 3 years old, he recognized that there were words in books; now he was able to identify individual words when requested. He was also able to track text in books where there were only one or two sentences on a page.

Sean also enjoyed the writing program on the computer. He liked to select a graphic and then tell about it. As he dictated, I wrote the text on the screen. We then read the text together and then he read it alone. I was using a language-experience strategy here. When Sean was pleased with the text and illustration, I printed copies for both of us. When Becky came back, he would show her his story and read it to her. Figure 7 is one of Sean's stories about fish. His nonfiction interest showed up in his writing; he liked to write factual information about the clip art he chose.

Figure 7
Sean's Computer-Generated Story

Sean
    The fish is in the water. He is jumping out of the water.

Understandings of Sean's Literacy at Age 4

During this year, Sean built on his previous literacy knowledge and had new understandings that included the following:

- recognition of the letters of the alphabet;
- the ability to write some letters;
- using letters for writing, rather than scribbles;
- the ability to use some initial consonants correctly;
- recognition of words in print and the ability to identify specific words;
- a continued interest in nonfiction;
- the ability to make intertextual connections among characters in one book with those in another (for example, Goliath with a dinosaur); and
- the ability to compose stories with the help of dictation.

Sean's development throughout this year placed him more as a beginning reader than as an emergent reader. He knew the alphabet, started to recognize the relations among letters and their sounds, and could track print and identify individual words. However, he still needed predictable text and he relied on memory for reading. He was not yet able to read material independently. Although his ability to decode text independently had not developed yet, his comprehensive knowledge was extensive. He expected that a reader would help him understand new vocabulary. He did not simply recall, but interpreted text. This was seen clearly when he disagreed with the story of the grouchy ladybug. He also was making intertextual connections. He compared Goliath to a giant and he said that a rabbit in one story was similar to Peter Rabbit from his Beatrix Potter collection.

Final Thoughts

> Ob was gentle with him and with me. He would lean with Cletus over a glass case in the museum...as they read the words off an old yellowed newspaper. (Rylant, 1992, p. 81)

Being a part of Sean's life for 4 years allowed for a view of the literacy learning of a child who was precocious with his understandings. Understanding Sean as an individual literacy learner destroyed the myths about children prenatally exposed to crack/cocaine. Sean was never distracted; he was always focused on our interactions. He tuned out the behaviors of numerous foster brothers and sisters as we worked together. He also tuned out the words and music from the radio that was always playing. He tested in the above-average range on all psychological and physical tests, something that many people feel is not possible for children with his prenatal history. And he became a beginning reader and writer before age 5 and before formal schooling.

In addition, Sean provides a detailed portrait of a child who experienced high poverty, destroying the myths often centered on the home literacy experiences of such children. Sean's literacy demonstrated what often has been observed in research literature, that children from poor backgrounds are supported in literacy learning at home (Anderson & Stokes, 1984; Pelligrini, Perlmutter, Galda, & Brophy, 1990; Purcell-Gates, 1996; Taylor & Dorsey-Gaines, 1988; Urzua, 1986). Although Sean's parents had limited financial resources, they read with him on a daily basis and they diverted funds from other needs to purchase books for him. Unlike the stories of poor children who come to school experiencing book reading episodes infrequently, Sean has had many such experiences. In fact, he had understandings beyond stories that included nonfiction text.

As Sean's parents considered his academic future, they were willing to spend the time necessary to educate Sean at home. Although there are both strengths and problems associated with such schooling, this dedication demonstrated their commitment to their children's education. To support this at-home learning, Becky and Ron were saving for a computer so that Sean could continue his experiences with reading and writing. They were also checking into advertised programs to help Sean develop a stronger sense of sound-symbol relations. They planned on buying a phonics-based program to enrich his knowledge of letters and his ability to decode words.

Although I began my study with Sean because of his prenatal history, he has allowed for an exploration of the literacy development of a child who found reading an easy task. He demonstrated what it means to be safe, in that he was unwilling to take risks with reading, writing, and drawing. Although he had acquired much knowledge about literacy, he was reluctant to share it until it was perfect. His safe style most likely limited what I came to know about his literacy. Realistically, he knew more about reading and writing than he was willing to share. After all, it had to be correct before he let his parents or an outsider become aware of what he knew. In a letter that Becky wrote to me after our visits ended, she said that "he is a perfectionist like me." Although we will not be privy to Sean's future development, it would be interesting to see how Sean reconciles his exceptional ability and his perfectionist needs.

CHAPTER 5

Billy: A Child for Whom Instruction Often Was Not Supportive of Literacy Learning

I'm sitting on my front steps
watching the world go by.
(Greenfield, E. [1988]. *Nathaniel Talking* [unpaged]. New York: Black
Butterfly Children's Books.)

This brief piece of a poem called "Watching the World Go By" reminded me of Billy. Billy was a child who always appeared older than his years. He was for the most part always well behaved and polite. He carried himself tall and straight. And even when he was in preschool, he seemed out of place because of his more mature appearance. It was not that he did not interact with other children or that he could not play roughly. It was the way he approached all school tasks seriously. It was clear that even when Billy was very young, school and doing well in school were important to him and to his family. His demeanor and dedication to doing well in school led me to consider this poem when thinking about him and how he appeared to be pondering his future even when he was 3 years old. Figure 8 shows Billy's self-portrait.

Getting to know Billy

Grandma grew up
in the nineteen-forties
she can still do the jitterbug.
(Greenfield, 1988)

Figure 8
Billy's Self-Portrait

Billy and his younger sister, Becky, were both members of the study. Billy fit the identified target group in that he was 3 years old at the beginning of the study. Additionally, he was African American and lived in a high-poverty area. Billy's grandparents were the foster parents for Billy and Becky, but their mother lived next door and there was hope that one day she would take over the responsibility for the children. During the period of the study, the children moved into their mother's house and then sadly, because their mother neglected them, they returned to their grandparents' home. However, Billy's grandmother, Lucille, was always hopeful that her daughter would one day be able to care for her children.

Although Billy's home was in a high-poverty area, it was located in a stable part of the community. There were several streets of homes that had been owned by families for many years. These homes were well kept and the community was proud of their efforts to maintain them. They were all freshly painted and had landscaping in the front yards. Even though the homes were quite nice, the larger neighborhood could be dangerous, and as a result, the children never played outside. There were never any toys outside to indicate that children lived in the home. The children had a small area in a family room and space in their bedroom for play.

The neighbors surrounding Lucille's home looked after one another and they extended this watchfulness to me. Whenever I visited, there were always two large men who stood outside the house. On my second visit, I was a bit scared by having them observe me. I was not very familiar with the neighborhood yet, and I was not sure if the situation was dangerous. By my third visit, when they again appeared, I realized that I was being protected. These men showed up on each of my visits over 4 years and served as protectors. They knew that others in the neighborhood would see me as a stranger and they determined that it was their role to protect me. They stood guard from when I arrived until I departed.

This family's community extended beyond the immediate neighborhood. They were very involved with a local church nearby. Lucille went to church services almost every day. She volunteered to lead many programs in the church, including a fashion show, and she was in the choir. The church had a day-care center attached and she sent her grandchildren to these programs each day. She wanted her grandchildren to benefit from the academic instruction and the religious instruction provided in this school. Although more will be said about these settings, they were grounded in African American beliefs. The teachers, staff, and all children were African American and a goal was to help these children build and extend their knowledge of their cultural histories.

During my first visit, Lucille filled in the details of Billy's early life experiences. He was born at home 2 months early and then taken to the hospital. Throughout her pregnancy, Billy's mother never received prenatal care. (As mentioned earlier, this situation is not unusual for expectant mothers who are using drugs. They are worried that the doctor will turn them in to the authorities for child neglect so they avoid medical treatment unless it is an emergency.) After his birth, Billy stayed in the hospital for 1 month and then came home to his grandparents.

In describing Billy, his grandmother first talked about his severe asthma. Billy often found himself in the hospital because of it. She said that when it was windy, she could predict that they would have to go to the hospital, which occurred about every other month. She then talked about his sleeping routines. It seemed that he was always the last one in the house to go to sleep and the first one up in the morning. He often was found walking around the house at night, which worried her. Continuing her description, Lucille said that

> Billy learns things fast. Will talk, talk, talk, when he wants to say something. He rebels in his own way. He plays well, sometimes in a world by himself, not paying attention to anyone around. Can't give him enough attention. His feelings are hurt easily.

When she talked about his early literacy experiences, it was obvious that she had spent a lot of time interacting with him. One of the questions that I asked each parent was whether a child had a favorite book. Lucille laughed at this one and said, "We have too many books for him to have a favorite." She then elaborated on his literacy knowledge. He could recite the alphabet and he recognized almost all the letters. She indicated that "He loves to have books read to him—at least two a week." She also complained that he watched "too much television." She estimated that he watched about an hour a day.

On most of my visits, Lucille cooked as I worked with the children. She often talked about events at the church in which the children participated. She loved getting them dressed for the big fashion show, for example. Billy wore a tuxedo for that event. The children participated in every event that was sponsored by the church and included children. Sometimes these were huge church socials like the fashion show; and other times, they simply participated in church services. Involvement with church was an integral part of this family's life.

Tied to these religious beliefs was an expectation that the children would do their best in school. When the children were in preschool, this expectation was shared in the home, in school, and in the church. Children were recognized in these different contexts for their work in school. For example, during church services the pastor mentioned children who had done well in school. While Billy was a preschooler there were close connections among home, school, and church. These connections were stretched and in some cases torn as Billy moved into and through his public school experiences.

Billy's Literacy at Age 3

Billy in Preschool

I see my future
clear as I don't know what
not all the things around me
not furniture or houses
or sidewalks and stuff
I just see me.
(Greenfield, 1988)

Billy had been enrolled in the church preschool since he was 2 years old. There were separate classes for children based on age. There were separate classes for 2-year-olds and 3-year-olds, and 4- and 5-year-olds were combined into one room. Many parents of 5-year-olds enrolled their children in the neighborhood public school for kindergarten, rather than keeping them in the preschool where they had to pay tuition. Other than the differences in age, there were few differences among the classrooms. The curriculum in all the rooms was similar, as were the physical characteristics.

The rooms in the school were very small, especially because there could be up to 30 children in a single class. Each room had a teacher's desk, a cabinet for supplies, and two or three tables for children. There was no additional space in the room. In a few rooms, there was a chalkboard, but most teachers used a portable chalkboard that was moved from the hall to the classroom only when it was needed. There were no books, paper, pencils, puzzles, or crayons freely available to children. Teachers provided these materials to children only if they were a part of a lesson. On the walls in each room were the alphabet, the numbers from 1 to 10, and the shapes, colors, days of the week, and months of the year. These displays were the primary curriculum in each classroom.

Although there were slight differences in how individual teachers organized their days, there was a general consistency among the classrooms. The day started with a video. Then the children said the Pledge of Allegiance and a prayer. Following this, the children chanted the wall curriculum. They said the shapes, colors, and the alphabet. Following this whole-class chanting, each child had a chance to do the same chanting. All children sat quietly while one individual had a chance to display his or her knowledge. This routine generally took an hour to an hour and a half to complete. Children were expected to remain seated throughout the chanting. The only time they could move was when they were called to point to a letter, number, or shape on the wall. Following this routine, the children generally worked on a worksheet centered on number or alphabet knowledge. Then they had recess on the playground outside. If it rained, the children had recess in the classroom. They had to remain in their chairs and some toys were brought to the tables for play. The curriculum following recess varied with the teacher. Often they practiced for a program. If they were not practicing, they usually engaged in a memorization activity. These activities were grounded in having the children able to recall the exact words of a poem, prayer, or song. Then they had lunch and a nap. Following their nap at 2:00 in the afternoon, they were dismissed.

For the most part the teachers were volunteers from the church. There was a director who provided some suggestions for the curriculum for the teachers. The teachers had limited understanding of young children's literacy development, had limited supplies, and had to work in crowded spaces. Several of the teachers had not graduated from high school. Although these limitations were troublesome, there were strengths demonstrated in this school. The teachers were familiar with the families and had a commitment to helping these children do well in school. On each occasion that I visited the school, the children were well behaved and focused on the lessons. They always tried to do their best because this was a clear expectation in this school. Parents, the director, the pastor, and volunteer grandparents were always there to help the children learn. Children's learning was seen as a community effort, not just an individual event to be celebrated or criticized. On many occasions, I witnessed the teachers, pastor, director, and parents commenting publicly on a child's achievement.

On my first visit to see Billy at school, I arrived during breakfast time. The children were all in the school cafeteria finishing their cereal. There must have been 150 children sitting in this room. Teachers were walking among the children keeping them under control. Billy was sitting on the right side of this room, crowded on a bench with other children. There was very little space between each child. He had finished eating and was spitting milk in and out of his glass. A teacher quickly reprimanded him for this behavior. Then he talked to a friend next to him. They whispered in each other's ears. As Billy engaged in this behavior, he had his eyes on the teacher. He was aware where she was and the possibility of his being caught and punished for inappropriate behavior. He always sat up tall when she glanced in his direction.

As I observed Billy and the larger room in general, I found that I also was being closely observed. Many of the children were staring at me. There was no way I could truly blend into the background in this school as I was the only Caucasian in it. As the children were dismissed to go to their classrooms, many of them came by me to line up, even though I was not in the path of the developing line. They touched me and smiled. Several asked if I was a teacher here. The teachers had a hard time getting the children to focus because they were much more interested in the stranger in their school. Billy also was watching me closely and I think he was surprised when I followed his class back to the classroom.

As the children entered the room, they quietly found a place to sit. Most of the children went to the same seats each time. I tried to find a corner to sit in, but I found that this was often impossible. Each time I observed in this school, I had to move frequently to allow for students to be able to sit at the tables. Space was limited and everyone was mindful of this.

The children often began the day by watching a video. These videos could last from 20 minutes to an hour. Although Billy never fell asleep during them, other children did. When the video finished, the teacher occasionally engaged the children in discussion about it. Following the video, the teacher began the instruction described earlier. The children were expected to sit up straight in their seats as they chanted the curriculum on the wall, and they did. Billy's voice was often louder than the others as he was familiar with the alphabet, shapes, and numbers. Once the whole-class recitation was complete, individual children were asked to recite the alphabet. Following this process, individual children were called on to point to the letter that started their first name. Billy seemed to enjoy this process and he could identify the initial letters of all the children in the class. When a child was unable to point to the correct letter, Billy often was called on to show the child the letter. Additionally, Billy was able to spell his name by pointing to the alphabet letters on the wall. He pointed to the *b*, then the *i*, and so on until his name was complete.

Once the children chanted everything that was on the wall, they worked on a single worksheet. The teacher passed out the paper and one crayon. Most of the worksheets required coloring and no reading or writing. The children colored in the shape, the letter, or the number. On a few occasions, the children were given puzzles to put together during this time, and twice during the year, I saw the teacher read a story to the children. These stories were religious in nature.

It was clear that Billy was seen as a leader in school. The teacher told me on numerous visits, "Billy is a leader in here." Billy also was told this by his teacher and the rest of his community, and it was clear that he acted this part in the classroom. He was always the loudest in chanting and he was always ready to help another child. However, Billy also was shy and on some occasions, especially when many adults were present, he spoke quietly and tried to move from the forefront of attention.

Billy at Home

Observing Billy at home allowed me to learn more about his literacy knowledge. He knew the difference between drawing and writing. In Figure 9, his self-portrait and signature are distinct, and his signature definitely represents cursive writing. But Billy was not comfortable when I asked him to write because he never had this experience except during my visits. His teachers never asked the children to write, and Lucille provided only coloring books for the children, which were expected to be colored in neatly. They did not have paper and crayons or pencils for experimentation. Billy and Sean (see Chapter 4) exhibited similar behaviors when asked to write and draw but the reasons behind the behaviors differed. Sean would not write or

Figure 9
Billy's Drawing and Name Writing

draw because he expected his representations to be perfect, careful copies of reality. Billy, on the other hand, did not have the opportunity to experience drawing and writing and felt uncomfortable with these tasks. Another difference was that Sean had access to writing materials, and Billy did not.

Billy enjoyed looking at the books that I brought when I visited. He never seemed to prefer any of the books, but would look at them all. Even the books I brought on previous visits received no special attention. He was willing to read the books to me and he did this using storytelling and book language. He memorized some repeated phrases in books, such as "What do you see?" from *Brown Bear, Brown Bear, What Do You See?* (Martin, 1967), but he did not memorize complete texts during this year.

Understandings of Billy's Literacy at Age 3

Billy was certainly within the emergent-literacy category at age 3. He also had knowledge of books and letters, which showed his growing awareness and emergence into the beginning reader and writer category. Billy knew

- that there were differences between drawing and writing;
- how to spell his name;
- that books have beginnings and endings, how pages are turned, and that pages have tops and bottoms;
- how to retell a story using book and storytelling language; and
- the mapping of letters and sounds.

Billy's literacy development is particularly interesting because his school might not be considered as adequately supporting and providing the necessary background for this development. The curriculum was certainly an initiation-response type: The teacher said a letter or numeral and the children responded. There was little engagement with text. Children were expected to be quiet unless they were chanting. There were few paper-pencil activities, and there were no books available to children. However, there were clear expectations that children could and would learn the curriculum. Although the teachers did not see value in books or did see value but did not have any materials, they did expect children to know the alphabet. They also expected children to learn the initial consonant in their name and how this matched the sound and symbol of the letter on the wall. Is this enough for children to develop as readers and writers? This was a question I pursued as I continued to observe Billy in this environment.

Billy's Literacy at Age 4

Billy in Preschool

Billy returned to the same preschool when he was 4 years old. He moved into the class for 4- and 5-year-olds. There were about 30 children in this class, which had several teachers throughout the year. The first teacher left, then there were substitute teachers, and finally a teacher was hired who completed the year with the children. A grandparent helper was the only consistent adult in the class throughout the year. However, even with varied teachers throughout the year, Billy retained his position as the class leader. I was impressed that he was able to maintain this role because there were both 4- and 5-year-olds in this class and he was one of the younger students. At the end of the year, his teacher said that "Billy is the brightest child in the class by far. He knows everything on the wall."

The curriculum was the same as it had been in the previous year. There were higher expectations in this class though, as the children would leave either as 5- or 6-year-olds to enter public school. I often heard the teacher say to the class, "In order to go to kindergarten, you need to know your colors, numbers, alphabet, and shapes." One thing I observed in this school was that there was a consistency among what the teachers felt was important for children to know when going to kindergarten and their school curriculum.

As in the past year, each day began with a video. On several occasions these videos lasted longer than an hour. On one occasion, after seeing a video about the Three Little Pigs, the teacher engaged the children in questions about the story. Billy was one of the few children who had his hand up for each question the teacher asked.

Each child now was expected to spell his or her whole first name by pointing to the letters in the alphabet. The children had practice with this type of name spelling but they had no practice writing their names or letters. I saw writing practice of the initial letter in each child's name on only one occasion, after the teacher saw me ask Billy to write his name for me. Although it was never directly articulated by any of the teachers, it seemed that writing was expected to be "correct." Therefore, the children were not encouraged to experiment with writing, not even with the writing of their name. The poverty of the school was compounded with this belief. There just did not seem to be any money to allow children to have paper for experimentation. The children had only one worksheet to write on each day and they always had something specific that needed to be done on the reverse side. Other than these papers, there was no paper in evidence in the school.

Beyond alphabet knowledge and name-spelling knowledge, the teacher included some simple word study toward the end of the year. For example, she wrote *at* on the board and asked the children to say "at." Then she put a *p* in front and asked them to tell her the new word. Billy said "rat" for this word. Then she put an *f* in front and again asked the children the word. For this one, Billy said "fat." He seemed to understand the word play. Then she changed it to *rat* and again Billy identified it. On the last reworking of this word, she wrote *sat*. Billy guessed "snake" for this word. Here he relied on his knowledge of the initial consonant and abandoned what he had learned about the vowel and what comes after.

Following this word play, children were called to the board and asked to write their names. When Billy was called, he went to the board smiling. He spelled his name orally but was unable to write the letters because he had never had practice doing this. On my next visit to Billy at his home, I asked him to draw a self-portrait and to write his name. Figure 10 on page 86 shows the results of my request. He was able to draw a self-portrait although it is missing a traditional head. The head on his person is off to the side. He then refused to attempt to write his name until I made a *B*. He imitated my *B* but never attempted any of the other letters in his name.

After this attempt, I showed him some letters on a paper. For each, I wrote the letter and asked him to identify it. He had no problem identifying the alphabet letters. I then asked him to write the words *bed* and *ship*. He refused to write but was willing to dictate the letters to me. He spelled bed as *bkn*. He knew the initial consonant but not what came after. For *ship*, he sat and puzzled for awhile. He kept saying "ship" in an attempt to figure out the initial consonant sound. The digraph caused him difficulty during this process. Then he said *d* and *c*. The *c* is a feasible representation for the *sh* digraph as *c* can have an *s* sound as in the word *circus*. After these two words, Billy said that he would spell words that he knew for me. He dictated the spellings for *Dan*, *pan*, and *can*. This sample of writing is shown in Figure 11.

Figure 10
Billy's Self-Portrait and Writing of the Initial
Consonant of His Name

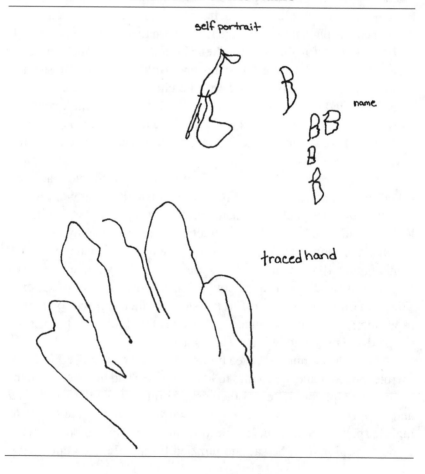

self portrait

name

traced hand

Figure 11
Billy's Letter Recognition and Dictation of Spelling

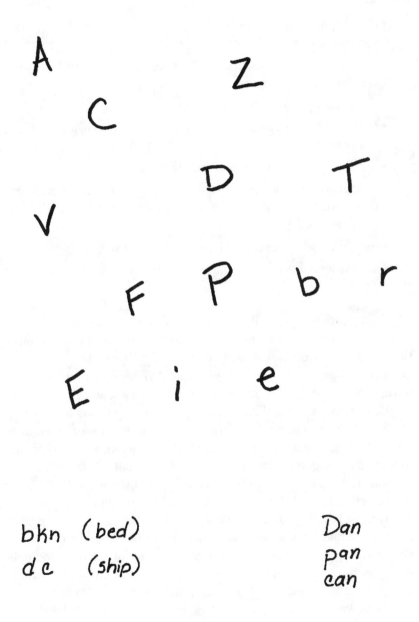

Understandings of Billy's Literacy at Age 4

Billy's knowledge of literacy during this year included the following:

- development in his ability to create a self-portrait. It was no longer a scribble;
- the ability to spell his first and last names. He was able to write the first letter of his first name;
- awareness of a book's organization;
- the ability to point to words in text on pages of text without many words;
- the ability to memorize predictable text;
- a refusal to reread text on several occasions because he knew that words carry the meaning in stories and he was unwilling to guess at words;
- the ability to represent initial consonants in words; and
- an exploration of consonant-vowel-consonant (CVC) word patterns.

At 4 years of age, Billy was a beginning reader. He knew that stories and videos needed to make sense, and he could answer questions about the stories he heard and the videos he watched. He also had knowledge of letters and letter sounds. What was troublesome to me as I observed throughout this year was the lack of writing opportunities. Billy rarely had chances to practice any of his knowledge about letters or to practice writing his own name. I wondered how this lack of experiences would support him in kindergarten. His grandmother had decided to place him in a public-school setting for kindergarten. Although he would be attending a neighborhood school, it would certainly be different from his years in preschool.

During Billy's year as a 4-year-old, there was an uncomfortable experience that affected the family and me. Lucille decided to bring Billy to the public school for assessment. Many of the foster parents were encouraged to get this assessment for the children in their charge, and Lucille called the district and arranged it. When the assessment was completed, the recommendation was that Billy should attend the public school's preschool so that he could have additional work with language. The district felt that his language development was delayed. Lucille responded that he was "most likely shy during the assessment with a stranger and they needed to see him in church to see that his language was just fine." The school district persisted and expected that Lucille would enroll Billy in the preschool program.

At this point I received a call from Lucille. She explained what had happened and that she was worried. She thought that if she did not do what they wanted, they would take Billy from her and place him in another foster home. Yet she wanted to keep Billy in his current preschool until kindergarten. She wanted me to call the school psychologist, which created quite a dilemma for me. I agreed to call the psychologist, listen to the reasons he wanted this placement, and to ask him to consider the other values of the family. As I talked to him, I realized that he did not know how complex the situation was and the implications of his recommendations for this family. After our discussion, he revised his recommendation and suggested that Billy remain in his school for the duration of this year. Then in kindergarten, Billy was placed in a Chapter 1 program for half the school day. This revised decision allowed Lucille to keep Billy where she felt he was best served for preschool and to have him in a full-day program in kindergarten. Additionally, she trusted the school district which supported her needs in this decision.

Billy's Literacy at Age 5

Billy in Kindergarten

Children in Billy's neighborhood typically attended kindergarten in their home neighborhood and then they were bused to other sections of town for first through fifth grades. In sixth grade all the children in the city attended sixth-grade centers in this community. This has been the approved integration plan for the city, a plan that had been implemented in the 1970s. However, during the year before Billy was in kindergarten, the plan was revised. The sixth-grade centers, including the one Billy would attend, were expanded to include all elementary grades. This decision was made so that African American children could go to neighborhood schools. Parents could decide to keep their children in their home neighborhood during elementary school or send them to middle-class schools throughout the city. As a result of this revised decision, Billy's school had been fully renovated. Although the outside of the classrooms showed their age, even with a fresh coat of paint, the inside of each classroom was renovated to modern standards. Billy entered a beautiful, large kindergarten filled with books, puzzles, paper, computers, and toys: A classroom environment very different from what he had experienced in preschool.

Billy attended the traditional kindergarten for this school district in the morning. He had 20 children in his class for 2½ hours each day. Following this session, he went to lunch and recess and then attended a Chapter 1 class for the afternoon. This class usually contained about 15 children, and the kindergarten and Chapter 1 teachers collaborated so their literacy curriculums were similar. The teachers engaged their students with many shared-book experiences. They also used guided reading, usually done in small groups. Each child wrote in a journal daily and there were other bookmaking experiences. The children had skill instruction daily that most often focused on the alphabet and the sounds of the letters. This instruction was extended in the children's use of computers. Most of the programs on the computer focused on sound-symbol relations. In addition, there were many drama and cooking experiences.

Billy's classmates and teacher were all African American. The teacher, Mrs. Campbell, lived in the community and knew many of the children and their families outside of school. This always was evident in the group time that began each day. The children could talk about themselves or share a treasure that they brought from home. Mrs. Campbell often shared her own experiences and she commented on the children she had seen outside of school. They always smiled when they were mentioned. She even had nicknames for each child. Whenever she called a child by his or her nickname, the whole class giggled. What I noticed on every visit was that Mrs. Campbell was able to have fun with her students while also having high expectations for them. She confided that she was worried about this group of children because at least 50% of them had been exposed to drugs. She also said that "they were low functioning and lacked language. They don't know the names of things like turkey and lion." Although Mrs. Campbell was especially worried about this group, she had the support of the parents of these children. Of the 35 parents, 27 participated in the first set of conferences. Even though this was an impressive turnout, she was not pleased. She expected to see all of the parents at the next round of conferences. She knew how important it was to get the parents involved and to help them see how they could help their children at home. Each day, each child took a book home to be read. The parent was expected to sign a note that they had read the book together. Then on the next day in school, the children would talk about the books they shared with their parents.

After I watched this classroom in action, I asked Mrs. Campbell about Billy. She said that "he is doing well and he likes to talk." This was evident in my observations as well. Billy was always ready with an answer and he enjoyed talking to the children next to him. This talk was sanctioned when the children worked together in small groups and was very different from the expectations of quiet in his preschool classrooms.

The routine in the classroom began with the children forming a circle for sharing. After this, the teacher moved into explicit sound-symbol instruction. This session ended with the children sharing a Big Book that had been read on a previous occasion. The children joined in with the reading with the teacher. After this whole-group time, the children moved into centers. One group worked on journals, another group visited computers, a third group worked on an activity (usually an extension from a shared reading), and the last group worked with the teacher. She involved the children with shared reading, guided reading, or a language-experience activity. For example, during Halloween, each child dictated a story to go with a Halloween picture he or she had created. Billy dictated,

> We went in the haunted house. All the monsters were scaring us. We ran out. We went trick-or-treating. We went home. We went on the playground. We went and played in the backyard, and we saw a pumpkin.

After several readings of this dictation with the teacher, Billy was able to read it independently. He always smiled when a visitor asked him to read one of his dictations.

In addition to dictation, Billy and the other children were expected to write about the pictures they drew in response to the stories that were read to them. At the beginning of the year, Billy was reluctant to do this. He was not comfortable drawing, and writing was a painful process for him. However, with encouragement from his teacher and the reality that writing was a daily expectation, he began to more freely participate in these activities.

Billy's teacher realized in October that Billy knew "all the letters of the alphabet and all the sounds." Soon after, she involved him in instruction focused on CVC words. Billy enjoyed this instruction and was able to decode most CVC words by the end of the year.

Understandings of Billy's Literacy at Age 5

At the end of the year, I asked Billy how he had become such a good reader. He said, "I learned to read at school by reading books." Even though Billy had had an enormous amount of skill instruction, he saw the critical event in his learning to read as "reading books." At the end of kindergarten, Billy had learned the following:

- that spoken words and text match. He had developed full concept of word in print;
- to read the words in text independently. He read in a word-by-word fashion;
- to write the letters that he knew and connect sounds to build words; and
- to write words using initial and final consonants and a vowel.

His growth in literacy during his kindergarten year placed Billy in the beginning reader and writer category. Although some children acquire this literacy knowledge in kindergarten, it is seen more typically in first grade. It is also important to remember that Billy was a minority child attending a school that might be designated at-risk because of the backgrounds of the majority of its students. Additionally, Mrs. Campbell was worried about this group of children. She saw them as not as strong as previous classes that she had worked with. Yet even with these conditions, Mrs. Campbell, with the help of parents, was able to have the majority of the children in her class leave with a wealth of literacy knowledge. Although not all the children were at Billy's level, no child left without full knowledge of the alphabet and the sounds of the initial consonants. They also left with many book-reading experiences. Mrs. Campbell read to the class several times each day. In addition, they worked with her daily either with a book or focused on a dictation. These activities and instruction allowed them to leave this class strong in literacy knowledge. This situation is very different from the experiences of other children attending similar schools. She reminded me very much of the teachers described by Ladson-Billings (1994) who were particularly successful teaching African American children.

Billy's Literacy at Age 6

Billy in First Grade

Lucille chose to have Billy stay at his neighborhood school for first grade instead of attending a school in another part of town. On my first visit to see Billy in first grade, he was in a team-taught class. There were 40 children in the class with two teachers. This class was too large to meet the state expectations of class-size reduction in the primary grades. Ideally, there would be about 16 children to each teacher in the first grade. Therefore, the teachers were creating lists of children who would move to a new first grade when a teacher was hired. Billy was on this list but he spent the first 3 weeks of school in this classroom.

The teachers used a similar curriculum as Billy had experienced in kindergarten. The movement among centers and the expectations at centers were also similar. Billy and the other children seemed to be comfortable in the new first-grade setting. Although they were comfortable, they were also very crowded. On this day, they were preparing for a "Stone Soup" party, which was planned after the children had heard the story *Stone Soup* (Brown, 1947). They were discussing a visit to a grocery store to get the ingredients for their soup. All of the parents were invited on the day that the soup was made. The children and teachers were very excited about this event.

When I again visited in October, Billy was in his new classroom. The best word for this class was chaos. The 15 children all sat in desks that were isolated from one another. The teacher and her husband were in the room. The teacher was having trouble with discipline and she called in her husband for help. The best way to share the seriousness of her management problem is to share directly from my field notes from that day:

> The teacher screams red light and then she wants the kids to be quiet. Billy is chewing gum and talking back to the teacher as are the other

kids. Five children left their seats. Three are in the back of the room, one is on a bookcase, and one is getting his backpack and saying that he is leaving. Billy pushes his desk over. Nothing happens. The teacher finally says that that was a good thing to do as the class is now paying attention. Her husband keeps on putting check marks next to children's names, written on the board. None of the children pay attention. One child goes up and erases some of the checks. Teacher says that one child is running out of points to lose. At this point, a child leaves the room. No one follows him. The kids are kicking chairs, sharpening pencils, and the teacher tries to start a lesson focused on the calendar. She yells, "No recess." A child gets up and hits another with a pencil. Nothing happens. Teacher says, "I have been trying to be nice, now I am going to get angry." One child stands on her head. Another child pokes a child with a staple. Two kids are fighting. Children are dismissed for recess.

I was stunned. I could not believe what was happening. I could not comprehend that a first grader could walk out of school and no one paid attention. I could not believe how quickly these children whom I had observed for 1 year could become out of control. While making a futile attempt at control, the teacher tried to have the children do routine calendar activities. I was shocked to see her have the children name the months and days, and then proceed to name the letters of the alphabet. I felt that I was back in Billy's preschool with the wall curriculum. This bulletin board was the only one completed in the room. The rest of the room contained desks and chairs, but no books, paper, pencils, or crayons. After the calendar and chanting, the children were given a paper with their names on it. They were to practice writing their names. When this was done, they were given a picture of a pumpkin to color. In addition to the name writing and coloring, they were to practice their spelling words which were all part of the *ad* family (*bad, dad, lad, mad, pad,* and *sad*). I stayed in the room for an hour, and it seemed like a lifetime. I left wondering how I could ever visit again.

Lucille evidently had visited this classroom too, for she called me at the end of October to tell me that she had enrolled Billy at another neighborhood school. She did not expand on her reasons for this move, but it was clear in her tone that she was not pleased with Billy's new teacher. This school was a new school built in the area. This time, Billy was placed in a combined first- and second-grade class. Unlike Billy's previous first-grade teachers, this teacher was

African American. This move was not a positive move. Billy's new teacher believed that children should be able to copy from the board. Each day, the children had several sentences to copy. Billy had never been expected to copy from the board and he found this task difficult. The teacher told me, "I am worried. He cannot copy from the board. I am going to have him tested." She communicated these worries to Lucille who started to come to class each day to help Billy with the copying exercises. Lucille felt that copy work was appropriate for first graders and she wanted to provide the necessary support for Billy. Once these initial sentences were copied, the children copied other sentences with grammar and punctuation mistakes in them. They were expected to copy the sentences and correct the mistakes. They then wrote spelling words three times each. Following this, they did a handwriting sheet. The reading instruction was centered on the basal and the worksheets that accompanied it.

With the constant support of his grandmother, Billy was able to succeed in this grade. At the end of the year, the teacher said that, "Billy is doing better in school. He cries when his work is not right." Clearly, Billy's determination to be successful in school again proved strong. He figured out how to complete the work that was expected and ended the year with good grades on his report card. The teacher no longer thought about having Billy tested for extra academic support.

Understandings of Billy's Literacy at Age 6

There was no additional growth in literacy documented during this year. Billy remained a beginning reader and writer as he had in kindergarten. When I reflected on why this might be, I pondered two possible reasons. One included all of the moves he experienced. With the exception of his first month in school, Billy had to learn to exist in very different classroom contexts from those he had experienced previously. In his second classroom, no child could learn. This was the worst classroom climate I had ever seen. The children seemed to be pushing all limits of behavior to see when the teacher would be concerned with them. My second explanation is centered on the curriculum in his final first-grade experience. The teacher had a very different curriculum, one that Billy had never experienced. My guess was that he spent all of his energy trying to understand and meet the expectations of this class. This concern allowed him little energy to add to his literacy understandings. I think this is illustrated in the teacher's comment that "he cries when his work is not right."

When I worked with Billy at his home, he seemed more relaxed. He enjoyed reading stories to me, especially predictable text. He loved looking for the flea in *The Napping House* (Wood, 1984). And he began to enjoy drawing and writing with me. During my last visit, I asked him again to spell the words I had requested while he was in kindergarten. This time he willingly wrote *bed*, *ship*, *drive*, *bump*, and *when*. His writing of these words, shown in Figure 12, demonstrated his knowledge of initial and final consonants, and his experimentation with short vowels.

Figure 12
Billy's Spelling

Final Thoughts

Like Sean, Billy was sophisticated in his literacy knowledge. Unlike Sean, he did not have consistent support with his development, nor was his instruction always exemplary. Billy's preschool experiences were often difficult for me to observe. I had a hard time understanding how little the curriculum changed from class to class and how impoverished the school was. I often thought about how different this experience for children might be if they just had books and paper and pencils. However, the teachers and parents saw value in the preschool curriculum. They saw the curriculum as preparing the children for kindergarten and they saw that their religious beliefs were shared with the children. The preschool was an extension of family and church. There was no dissonance experienced by the parents, children, or teachers. And the children did learn the expected curriculum. No children left this preschool without mastery of it.

Although the curriculum of this school did not in any way match the International Reading Association's (1985) or the National Association for the Education of Young Children's (1988) position about early literacy experiences, the children left this school as successful learners.

The congruence between home and school was not seen consistently in the public schools that Billy attended. His kindergarten experience was a model of what is described for exemplary practice for the early learning of children. In addition, his teacher modeled many of the characteristics described by Ladson-Billings (1994) as necessary for the success of African American students. In particular, she was a master at providing "effective teaching [which] involves in-depth knowledge of both students and subject matter" (p. 125). She often commented on the experiences of children inside and outside of the school. She used this knowledge constantly within her lessons. She was also a master at creating a permeable curriculum, one that allowed school to enter the homes of the children and that allowed the home experiences of the children to enter school (Dyson, 1993).

Billy experienced a literacy curriculum that was not exemplary in the first grade. In addition to this limited model, Billy did not have teachers who shared with children the conviction that they could be successful. These teachers seemed to focus more on what the children were having difficulty with than what they could do well. They also did not have an understanding of the literacy knowledge or home experiences of the students. All the children in these classrooms were treated as though they all shared the same knowledge or lack of knowledge. This belief was evident in the requirement that all children practice writing their names, when most could do this well. It also was demonstrated in having all of the children copy sentences from the board. Although this was a difficult task for Billy, it was impossible for several children in the class who still were not aware of letters or their sounds.

Billy's story certainly moves us beyond the focus on children prenatally exposed to crack/cocaine. His literacy instruction became most important to me, especially while I observed him in preschool. I saw firsthand how a family's religious beliefs structured the preschool experiences for this child. I also witnessed exciting literacy practices that built connections between home and school. And I saw humiliating, awful classroom experiences that tend to happen most frequently in schools serving high-poverty children.

Billy again taught me the value of resilience. He moved from the security of his grandparents' home to his mother's home. His grandparents' love helped him deal with his mother's situation. She lived next door and continued to use drugs throughout the study. She vacillated among taking care of him, neglecting him, and ignoring him. He left home to be nurtured in a school based on his grandparents' beliefs and that continued to stress the values they instilled in the home. From this security, he entered public schooling. Although not all of his experiences were positive, he continued to be a leader and a child who valued doing well in school. He was able to be successful, despite the inconsistency experienced in his classrooms. And through all of his schooling, his grandmother was there to support him. She even visited school each day in first grade to ensure his success.

Billy's story allowed me to shed some of my biases about literacy instruction. Although I would still like to enrich his preschool experiences, I learned that learning about literacy is more complex than books and paper. Billy was able to develop his knowledge about literacy because of the support he received at home, in school, and at church. This foundation proved to be sufficient for the more sophisticated understandings of literacy that he would develop.

CHAPTER 6

Melina: A Child Who Loves to Learn With Friends

This day was the most wonderful day in the world! The sun shone, the sky was blue, and Miss Binney loved her.

(Cleary, B. [1984]. *The Ramona Quimby Diary* [unpaged]. New York: Morrow.)

Melina always seemed happiest when the people around her showed their pride and love toward her openly. She smiled in classrooms where the teacher complimented her on her work. She beamed when her friends, especially her best friend, were near and followed her directions. She hugged her grandmother when she talked about how beautiful and bright she was. People are important to Melina, especially her family, her teacher, and her best friend. When these people were all supporting her, she had a wonderful day; her smile was huge and it was the first thing you noticed about her. But when her grandmother or teacher displayed displeasure with her, it was evident by the frown on her face and sometimes the tears streaming down her face. Her feelings of sadness were always evident when her best friend was not near. She pouted and stayed by herself through a whole school day. Melina's self-portrait appears in Figure 13 on page 100.

Getting to Know Melina

The hardest part of her name, she soon discovered, was getting the right number of points on the *M* and *N*. Sometimes her name came out

RANOMA, but before long she remembered that two points came first. "Good work, Ramona," said Miss Binney, the first time Ramona printed her name correctly.

(Cleary, B. [1968]. *Ramona the Pest* [p. 74]. New York: Dell.)

My first meeting with Melina was at her home. Melina and her sister, Anna, were both in my study. Like Billy (see Chapter 5), Melina fit the target group; she was 4 years old when the study began. She also is African American. Melina lived a few blocks away from Billy but they did not know each other. The houses near where she lived

Figure 13
Melina's Self-Portrait

also were well cared for. Melina's home had a fence around the front yard, grass and flowers in front, and a large driveway. Like Billy's home, there were no toys in the front yard. All of Melina's and Anna's outside toys were in the back yard. In all of my home observations however, the two girls rarely played outside. They seemed to be most comfortable in the family room or kitchen.

Melina's house was quite large inside. There was a living room and a family room. The kitchen was in the center of the house and it had a large table for family meals. There were also several bedrooms, including Melina's grandmother's room, which was next to the kitchen. Many of the family conversations occurred in Melina's grandmother's room with the whole family sitting on the king-sized bed. Melina's grandmother, Bertha, was the foster parent for Melina and Anna. During the study, Melina's youngest brother also came to live with them (at the beginning of the study, he lived with another foster family).

Melina enjoyed a large extended family. Her great-grandmother lived in the house along with an older disabled uncle. Both of these people required help with dressing and eating on a daily basis. Bertha's other children were often in the home helping Bertha. One of the older children was in the home each night as Bertha worked as a school custodian in the evening. Moreover, they often watched Melina and Anna and helped get the girls to school and to appointments. Melina's and Anna's natural mother visited as well although she took over the care of her daughters or son infrequently.

During my first visit, Bertha talked to me about the difficult decisions she had to make with her own daughter. She said that Melina's mother started using drugs as a teenager. When Bertha learned that her daughter was pregnant with Melina, she called in the authorities and had her daughter arrested, feeling that if her daughter were in jail, she could not use drugs. Unfortunately, however, Melina was born in jail with drugs in her system; her mother had continued her drug use while in jail. The positive side of Melina's mother's incarceration was that she received prenatal care and Melina was a full-term baby weighing 8 pounds 8 ounces at birth. Soon after Melina was born, she was brought to Bertha and she became responsible for Melina as her foster mother. When Melina was 1 year old, Anna was born and again Bertha took responsibility. Two years later, another child was born, and once this boy was 1 he also became part of Bertha's family. Bertha and her family provided all the care for these children. All the young children had asthma, and as a result there were many trips to doctors and occasionally to the hospital when there was a serious asthma attack.

On each occasion that I saw Melina, I was always struck with how well she was dressed. She loved to wear dresses with socks and shoes to match. She also had her hair done with braid extensions attached that were decorated with beads or ribbons to match her other clothing. Melina loved to receive compliments about how beautiful she looked. It was clearly important to the family and to Melina that she be well dressed and have a matching outfit.

During my conversation with Bertha, she talked to me about Melina's involvement with reading and writing, Bertha smiled at how smart Melina was. Bertha told me that, "she had 97 on a test the Head Start teacher gave on letters, numbers, and colors." She also said that Melina was "a loner....When she is in school, she plays by herself or with one friend. She is lost when her friend is not there." Bertha said that she is teaching Melina to write her name and to write the alphabet letters. She said that the *n* is the only letter causing her trouble.

Bertha told me that the children had a few books but there was not much time for reading. She read to Melina sometimes on the weekend. She described Melina as a "picture reader." Melina asked to have a story read and then after each page was read, she would tell the story based on the illustrations. Bertha was pleased that Melina, even at age 4, was teaching her older cousin to read and write. "Melina acts like she is a teacher and tells Kisaea the letters and then has her repeat them. Kisaea is in the first grade and doesn't know her letters yet."

When I visited this home, I was never sure who would greet me. Sometimes, it was Bertha and at other times it was one of Bertha's children who was in charge. The children never seemed bothered by the multiple caregivers. The only complaint that I heard was from Melina's aunt who said that she was angry that the children treated their mother "like a star." She said that whenever she walked in with a new boyfriend the children would cluster around her like " a movie star." She wanted her sister to start taking responsibility for her children. She hated the idea that the children looked up to their mother, especially with her lifestyle.

As was true in my visits to other homes, by my third visit I was allowed to move from the living room to the kitchen. The kitchen was the center of most of the activity in this house. Sitting at the kitchen table with Melina was the most comfortable place to be and the place where family members felt the most free to talk to me. As I continued my visits, I was often brought into family discussions. While we engaged in talk, Melina was always pleased to continue looking at my books or to draw or write. She occasionally looked at us and commented and then returned to her reading or writing.

During several of our conversations, Bertha asked about becoming a teacher. She had finished 2 years at the community college and wanted to know more about this profession. Throughout the study this conversation continued but she did not begin a teacher-education program.

Melina's Literacy at Age 4

> Ramona wished she had a *K* in her name, so that she could give it a nice straight back. Ramona enjoyed Miss Binney's descriptions of the letters of the alphabet and listened for them as she worked.
>
> (Cleary, 1968, p. 74))

Melina in Preschool

Besides the literacy events at home, Melina and Anna went to Head Start each day. This center, which was close to Melina's home, was old and in need of repair. The doors were hard to open and had been painted over numerous times, resembling a collage with all of their colors. Once inside, there was always a volunteer, usually a parent of one of the children in the program, to greet you and direct you to the right classroom. The children's rooms were on the perimeter of this circular building. Many of the rooms opened to one another and the teachers occasionally combined the children for activities. There were approximately 300 children in this center on a daily basis and most of the preschool classes had about 20 children in them. Each class had a teacher and a parent helper. In addition to the preschool classes, there were classes for adults occurring at the same time. Many young mothers were enrolled in these classes and they brought their infant children with them. The building was always full of activity, however, the adults and children never seemed bothered by the steady hum of noise.

The preschool classrooms were organized around centers. The dominant centers were blocks and housekeeping, but there were puzzles and a library too. Many of the puzzles were missing pieces and most of the library books were tattered and very old. Although there was a bookcase and a rocking chair in the library center, the few books that were there did not make this a particularly inviting center. Beyond these centers, the teacher usually had an art or cooking center that varied on a daily basis.

The routine in the classroom was fixed. The children started the day with breakfast. After breakfast was the hand-washing and teeth-brushing routine. Following this, the children sat in a circle on the carpet. They sang songs, including a fluoride song during which they received fluoride tablets. Once the songs were completed, the children selected a center and informed the teacher of their choice. The remainder of the morning was spent in centers. During the morning, there was an outdoor recess. Near noon, the children washed their hands and had lunch. Dismissal followed lunch.

As I observed and talked to the teachers, I learned that their curriculum was centered on health (washing, brushing teeth, and eating) and on teaching children how to behave well. I rarely saw a book-reading event. When I did, the book was most often centered on a topic such as responsibility. On a few occasions, the children were provided with paper and crayons and were allowed to draw. I never saw a teacher give a child a pencil and ask him or her to write.

Watching Melina in her Head Start class was always an interesting experience. I learned much about the social network in her class, especially the girls' social network. Melina was a leader among the girls. Although she was happiest when her best friend, Ebony, was next to her, the other girls also clamored to be her friend. They followed her to the doll center, hoping that she would give them a doll to play with, which occasionally she did. When the children were expected to sit on the carpet, Melina walked to the circle area slowly. She wanted to make sure that she would sit next to her best friend. If she did not, she sulked through the entire circle experience. Although the other girls in the class wanted her attention, she shared it only with one friend. Melina's teacher was aware of this situation and was "working with Melina to make more friends." She had not been successful however.

As I watched Melina interact with the teacher, it was clear that she always paid attention. When the teacher asked a question, Melina's hand popped up. As a result, the teacher called on her frequently. Melina also was persistent with the projects prepared by the teacher. Even if all the other children in the class were done, Melina continued to work on her project until it was completed. For example, when they were assigned an Easter basket project, most of the children quickly glued the paper to a basket and were off to another center. But Melina spent an hour and a half gluing the paper to her basket in an intricate design. She stopped only when she felt the project was complete. She was not bothered that all the other children were involved with another activity and remained focused and involved until she was satisfied with her work.

At the end of the year in this preschool center, the teacher individually assessed the children in language. She told me that "Melina has 100. She does well on all of these tests."

Melina at Home

As I worked with Melina at home, I learned that she wrote her first name easily and often experimented with the letters. Her experimentation with her name is shown in Figure 14 on page 106. She had a hard time making the *n*, and this letter often was left out when she wrote her name. She could count to 23 and sometimes higher. I discovered this counting ability when she drew a picture of herself and carefully counted the braids she put on her head (see Figure 15 on page 107). As she wrote the names of the other members of her family, she always had the initial letter of their names correct. After the initial letter, she guessed the rest.

Melina enjoyed the books that I brought on each visit, although she never indicated that any one of them was a favorite. We often looked at *Fizz and Splutter* (Melser, 1982). She enjoyed this book because she could identify all the letters that were highlighted on each page. She also noted that the pictures on each page began with the letter that was highlighted. During this year, she began to refuse to reread books to me. On one occasion, I asked her to read *Brown Bear, Brown Bear, What Do You See?* (Martin, 1967). She had not heard this book before and she told me, "I can't read." I then read the book to her one time. After this, she read the whole book to me accurately, having fully memorized it after my single reading.

Figure 14
Melina Experimenting With Name Writing

melin
Melia
Melia
Meli
Melia
Melia
Meli
Melina
Melia

Understandings of Melina's Literacy at Age 4

After observing Melina at home and at her preschool, I noted the following literacy understandings. Melina knew

- how to draw a self-portrait (she had moved beyond using scribbling to represent herself);
- how to write her first name;
- that books have fronts and backs, how to turn pages, and that each page has a top and bottom;
- that books have a special language, different from oral conversation (she retold books using book language);

Figure 15
Melina's Self-Portrait and Drawing of Her Family

her family

Anna

mila

5-16-91
Melina

- that books had text or words that she could not read independently (she thus refused to read unless she had memorized the text); and
- that words began with specific consonants (she had developed sound-symbol awareness for the initial consonants in words).

As a 4-year-old, Melina was clearly toward the end of the emergent-literacy category. Her awareness of letters and their sounds demonstrated her phonemic awareness and her approaching move to the beginning-reader-and-writer category (Hiebert & Raphael, 1998). Melina's development was very intriguing. She had minimal exposure to book-reading events at home and at school. She did not have paper and pencils available for experimenting with writing or drawing, yet she understood a considerable amount about written literacy. Her knowledge was documented through her in-school testing and my less formal observations.

Melina's Literacy at Age 5

Melina in Preschool

Melina returned to the same preschool the next year. She joined a group of 5-year-olds in her new classroom. As in the previous year, she had about 20 other children in her class. The structure of the class replicated the curriculum from the previous year. The children started with breakfast, followed by teeth brushing and hand washing, and then group singing. At the conclusion of this routine, the children selected a center for the remainder of the morning. The centers on most occasions were blocks, housekeeping, puzzles, and library. Each day, the teacher created an additional new center that she invited children to use. These centers usually involved a project, often related to the season, or the project might be as simple as a free exploration with clay. As I observed through the year, the teacher infrequently read to the class and there were few opportunities to explore with writing or drawing materials.

During this year, Melina expanded her group of friends. She still had a best friend, but she also interacted with a group of about five girls. They went everywhere together. If Melina was in the housekeeping center playing with a doll, the other girls were there too. If there was a puzzle to be done, all five worked on the puzzle. Their favorite center became the library area. This was a place that few other children visited, so they had it to themselves. Melina or another child would sit in the rocking chair and pretend to read to the other girls. On one occasion, Melina pretended to read a story to this group about a ballerina. When a boy tried to join in, he was told that "only girls are allowed!"

In addition to reading to one another, this group of girls enjoyed pretending that they were cheerleaders. They often used pompoms and practiced cheers. When they practiced, many of the other children would sit near them and just watch. After the children in the class became familiar with the cheers, they would join in.

Toward the end of the year, the teacher brought in alphabet stamps for the children to experiment with. Melina and her friends enjoyed stamping their names. As the children looked for the appropriate stamp, they talked to one another. Sometimes one child asked another child to find a specific letter, but usually the girls' social network was more important to them than the identification of a letter. There was much discussion of whom was which girl's best friend. I watched as each girl pointed to Melina and claimed to be her best friend. One child said, "Melina is my best girlfriend. She's my sister." Being a best friend was the single theme that was repeated throughout the year. It was more important than any of the curricular issues occurring in this class. Friendship was the dominant concern.

Melina at Home

During my home visits, Melina enjoyed reading the books that I brought. We continued to read *Brown Bear, Brown Bear, What Do You See?* She told me that *brown* and *bear* began like her friend Brianna's name. Her focus on letters and sounds stayed with the initial consonant. She did not overtly share any knowledge about vowels during this year. When she wrote, she tried to figure out the first consonant and then she used random letters to represent the remainder of the word.

When we read any book the first time, she was reluctant to read it to me. She consistently told me that she could not read. Once she had heard the book and had it memorized, she willingly read it to me. However, she did not consider this reading. I frequently told her that I was impressed that she could read, but she always responded with "No, I can't read yet." Although when I gave her this compliment, she always smiled.

However Melina's confidence in her reading grew during this year. Bertha told me that Melina liked to read to her, something that she was unwilling to do before. I observed this behavior on several visits. Melina read a book with me and then immediately took it over to a member of the family and read it to him or her. She enjoyed the hugs and positive comments that she received from the family member. Like Billy's family, this family constantly complimented Melina on how smart she was. Melina appreciated these comments and acted the role of a smart child.

Understandings of Melina's Literacy at Age 5

Melina's literacy development was subtle during this year. There were no dramatic shifts in her previous understandings about reading and writing. However, many of her tentative understandings were established more firmly. For example, she knew

- how to write her first and last name;
- how books were organized (she was aware of the importance of text);
- that individual words match to speech on most occasions (she became confused with this concept when there were many words on a page);
- how to memorize a predictable text after a single reading;
- that she did not know how to read books without them being memorized (she was aware that she could not decipher words without support from a more capable reader); and
- how to represent initial consonants.

Perhaps there would have been more significant literacy development for Melina during this year if the school or the home supported her literacy development. I continued to wonder how Melina was learning about literacy.

In school, the focus was on behavior and health, not literacy. There were few to no book-reading experiences. Occasionally, an adult volunteer sat in the library and read to some children. However, these occasions were few and far between, and only those children who happened to be in the library benefited. In addition, there were few times when literacy was directly explored. The teacher brought in letter stamps and provided paper at the end of the year, but there was no direct instruction about the names of the letters or how they might be combined to spell words. By any standard, this classroom would not be considered literacy rich.

What is unfortunate about this school situation is its combination with Melina's home environment. Although the adults in her home were happy to listen to her read, there were few books in the home. There also were no paper or pencils with which to experiment. Melina was definitely ready for extended periods of time that focused on book reading, sound and letter exploration, and writing. However, these opportunities were never provided to her. In Melina's situation, the school would be expected to provide these critical learning experiences. Unfortunately, her preschool did not yet see these literacy experiences as important for young children.

Melina's Literacy at Age 6

Melina in Kindergarten

Melina entered the public school kindergarten near her home. This school was similar to Billy's in that it had been remodeled recently to meet current standards. Melina entered a school with a new facade that now included a full elementary in addition to a sixth-grade center. Her classroom was in the front of the building and could be entered without going through the main part of the school. Her school day was 2½ hours in length, which is typical of kindergartens in this district.

Melina's teacher, Ms. Hasada, greeted the children at the classroom door each morning. She expected them to provide a welcome to her as they entered the room. After the children entered, they were to sit on the carpet for the first lesson of the day. On most days, this lesson centered on the alphabet. The core aspect of the kindergarten curriculum was the letter of the week. Each week the bulletin board changed to reflect this focus. The children began by identifying the letter and the sound. The teacher then asked the children to read words that began with the letter. She was required to provide extensive support for the word-reading part of this lesson because most of the children had no idea what word might be written on the card she held up. In fact, most of the children could not yet write their first names and they were unaware of the names of the letters in the alphabet.

This instruction usually went on for about an hour; many of the children became restless during this time and were sent to various locations in the room until they "could behave." Ms. Hasada frequently complained about the behavior of her students and worried about their lack of control during her instruction. She did not seem to consider that an hour of instruction centered on letters, sounds, and words might be too much to expect from most kindergarten children and saw the problem with classroom discipline as student owned. All problems originated with the children, not the organization or the curriculum within the class. This orientation of viewing the child as the problem is not unique to Ms. Hasada; Delpit (1995) and Ladson-Billings (1994) have described it as well. Unfortunately Ms. Hasada never revamped her curriculum because she did not see it as a problem.

Another unfortunate aspect to Ms. Hasada's teaching was that she called only on children who knew the answers to her questions. These children were seen as the classroom stars. Melina was a member of this group and was called on four to five times in each lesson to provide a response about a letter or a word. As would be expected, the children who were not called on never paid attention to any of this instruction.

Following this lesson, the children moved to tables to complete worksheets that centered on the letter of the week. They spent the remainder of the morning in this activity. Beyond the classroom curriculum, the children had weekly music, art, physical-education, and computer lessons. When they visited the computer room, the programs that were chosen for them all centered on alphabet and sound-symbol knowledge.

There were few books for the children to explore in the classroom. The most I ever saw were five books stacked on a table. There was no classroom library. Occasionally, the teacher read to the children but she found this a frustrating activity because the children would not listen to the book. When I observed her read to the class, the book she chose was long and had no predictable pattern. She was correct in her assessment of the class, which did not listen to her read beyond the third page of the book.

Melina was a successful student in this class. In November, she was picked as the student of the month. This choice was made by the teacher based on a child's behavior. When I talked to Ms. Hasada about Melina, she told me that "she is at the top of the class. She knows all of the alphabet sounds. She is very cooperative."

When I went to observe Melina after the winter break, she was in a new classroom. I never found out the reason for this move. Bertha told me that the school moved Melina and that she did not request the move. When Melina's sister entered Ms. Hasada's room the following year I talked to Ms. Hasada, but she had no reason to offer about Melina's move except that she thought the school was trying to equalize the size of the kindergarten classes.

In the new room, Melina went to kindergarten for a full day. There were about 15 children in this class. The teacher, Ms. Dailey, was new and had just finished her teacher-education program in December. She was hired during her last week of student teaching.

The environment in this room was very different from Melina's previous setting. There was a library and books were everywhere. The teacher had poems written on the board. The children were expected to read a poem with the teacher and then talk about it. One day, I listened in to a discussion about a poem with ducks in it.

Michael: The big one eats too much.

Ms. Daily: Why do you think the black duck can quack quicker?

Hikmat: He is bigger.

Maria: He is the mom.

Melina: The black duck is older than the blue duck.

Jaryd: The blue duck is the baby. He is about 4 years old.

This discussion continued until the children had worked through their understandings about the ducks in this poem. The quality of this discussion was impressive. The children used their background knowledge and their discoveries from the poem and its illustrations to respond to the teacher's questions. The teacher allowed the children to talk through an issue before she intervened with another question.

In addition to the poetry experiences, the children composed a daily message. Children orally volunteered important events that they had experienced recently. The teacher chose one and wrote it on a chart. The children helped compose words by contributing letters for the teacher to write. When the message was complete, the children read the text together. This message stayed on the board throughout the day and children periodically went to the board to read it. Beyond this writing, there was a writing center in the room where the children wrote their own stories. A few children preferred to dictate to the teacher. Following their dictation, they illustrated their stories.

In addition to these activities, there were other centers in the room. There was a listening center, a reading center (most often the books in this center were based on phonics principles; the vocabulary was controlled), a computer center, and an art center. Children had time to go to centers each day and they also were expected to complete worksheets. These worksheets contained color and number words and letter-sound practice.

As the year was coming to a close, the teacher worked with her students on writing and reading CVC words. She wrote a word on the board and the children read it. She then wrote words that were in the word family for the children to read (for example, *man, fan, ran*). After the children could read these words easily, she combined them with other words and created sentences. The children then read these sentences together.

In addition to emphasizing sounds and words, the teacher read to the children several times each day. The children also explored books with the teacher in small groups. These were most often simple, predictable stories. There were numerous occasions during the day for the children to explore books independently or to read the poems or charts around the room.

As might be surmised, Melina's literacy development was enhanced in this environment. Her teacher noted that "she is doing really well. She is getting more outgoing and even comes to the front of the room to sing or read."

Melina at Home

New literacy understandings were evident in my visits with Melina at her home. She no longer was hesitant to read. She could read independently books she had not explored before. When I asked her to write the words from the developmental list (see Figure 16), the results indicated that she was at a letter-name stage of development. She chose to spell words that she knew from her kindergarten class first. Once she finished writing *sat*, she was ready to explore the words I requested of her. She spelled *bed* as *BAD* and *ship* and *SEP*. These spellings are typical of children with her literacy knowledge. She knew the beginning and ending consonant, she was just confused about the short vowel. But an important benchmark of children at this stage is the inclusion of a vowel in each word (Bear & Barone, 1989; Bear et al., 1996) and Melina did this. She was also willing to write about the stories she read. Figure 17 on page 116 is an example of this writing. We had read *Brown Bear* again. When we were done, Melina wrote about the cat in the story. This writing demonstrated her ability to express herself independently; each word was easy to read and easy for her to write.

When I asked Melina about her ability as a reader and a writer, she talked about books first. She said that she had "too many favorites" to tell me about one. Then she said that she learned to read because

Figure 16
Melina's Spelling

Figure 17
Melina's Writing

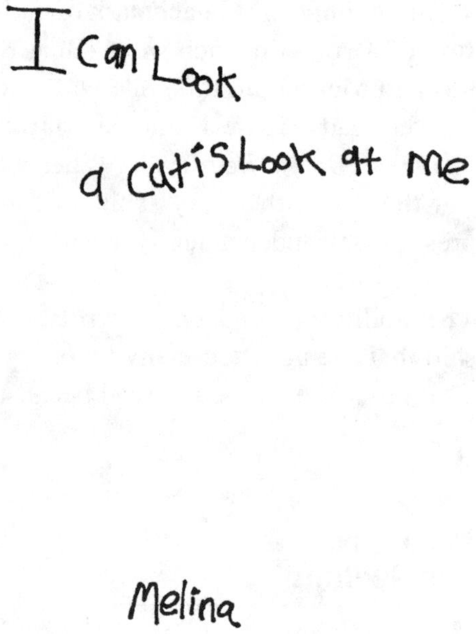

I can Look

a cat is Look at me

Melina

"my teacher taught me in kindergarten when she wrote on the board and I had to read everyday."

Understandings of Melina's Literacy at Age 6

The most noticeable difference in Melina during this year was the explosion of her literacy knowledge. In a classroom that indirectly and directly supported literacy, Melina's previous understandings about literacy led to new accomplishments. During this year, she learned

- about the synchronicity of speech and print;
- how to read independently in a word-by-word fashion;
- that text carries a message (she explored poems and stories with the teacher with a focus on meaning);
- that words can be represented with initial and final consonants and a vowel;

- how to read sight words such as *the*, *like*, *is*, *and*, *I*, *see*, *look*, *said*, and *are*; and
- how to express herself through writing.

Melina left the category of emergent reader and writer during this year. She was a beginning reader and writer at the end of kindergarten. This development is not typical of most children in kindergarten (Phillips, Norris, & Mason, 1996). The expectation would be that they would still be considered in the emergent category. There were questions that remained with me at the close of this year: Would this development have happened if Melina had not moved from her first kindergarten experience? Would Ms. Hasada's list of words and worksheets been sufficient for this development? Although these questions remained, my belief was that this new environment provided the foundation necessary for Melina's development. Melina might have become an independent reader in Ms. Hasada's classroom, but she would have had no extended text to read. She would have seen reading as isolated words. This definition of reading would have required expansion as she eventually engaged with stories and content material. As a result of her move to the second kindergarten environment, Melina learned that it was necessary to decode text to read and that text carried meaning.

Melina's Literacy at Age 7

Melina in First Grade

Melina remained in the same elementary school for first grade. Her classroom had 17 children in it. Mrs. Tabner, her teacher, organized her classroom in a traditional way. The children all sat at desks and were expected to be quiet while they worked. She had no classroom library because the only materials she used for reading instruction were basal texts and workbooks.

The daily routine began with the children writing in journals. The children wrote each day, although the teacher never read their writing. Following journal writing, the children worked on their spelling words. Some days they wrote their words three times each, other days they used them in sentences, or they put them in alphabetical order. On one day each week, they wrote their words on the classroom computer. The entire class had the same spelling list. After spelling, the children worked as a whole class on a basal story. Mrs. Tabner talked about the content of the story. Following this introduction, each child had a chance to read part of the story orally while the rest of the class listened. After the story, the teacher asked the children a few questions about it. After the story was finished, the children were expected to complete the accompanying worksheets. This work usually lasted until lunch. After lunch, the children learned about math concepts and they had their special classes of art, music, computer, or physical education.

Mrs. Tabner had high expectations for all of her students. She continuously moved among them as they worked, complimenting those who were doing a good job, nudging those who could do better, and reprimanding those who had not shown sufficient effort. The children valued these comments and wanted to do their best for her. During all of my visits, I saw children start work again if Mrs. Tabner said they were not doing their best. The children never complained and wanted to give her their best work; they knew she expected it and they did not want to disappoint her. On one occasion, I saw her interaction with a child who disappointed her. She took this child aside and let her know that she knew this was not her best work. Her conversation with this child was lengthy and it was clear in her message that for this child to be successful she had to do better than what was expected of other first graders. While this conversation took place, the children in the classroom definitely were listening. This teacher's message to these children was that she knew they could learn and she would not accept anything less. There were no excuses for not doing homework or for sloppy writing. She had high expectations for their success as students and later as adults. I noted that at the beginning of the year some children forgot their homework. By November, this never happened. All of the children remembered to hand in their homework each day.

I read Melina's journal on each of my visits. At first, she copied from the words in the room. In August, she wrote the following:

> My name is Melina. circle, pink, oval, triangle, yellow, black, blue, white, brown, purple, green, good, Tuesday, Thursday, good (punctuation added, all words were spelled correctly).

In November, she copied environmental print and expressed her own ideas, writing

> Today is Thursday the 13th, I like pigs. You like thirteen fishs. I like thirteen dinosaurs. Thirteen is a number. Do you like the number thirteen. Yes i like the number thirteen. I like the number. (punctuation added, all words spelled as represented)

By April, Melina no longer copied; she wrote her own ideas. An example of the entry she wrote about her mother follows:

> I loeve my mother because she takes me to the store. She is nice to me. I love my mother because she hugs me. I love my mother because she takes me to the store. I love my mother because she is the best in my world. (punctuation added, all words spelled as represented)

These writing samples demonstrate Melina's growing ability to represent her ideas through writing. They also show her ability to represent words. She has moved beyond her knowledge of CVC words and is now able to represent long vowel words like *takes* and *nice*.

The spelling curriculum began with sight words like *a*, *and*, *can*, *it*, and *be*. By November, the children were exploring long-vowel words like *nail* and *vase*. Melina was able to get 100% in each weekly spelling test.

Melina was also able to keep up with the basal reading. She was one of the few children who read fluently when called on to read from the basal to the class. Her reading of the basal was fluent even when it was the first time she saw the text.

Her literacy capabilities were noted by Mrs. Tabner, who often complimented Melina in class and always told me about how well she was doing. She said, "Melina is doing well. She wants to be at the top of the class."

Melina at Home

When I visited Melina at home at the end of first grade, she wanted to show off her reading and writing skills. She read some of my picture books, but wanted to know why I did not bring longer books. She said that she liked books about *Frog and Toad* (Lobel) now. Then she wrote a story for me (see Figure 18 on page 120). She completed this story in less than 5 minutes. Each word that she attempted to spell was correct. She did not hesitate with words like *brothers* or *play*. She knew how to write these words automatically.

Bertha was still worried about Melina's development, even though she was doing so well in school. She thought she might buy Melina a commercial program to help her with sounds. We talked for a bit about these programs. I encouraged her to visit the library with the children over the summer even if she decided to buy one of these programs. She also decided to enroll the children in a book club. She thought they might enjoy having their own books. Throughout this year, through the encouragement of Melina's teacher, Bertha learned that she was expected to help with reading instruction. At first this was a surprise to her because she expected the school to be responsible. But with Mrs. Tabner's continued conversations about the importance of parents helping their children learn to read, she was willing to participate.

Figure 18
Melina's Story

I like to play. I like my brothers, Jovaris and Mal. I like to read books.

Understandings of Melina's Literacy at Age 7

As seen during Melina's kindergarten experience, Melina's growth during this year was incredible. She learned

- how to read fluently;
- how to write with ease; and
- how to represent long vowels.

Although this list appears short, these learnings are complex. Most children do not achieve this level of competency with reading and writing until the second- or third-grade year (Bear et al., 1996).

The other advantages that Melina experienced during this year were her teacher's high expectations, not only for her, but for the other children in the class. Although there might be quibbling about the way this teacher organized her room for literacy instruction, she certainly created an environment where learning was important and *all* children were expected to be successful. Additionally, Melina's grandmother came to value the importance of her role with literacy instruction. Melina's home environment now included books and a phonics program.

Concluding Thoughts

Melina's story is similar to Billy's and Sean's in that she was also a successful literacy learner. Yet her preschool experiences were different from Billy's, whose preschool curriculum was centered on skills. Melina's preschool focused on health and behavior. Neither of these experiences would be considered as being particularly supportive of literacy learning. Like Billy, but unlike Sean, Melina's home culture did not include many books. There were few occasions when Melina and Billy experienced book-reading events in their home.

Perhaps in reflecting on Melina's story, the attitude of her parents, in this case her grandmother, becomes critical. Although Bertha did not explicitly support Melina's literacy growth, she expected that she would be a successful student in school. This same attitude was shared in Billy's home and he also experienced success in most of his school experiences. Melina was able to adapt to her teachers' expectations.

She and her teachers always viewed her as a successful student. As Mrs. Tabner said, "She wanted to be at the top of the class."

Melina's story truly lets us see the value of a teacher and how important a teacher can be in the life of a student. Ms. Dailey's literacy curriculum expanded her students' ideas of what literacy might include. They no longer saw it as limited to letters and sounds and realized that literacy involved reading text and making sense of what they read. Although Mrs. Tabner's definition of reading was limited to a basal and worksheets, she enriched her students' lives by having high expectations for them. Melina was ready for these expectations, so Mrs. Tabner's job was not difficult, but Mrs. Tabner held these expectations for all of the children in her class, children on whom others had already given up. These children rose to her expectations and they all left her class at least as beginning readers and writers.

Melina's story solidifies the idea that children who were prenatally exposed to crack/cocaine are capable of being successful in the classroom. Her story also alters the notion that these children will become sociopaths who are incapable of bonding with adults and other children (Odom-Winn & Dunagan, 1991). Throughout all of my encounters with Melina, friends and family were important to her. In fact, she was considered to be the social leader in all of her school experiences. I never visited her when there were not several girls clamoring to be her best friend. Friendship is the central core of Melina's story.

CHAPTER 7

Curtis: A Gifted Child Who Loves to Learn

By the time she was *three*, Matilda had taught herself to read by study-ing newspapers and magazines that lay around the house. At the age of *four*, she could read fast and well and she naturally began hankering af-ter books.

(Dahl, R. [1988]. *Matilda* [p. 11]. New York: Puffin)

Matilda and Curtis do not share the same home circumstances or gender, but they do share a love of reading. Throughout all my inter-actions with Curtis, I learned what it meant to love to learn and espe-cially to love to read. When Curtis misbehaved in school, which he did often, the teacher had only to withhold learning and he conformed quickly. He never wanted to miss an opportunity to listen to or read a book. Matilda and Curtis also shared a precociousness with reading. Curtis, whose self-portrait appears in Figure 19 on page 124, became a fluent reader during his first-grade year.

Getting to Know Curtis

Matilda's parents owned quite a nice house with three bedrooms up-stairs, while on the ground floor there was a dining room and a living room and a kitchen. (Dahl, 1988, p. 22)

Curtis's family was the first family I met when I began my study. They lived in a ranch house with a large front and back yard. Unlike

Figure 19
Curtis's Self-Portrait

most of the other homes I visited during the study, there were toys in the front yard. Most of the time these were bikes; Curtis and his two brothers liked to ride in the neighborhood. The living room and dining room in his house were not places where children played. They were formal rooms set aside for visits. There was elaborate furniture in both of these rooms and each of the tables had numerous breakable items on them. Curtis and his brothers played in their bedrooms, which they were expected to clean each day before going to bed.

On my first visit, I was greeted at the door by Curtis's mother, JoAnne, a tall African American woman. JoAnne started our conversation and she continued at a fast clip for over an hour. She began by telling me about herself and her family in general.

JoAnne had two grown sons. After they left home, she became the foster mother to three young boys, all of whom were identified with special needs. Johnnie, the oldest of the foster children, weighed 1 pound when he was born. He had learning difficulties and JoAnne spent several hours each day helping him with his schoolwork. Curtis was the middle child, and Nashon was the youngest child, who also had learning and physical needs. Johnnie and Nashon were African

American children and Curtis was biracial. JoAnne, her husband, and her two older sons cared for the younger boys. JoAnne's sons took the boys to karate lessons and took them camping. Her husband played baseball and other sports with them.

JoAnne is known as an activist in this community and the larger urban area. I observed this on several levels throughout the study. My first observation centered on JoAnne's creative way to keep up with the activities of the children in the neighborhood, which was populated by families who had resided in their homes for many years. However, several of the homeowners had started to rent their homes. JoAnne was worried about the changing neighborhood and its potential effect on the boys. She decided that the best way to protect them was to open a small convenience store with soda, candy, pizza, and sandwiches in her home. She opened the store just after school each day, and as would be expected, the neighborhood children all stopped by on their way home from school. JoAnne saw this store as a way to stay informed about what was happening in the neighborhood. She also noted children that she thought were "trouble" and she insisted her boys stay away from them. She used this opportunity to talk to the neighborhood children and learn of any potential problems.

My second observation demonstrated her involvement on a much larger scale. In addition to her neighborhood involvement, JoAnne visited every school-board meeting and city meeting dealing with schools. She was often on television sharing her views about the kinds of schools that should be available to the children in her neighborhood. JoAnne complained that parents in her community could not participate in their children's schooling because the children were bused to schools far from home. She wanted the sixth-grade centers described in Chapter 5 to become full elementary schools. She wanted a new elementary school to be built in the neighborhood. And she wanted these schools to have predominantly African American teachers and an Afrocentric curriculum. Her message was powerful. She rallied many city leaders and her neighbors to support her project. After a year of her persistent hounding of the school board and the city, the school district agreed to her requests. During the next academic year, the sixth-grade centers were remodeled and included full elementary programs. A new school was built, and these schools were filled with African American teachers who taught an Afrocentric curriculum. Later, as I read Ladson-Billings's book (1994) about successful African American teachers, I saw one of the qualities, education self-determination, as an apt description of JoAnne. This quality focused on a person's ability to complain about and then change the status quo in education. Ladson-Billings talked about this quality as one that is frequently used by middle-class parents to shape the schools that serve their children. She noted how important this quality was to the success of teachers when they worked with African American children. Certainly, JoAnne understood education self-determination. She not only complained about local education mandates, she also sought to change them, and she was successful.

After a lengthy time listening to JoAnne talk about her store and the changes she wanted to see in the local schools, I was able to nudge her to talk about Curtis. She told me that "he is beautiful. He's like a genius, stubborn as a mule. Wants all of the attention." She gave many examples of times when Curtis did not get the attention he wanted and engaged in inappropriate behavior to get the attention he craved. One example focused on bathing: "He has to be the first one in the bathtub. When he is second, he will just start yelling. I usually ask him, 'Why would someone who is so beautiful behave this way?' He always says that he doesn't know."

Curtis has lived in her home since he was an infant. He was a full-term baby and was identified with prenatal drug exposure. JoAnne told the welfare office when she took Curtis and his brothers that she expected these boys to stay with her until they were 18 years old. She said that she "was not going to stay awake at nights taking care of them to find out that welfare decided to move them. I told them to give me the boys and leave me alone." It seemed that as with the schools, state welfare knew when to sit back and listen to JoAnne.

She then went on to describe Curtis in general and his literacy learning in particular. She said that he "learns fast. If he's not familiar with a toy, he only has to be shown once, then he understands." She went on to talk about how Curtis learned to ride a two-wheeled bike. Johnnie had a two-wheeled bike and rode it in the neighborhood, while Curtis was given a two-wheeled bike with training wheels. Curtis was not happy about this. At 4 years old, he broke off the training wheels and taught himself to ride the bike in a day.

Curtis loved books. He begged JoAnne or his dad to read to him about four times a week. After he listened to a story, he told it back to the reader. JoAnne said that he now liked to listen to long stories, rather than picture books. She showed me several of the books from the "I Can Read" series that he was currently reading. These books are typically used during the second half of first grade or at the beginning of second grade by most teachers. She also showed me some of his writing that demonstrated that he could write all the letters of the alphabet. He also liked to spell words to her like *cat* and *bed*. She thought that Curtis knew so much about letters and words because he sat with her and Johnnie each night as she helped Johnnie with his schoolwork. She observed that Curtis loved to join them and play at school tasks.

She had enrolled Curtis at the local Head Start center. She said, "He loves to go to school. He is eager to learn." She talked about how he was surpassing Johnnie, who was 2 years older, in what he knew about reading and writing. She said that on most evenings, Curtis wanted to do Johnnie's homework and that she felt he most likely could do it well. Sometimes, she let both boys work the math problems together. She was sure that Curtis could add double digit numbers already. "I think he can just do it in his head."

Curtis's Literacy at Age 4

The nice thing about Matilda was that if you had met her casually and talked to her you would have thought she was a perfectly normal five-and-a-half-year-old child. She displayed almost no outward signs of her brilliance and she never showed off.... It was therefore easy for Matilda to make friends with other children. All those in her class liked her. (Dahl, 1988, p. 101)

Curtis in Preschool

Curtis attended the same preschool as Melina. The curriculum was centered on health and behavior issues (see Chapter 6 for a full description of this curriculum). He was in a class of 17 children. His teacher said, "Curtis is smart and he is stubborn. He gets in trouble almost every day for being upset at not being able to do something." I asked her what she did with him when he acted out. She replied that she "just had to tell him he would not be able to go to the library or some other learning event and he got quiet." She worried about how teachers would respond to these outbursts when he got older.

As I observed Curtis in this setting, he most often chose to play with puzzles and books. He loved to do puzzles and was able to put together puzzles with at least 24 pieces. When he was not involved with a puzzle, he usually lay on a pillow looking through a book. He spent long periods of time on each page, perusing the illustrations and tracking print, often reading some of the words slowly.

On one occasion, I engaged Curtis and several other children in this room in drawing and writing. In Figure 20, Curtis drew his self-portrait. As he created this picture, he talked about several events that he had experienced. One of his squiggles represented him bike riding. He also wrote some letters on his page. He was unwilling to write anything else.

Curtis was the first child to realize that I was writing about him and some of his classmates on my computer. Each time I visited his class, he came over and looked at the screen on my computer. He always wanted to write his name and he was able to do this. He examined my keyboard carefully and found each letter in his name. He slowly typed in each letter and was pleased with the results on the screen.

Understandings of Curtis's Literacy at Age 4

As I observed Curtis at school and interacted with him at home, I learned that he could

- draw a self-portrait that was recognizable, not just scribbling;
- write his first name easily;
- understand how a book was organized: front and back, top and bottom of a page, illustrations and text;
- almost understand how speech and print match in text;
- understand that books have a special language (he most often used book language to retell a story);
- understand the sound-symbol relations among initial consonants in words; and
- enjoy the pleasure of interacting with a book and being read to.

At age 4, Curtis was moving toward the end of the emergent category. He was familiar with the alphabet, both its letter names and the sounds that map to initial consonants. He was beginning to identify

Figure 20
Curtis's Drawing and Writing

words in text, especially in books that he experienced on more than one occasion. He loved to be read to and to retell a story to the reader.

Curtis's home was unlike Melina's in that literacy was supported in the home more formally. JoAnne spent each evening working with

Johnnie and Curtis on school-related assignments. Through these engagements, Curtis learned about literacy and math, and he understood how his parents valued these skills. The only concern about Curtis was his behavior. Although he could hold himself together through the majority of a day, he typically had at least one outburst in school each day. His teacher and his parents worried about how he would conduct himself in public school. They did not want him identified with a behavior problem, so they worked continuously to change his behavior. They hoped that he would develop more self-control and a willingness to not always be the center of attention.

Curtis's Literacy at Age 5

Curtis in Kindergarten

Curtis went to a neighborhood school for kindergarten. He attended kindergarten in the morning and a Chapter 1 class in the afternoon. He did not qualify for the additional help in the Chapter 1 class, but his mother wanted him in school all day and she was able to convince the principal that he should be allowed to be in the program. Each of these classrooms had about 15 to 17 children in them.

The literacy curriculum in both of these classrooms shared both common elements and differences. Both classes used Big Books and shared reading of these texts. In the Chapter 1 class, the children completed open-ended extension activities following the reading of a Big Book. For example, they might write about the book, create a similar book, do an art project, or perform a play. This class also had an extensive library that children could access. The teacher talked to the children about letters and their sounds but only through the connected text of books. In the kindergarten class, Big Book and shared reading typically were followed by worksheet time that rarely corresponded to the book. The children completed handwriting and letter-sound worksheets, and the only book available to the students was the one Big Book that the teacher had just read. The skills instruction in this class was more explicit in that the children focused on a letter a week throughout the kindergarten year.

In both of these classrooms, Curtis often was asked to help other children with writing activities. He helped children write letters and identify pictures that began with a certain letter. He thoroughly enjoyed being placed in this helper role. He always beamed when the teacher requested his help for another student.

During teacher read-aloud time, Curtis always worked his way to the front of the group. He would begin by sitting on the floor and looking up at the illustrations. Usually by the third page, he was up on his knees commenting on the illustrations or touching them. For the most part, the teachers did not seem bothered by his behavior. As the year progressed, Curtis became familiar with the labels of *author* and *illustrator*. If his teacher forgot, he asked for information about the author and illustrator for each book read.

As I watched Curtis during work sessions in both classes, he always approached each task with great care. His kindergarten teacher said that "he expected perfection" on all of his assignments. I often saw him write, erase, and then write again until he made each letter in an exact duplicate of the model. He always loved showing his work to his teachers and gaining their praise about the quality of his work.

Curtis came into kindergarten knowing the alphabet and all of the corresponding letter sounds. This knowledge was extended during the year as he learned to represent CVC words. His kindergarten teacher often asked the children to generate words that began with the letter being studied. As the children provided these words, he wrote them on the board. Curtis often copied these words on the back of his worksheets. Then in his Chapter 1 class, he used these words and other CVC words in his journal writing.

At the end of the year, both of his teachers agreed that he was doing well. His kindergarten teacher added that "he likes to do dittos." His Chapter 1 teacher was pleased that he could spell the names of all the children in the class. She observed this as he wrote about each student in his journal. They both talked about his behavior. Although they concurred that his outbursts were "not fun," they indicated that there were fewer of them. They extended this by saying that his outbursts all centered on learning. For instance, if they gave him a short period to complete his work, he became upset because he could not do it well. They both allowed Curtis to stay in at recess and complete his work if this happened, and that stopped most of his tantrums. They indicated that his behavior was easy to modify because it all centered on his being able to be involved with learning. He never was disrespectful just to get attention.

Toward the final days of kindergarten, Curtis's Chapter 1 teacher asked the children to dictate a story about themselves. These were then posted around the room. Curtis's story follows:

> I am a five year old boy who is nice to people. I like to be happy. My mama makes me happy. I like her. sometimes, my daddy is mean. I don't like him then. French fires, hot dogs, and hamburgers are my favorite foods. When I grow up, I'm going to be a policeman so I can put bad mamas and daddys in jail. (All spellings are as they were in his dictated story as recorded by the teacher.)

This story gives us a glimpse into who Curtis sees himself as currently and what his hopes are for the future. He has also decided that when he is an adult he will punish those "bad mamas and daddys" by putting them in jail. His story is quite extensive for a kindergarten child. He is able to talk about himself and also speculate about the future. This type of story is unusual in the dictations of kindergarten children, especially without nudging from the teacher.

Understandings of Curtis's Literacy at Age 5

Curtis continued to build on his previous literacy experiences during his kindergarten year. He was fortunate in that he had a full-day experience during this year that allowed him substantial time for exploring literacy concepts. At the end of the year, he had discovered that

- he could write both his first and last names easily;
- he knew how a book was organized;
- he knew about the roles of an author and an illustrator;
- he had full concept of word in print, and could match speech and print;
- he could read independently in a word-by-word fashion;
- he understood how to represent words using the initial and final consonants and a vowel; and
- he could convey his thoughts through independent writing.

At the end of this year, Curtis was a beginning reader and writer. He had moved beyond the safety of predictable text and was able to read text independently without this structure. He and his teachers also had devised ways to help Curtis control his behavior. These teachers recognized that Curtis became upset only when he was not able to complete his work to his high expectations. By providing ways for Curtis to satisfy his need for perfection, his outbursts became less frequent. The persistent concern was whether other teachers would be as flexible as these teachers in providing such an outlet for Curtis.

Curtis's Literacy at Age 6

Curtis in First Grade

Curtis left the security of neighborhood schools when he went to first grade. Because the new school was not complete and the sixth-grade centers were still being renovated and were not yet in use as full elementary schools, Curtis was bused to a middle-class school for first grade. This school was about 15 miles from his home.

I first visited his classroom in August. His class consisted of 15 children who were predominantly Caucasian. Each child sat at a separate desk and there were centers around the room. The teacher, Ms. Mills, greeted me as I entered. Her first words to me were, "I am surprised that he doesn't have learning problems like his brothers. He is so smart." As our conversation continued, I learned that she had taught Johnnie several years ago and she was familiar with Curtis's younger brother as well. She had assumed that Curtis would also have difficulties with learning as did his brothers.

As I continued my observations, I never saw any children's work on the wall. The classroom never had a library with books available for children. Each week the centers were changed by the teacher. The centers included a listening center, an exercise center (children did physical exercise like jumping and skipping), a writing center (children finished a story starter), and an art center. The children visited these centers while the teacher worked with reading groups. They were expected to visit each center during the week.

There were three reading groups based on ability in this room. All instruction was from the basal text and the children typically read using a round-robin strategy. Each child had one or more turns to read while the other children listened. Each reading lesson usually began with the children reading sight words from flash cards and then they read their story for the day. When they completed their story, they worked on workbook pages together. When the children left this group, they returned to their seats to complete a packet of worksheets. These packets were the same for all the children in the class even though there were significant differences in the children's literacy and math capabilities. The packet usually had six papers in it: Two were phonics skills related, two focused on math, and two were activity papers like dot-to-dot sheets. In addition to the packet, the children had a copy page each day on which they had to copy sentences from the board. Sometimes they had to correct spelling and punctuation because the sentences were purposely written incorrectly. As they worked independently, they were expected to be quiet and to work alone. The children complied with this expectation.

Curtis was in the top group which usually was called to work with the teacher last. Ms. Mills said that this "reading group is the best working group." As Curtis completed his worksheets, he always peeked at what the children were doing in other reading groups. He liked to listen to the stories they were reading. He listened, returned to his work, and then listened again. Although the content of the independent work was easy for him, he was usually the last one done. His limited focus on this work was one reason why he took so long to complete these papers. The other reason was that he expected his work to be perfect. He spent as much time erasing as he did writing.

The literacy curriculum focused on the basal throughout the year. The children moved through these books systematically. As a supplement to these books, the teacher used a phonics workbook for her skills instruction. The children began the year exploring short vowels. In September, the children also were exploring short-vowel words on their spelling lists. Before Christmas break, they had moved to long-vowel pattern words on both their worksheets and their spelling lists. During the second semester, they explored *r*-controlled words, vowel digraphs, and endings like *ing* and *ed*. All of this word investigation was fun for Curtis. He bragged to the class that he "never had to study." He always scored 100% on his spelling tests.

On one occasion, I asked Curtis to spell the words from the developmental spelling list. In Figure 21 are the results of this request. By examining his spellings, it is clear that Curtis could represent most short-vowel words correctly. He also had begun to understand how to represent long-vowel patterns. He was able to spell *drive* and *train* accurately, but he was still learning about this concept as is demonstrated by his spelling of *float*.

As the year came to an end, his teacher said that "he was doing very well in school." She commented that he was her best worker and best reader. "He can read anything." It was interesting that during this year, Curtis stopped having behavioral outbursts in the classroom. He was even named student of the week on several occasions. It did not appear

Figure 21
Curtis's Spelling

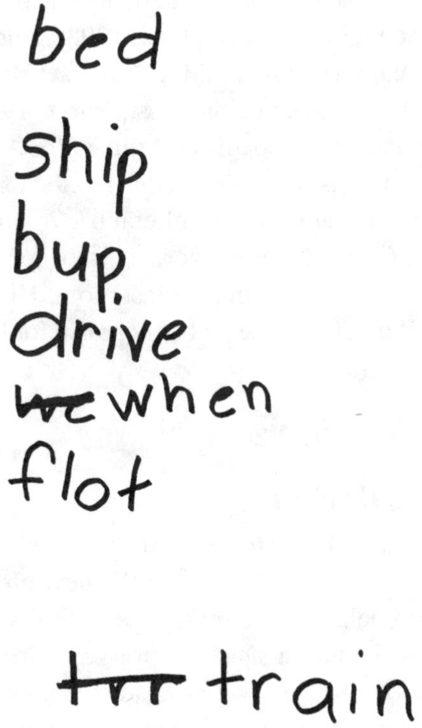

bed

ship
bup
drive
~~we~~ when
flot

~~trr~~ train

that his teacher had accommodated him in any way. For no explicit reason, Curtis no longer saw the need to become upset in this classroom.

Understandings of Curtis's Literacy at Age 6

Curtis's first-grade classroom was similar to his kindergarten environment, but not that of his Chapter 1 classroom. Access to books and to freely express oneself in writing were limited. The expectation was that children would read with the teacher in a small group and then independently complete worksheet assignments. In this environment and with the continued support of his parents, Curtis learned

- how to read independently in a fluent manner; and
- how to represent words using long-vowel patterns. He would be considered to be a within-word pattern speller.

This academic year proved to be successful for Curtis. His literacy development continued and he moved to fluency within the first grade. This development is typically not seen until the end of the second grade or during third grade (Hiebert & Raphael, 1998). Additionally, Curtis moved from his local school to a middle-class school, and he continued to be seen as the brightest in his class. Delpit (1995) and Ladson-Billings (1994) talk about how difficult this is for African American children and adults. Curtis was able to adjust to the expectations of his teachers even when they ignored his cultural background. And perhaps most important for Curtis, he no longer had to become out of control, even for short periods of time, in his classroom. His teacher saw no reason to be critical of Curtis; she had only praise for him as a learner.

Curtis's Literacy at Age 7

Curtis in Second Grade

Curtis had another school change in second grade. He moved back to his home neighborhood and attended the new elementary school that his mother had helped to be built. The school year opened with many special events including a celebration for Curtis's mother.

This school was unlike Curtis's first-grade school in philosophy. The school was led by an African American principal and the majority of the teachers were African American. In addition to the cultural and racial background of the teachers and administrator, the school was grounded in an Afrocentric curriculum. Each day, the children were involved in a class that investigated important African Americans. Beyond this class, the children were bombarded with messages about how it was up to them to be successful and that this was possible and expected. This philosophy was evident as a person walked through the halls of this school, in which each wall featured a famous African American.

Curtis entered a second-grade classroom led by Mrs. Cambell. This classroom overflowed with books. There was a library area for the children and there were books available to them throughout the room. Mrs. Cambell read to the children many times a day. Her readings were dramatic and involved the children throughout. As might be expected, Curtis was always at her feet as she read.

Before Mrs. Cambell read to the children, she had them put on visors. She told them that these visors would help them think. When they wore them they had "extra-special thinking powers." Before reading, during reading, and after reading, the children were involved with the story. Mrs. Cambell used the cover to focus predictions about the story and then she might stop in the middle and talk about it with the children. Following the story the teacher and children engaged in open-ended discussion. After this informal discussion, the children played "stump the teacher," asking her questions about the events or characters in the story that was just read. Their goal was to come up with a question that the teacher could not answer. The children loved this game and they especially loved when their teacher could not answer one of their questions. This strategy might be considered a variation of the ReQuest procedure designed by Manzo (1969).

On other occasions, after the teacher read, she engaged the children in critical discussion of the story by posing a question such as "Was Miss Nelson a good teacher?" The children had just listened to Allard's book (1977) *Miss Nelson Is Missing*. The children went back and forth on this issue and they finally created a chart showing good and poor teaching behaviors. Although Mrs. Cambell was not familiar with Commeyras's work (1990), this strategy replicated the dialogical thinking-reading lesson designed by her. In these lessons, children engage in debate focused on complex questions with no clear right or wrong answer.

In addition to these whole-group reading and comprehension activities, the children were expected to complete skill-based worksheets at their desks. The children all received the same packet of worksheets. For the most part, these sheets centered on phonics principles. Similar to first grade, the children also had copy exercises each day.

Continuing with his previous tradition, Curtis completed each of these sheets perfectly. He often stayed in at recess to finish his work. Curtis never saw this staying in as punishment. He found more pleasure in completing his assignments perfectly than he did in recess.

Throughout the year, I talked to Curtis about the books he was reading, the stories he was writing, and school itself. He told me that he "read too many books to have a favorite. I like the myths a lot." He then expanded on these thoughts and said, "I like reading. I like writing stories best at school."

His teacher had a lot to say about Curtis as a student. She said that she used reading to the class as a reward for Curtis. "He loves to read and he especially loves to read to our class." She needed to use this reward often when his mother suffered a heart attack. She said that "he was able to hold it together academically but he had trouble with his behavior" during this time. When JoAnne returned home, his behavior was once again under his control.

Mrs. Cambell recommended that Curtis be tested for placement in the gifted and talented program. He easily qualified as he achieved the highest scores possible. The tests were in the areas of learning (academic subjects like reading and math), motivation, creativity, and leadership. Mrs. Cambell said that he also

> maxed out on the district tests. He didn't miss one question on the criterion tests. These tests are really hard. I think he could skip a grade and be fine. He is that smart. He knows everything about a mythology unit we just finished. He cried one day when I ran out of time to read another myth. He loves to learn and is physically upset when he is unable to. I think he will be the president or mayor one day.

At the end of the year, Mrs. Cambell started to share French with her class. She read to the children and taught them new vocabulary each day. She said that the children loved playing with another language. She said, "Curtis loved it most of all. He retains each word."

Because of his interest and ability, she made tapes for him to take home over the summer.

Understandings of Curtis's Literacy at Age 7

During this year, Curtis consolidated his previous literacy learnings. He could now

- read fluently, even when he was reading a book for the first time;
- understand what he read both literally, inferentially, and critically; and
- begin to understand how multisyllabic words were structured. He explored root and base words and prefixes and suffixes.

This year was one of joys and trials. Curtis loved coming to a new school that was very important to his mother. He also lived through his mother's having a heart attack and the adjustments his family had to make as a result. Through all of this, with the support of his teacher, he developed as a reader and writer. He extended his understanding of reading through his teacher's comprehension strategy lessons. He enjoyed trying to trick her with his questions and he enjoyed the thinking required in the critical-literacy activities. His teacher also realized that he was a very special learner and had him tested for the district's gifted and talented program. He would begin working in this program during his third-grade year.

Final Thoughts

Curtis's story is different from the other stories in that his mother was such a successful activist. She dealt with welfare and let them know that these children were hers. The boys saw JoAnne as their mother. They were never worried that they would have to leave this home. They knew that she would not allow this. The other children in the study who were in stable foster care (not adopted) were never as sure as these boys that they might not be moved. Curtis was fortunate to have this stability in his young life. In addition to this stable environment, JoAnne and her family protected the boys (through her store) and supported their learning by working with them each day.

She also had books, paper, and pencils in her home for the boys' homework and for pleasure reading and writing.

JoAnne also valued the cultural backgrounds of her children and herself. She was tired and frustrated with the common beliefs about African American parents and their lack of interest in their children's schooling. She was willing to battle the school district and the city to provide elementary schools in her area. She also expected that these schools would provide instruction that was culturally appropriate. JoAnne visited the school each day once it opened and she held forums for parents. She wanted to make sure that they became a part of this school. She did not want the press to criticize these parents for lack of interest and further stigmatize this group of parents and children. Her crusade continued even after the school was built.

Curtis lived in this environment and as a result his academic success was valued. Curtis was a self-motivated learner from the first time I met him. The only time he had difficulty in school was when he had to complete an assignment too quickly. He took pride in each and every assignment that he was given. He did not complete some quickly and others slowly, each was considered done only when it met his perfectionist standards.

Although Curtis's emotional upsets in school might be seen as reinforcing the myths about crack/cocaine children, it must be remembered that generally he was not out of control. He only lost control when his learning was interfered with. All his teachers were able to deal with this behavior. By first grade, it had dissipated. It only returned again when his mother was seriously ill.

Curtis's academic behavior explodes the myths about these children. Not only was he successful, but he also always performed beyond the grade-level expectations. By second grade, he qualified for a gifted and talented program.

Curtis moved beyond his prenatal drug exposure and beyond being a biracial child to be a successful learner in all of his school settings. He moved to the front of the class in schools that were predominantly black or white. His racial and socioeconomic background did not become problematic for him. Curtis's teachers all focused on him as an exceptional learner. Even his first-grade teacher, who saw him as potentially learning disabled, set aside her prediction and considered him as a gifted learner. Curtis certainly is a special boy, one who may become "president or mayor one day."

CHAPTER 8

Ray: A Child Who Sees Reading as an Escape

Tough guys fight
All alone at night
Life doesn't frighten me at all.

(Angelou, M. [1993]. *Life Doesn't Frighten Me* [unpaged]. New York: Stewart, Tabori, & Chang.)

From the first moment that I met Ray, I worried about his life. Although he lived in a foster home with no indication that he would move to other homes, his home never seemed loving. His foster mother, Melva, kept all of her foster children at a distance. The children appeared to be only a job to her. I never saw her enjoy being with them. Melva's focus seemed to be on the clothes that needed washing or mending or the dinner that needed to be prepared. These were her primary worries.

Ray's school life, especially when he moved into public school, replicated this feeling of distance. The teachers who first came to my mind when I thought about Ray's school experience were not passionate about the children they taught. They went through the motions, but there was no excitement in their classrooms. I never witnessed any real caring from these teachers for the children they taught. The children went through their days working in isolation on reading and math papers. The only time they worked directly with the teacher was during small-group reading time.

Of all the children in the study, I worried about Ray the most. He seemed to be alone from the first moment I met him, and I rarely saw an adult share a close relationship with him. As I observed Ray, I noted how important stories and reading were to him. Perhaps as a result of having no close relationships with adults, Ray learned to read early; he loved to read. Ray seemed to be most free to express his feelings when he entered the world of a book. When watching him read, I often heard him giggle or gasp at what was happening in a story. He seemed to be most alive during reading adventures. Ray's self-portrait appears in Figure 22.

Getting to Know Ray

I've got a magic charm
That I keep up my sleeve

(Angelou, 1993)

Figure 22
Ray's Self-Portrait

I met Ray and his foster mother, Melva, at their single-family home on a busy street. The home was small and somewhat run down. It needed to be painted, some windows were broken, and the front yard was a burned-out lawn with no toys. Some of the homes on his street were filled with bullet holes or had been burned. I later learned that these were crack houses. Because there were so many of these houses close by, the threat of violence was always present.

My first visit was chaotic at best. As I walked in, Melva and a foster teenage daughter were screaming at each other. Melva had decided that this girl was "starting to fool with boys" and she would "have none of that in her home." She had called the Nevada State Welfare Department and told them that this child had to move. This was the day that the move was to occur. As I entered, her daughter was throwing all of her clothes in the living room in preparation for her departure, alternating between crying and yelling. Melva carried out her conversation with me while this was happening. She talked to me, yelled at her daughter, and then continued our conversation. As one might guess, I had a hard time keeping our conversation coherent and focused on Ray, who, along with another foster brother, played with blocks on the floor as we talked. They seemed not to be aware of the scene that was occurring.

Ray came to live with Melva when he was about 3 years old, moving into her home with his younger brother, Rashad. Melva quickly decided that the two boys were too much to handle and had Ray's younger brother moved to another home. She said that "Ray still misses his brother and wants to visit him." Although this was important to Ray, she complained that she did "not have enough time to take him for a visit." Rashad's foster mother had called to set up a time to meet at the park, but she did not think that she could ever find the time for such a visit.

Melva described Ray as being hyperactive:

He won't keep his shoes on. He needs new shoes every 3 months. He likes to play outside. He runs and hops and hollers in church. No one can control him. He has a mind of his own. He likes to experiment with everything. He walks around at night. He goes to bed at 7:00 but he doesn't fall asleep until 12:00 or 1:00.

She also talked about how Ray disappeared. When he was in trouble at home, he frequently walked out of the house and combed the neighborhood for his birth mother who had discovered where he lived and frequently came to the house crying for him. On these occasions, Melva had to walk through the neighborhood to find him. She said that "he always comes home crying and this is before I swat him for leaving." When I probed a bit about how she disciplined Ray, she indicated that she spanked him or withheld treats.

When I asked about other details about Ray's early life, she was unsure about them. She did not know when his birthday was or when he started to talk, for instance. From this discussion, we moved to a conversation about Ray and what she noticed about how he was learning to read and write. She shared how he loved to "play school" with the other children living in the home (I was never able to get an accurate number of how many foster children lived in the house). She also said that "he loves to pick up books." I found this interesting because I never saw a book in this home. However, she indicated that they went to the library each week where he checked out two books. She did not know if he wrote or if he knew the alphabet. She ended our conversation by saying how much he liked to watch television.

Ray's Literacy at Age 4

I just smile
They go wild
Life doesn't frighten me at all.
(Angelou, 1993)

Ray in Preschool

After our first visit, I most often saw Ray at the Head Start center near his home. Melva told me that she had to go to the classroom at least two times a week to help control Ray's behavior. I never saw her in all of my visits to the school, however.

Preceding my first observation visit, I talked to Ray's teacher, Mrs. Ricco. She said, "He has come a long way. He is settling." Mrs. Ricco indicated that Ray had difficulty behaving when he first arrived in this setting. He did not want to share and often took toys away from

144

other children. She was pleased that this behavior was changing and was thrilled that Ray knew all of his "alphabet letters." She indicated that he was the only student in her class who recognized them.

Although Ray was in the same Head Start center as Melina and Curtis, his room had more of a literacy focus. Although Mrs. Ricco spent a considerable amount of time each day on the prescribed program focused on health and behavior, she also enriched her room with a library center filled with books. She had personally purchased these books to share with the children. In addition to the library, she had a listening center set up each day with a popular children's story.

When I observed Ray in this classroom, he listened to a story read by the teacher or participated in listening to a taped story. Like several of the other children in this study, Ray moved to the front of the group whenever the teacher was reading. He wanted to be close so he could see the pictures. One day, the teacher was reading *The April Rabbits* (Cleveland, 1978), and Ray counted each rabbit with the teacher. He giggled when there were more rabbits on each page. At the end of the story, Mrs. Ricco asked the children, "What will they do?" Ray responded with "They got no mom. Maybe a fairy will help." The teacher replied to his suggestion by saying that "the fairy is not here today."

Ray's personal life was evident during his interactions during both book reading and center activities. For example, in his discussion about what might happen to the rabbits in *The April Rabbits* he immediately noticed that the rabbits "got no mom." Another example of this home-to-school connection happened when Ray was playing with Mike in the block center. The boys were building and using vehicles in their play. As they constructed they talked:

Mike: What are you building?

Ray: A castle. My daddy is in jail because he had a fight. This is a fire truck. Here are two helicopters.

Mike: Give me (referring to a truck).

Ray: (To the teacher) He has a truck on the table.

Teacher: Mike and Ray share the trucks.

I found it interesting that the children and the teacher never commented about the home situations that Ray so easily shared in school. No one even gave him a pat or a hug when he talked about having no mom or a dad who was in jail. His personal sharings were ignored in his school setting.

When I had a chance to sit with Ray and have him read and write, our conversation began with his telling me "I don't know how to read." I responded by asking him to tell me about the book *Fizz and Splutter* (Melser, 1982). The conversation that we shared about this book follows:

Me: Tell me about the book.

Ray: I don't know the words. (Responding to the *m* page. This page had pictures beginning with *m*.) Monkey, mom, mask, broom, monster, milk, mat, (responding to the *c* page) cake, carrot, camel, cow, coffee, cat, coat, eagle.

Me: How did you know that (referring to his identification of an eagle)?

Ray: 'Caused I saw one. (He continues identifying pictures on the *b* and *h* page) Pig, boat, bed, bug, cop, bucket, jungle, bell, balloon, bike, bee, book, ball, B, block, uh-oh, chicken, tree, water hose, helicopter, horse, bee house, towel. I saw a bee house on TV. (Continuing and moving on to the *s* page) hammer, knife, six, seven, lots of ships, sandwich, sock, hat, glasses, pin, S, fire, big bad wolf, letter, twelve, football, man, monster, fish, water fountain, people, the end. He looks like Freddie Krueger.

His retelling of this book indicated that he understood the metalanguage related to the concept of word. He told me when I asked him to read that he "didn't know the words." He recognized the words on the page and knew that he still did not have the ability to read these words independently, but he knew what they were called and that they were important to reading. He also was able to label all the pictures in the book, although not all of his labels corresponded to the intentions of the author, for example, when he called a *beehive* a *bee house* or a *hen* a *chicken*. Additionally, he made an intertextual connection between the illustration of the wizard in this book to the movie character Freddie Krueger.

Understandings of Ray's Literacy at Age 4

I learned quite a bit about Ray as a literacy learner throughout this preschool year, and realized that he knew

- how to represent himself in a self-portrait that was not considered to be a scribble;
- how to write and spell his first name;
- how a book was organized (he knew about the front and back of a book and how to turn pages, and he knew the difference between words and illustrations);
- how to recognize words on a page but could not yet coordinate reading and pointing;
- how to retell a story using storytelling and book language (he often refused to read because he did not know the words);
- how to use random letters and numerals to represent words; and
- how to recognize all the letters of the alphabet.

With the literacy knowledge that Ray exhibited during this year, he would be considered to be an emergent reader and writer. He was aware of the special language used in books, he appreciated the storyline of text, and he recognized the importance of the words in text. His development at this point would be considered appropriate or advanced for a child in preschool. The knowledge that he exhibited while in preschool is often the goal for children in kindergarten (Bear & Barone, 1998; McGee & Richgels, 1996; Templeton, 1995).

This development is curious because Ray did not have many books at home to explore. However, he did enjoy playing school with his foster brothers and sisters, and even his foster mother noticed how much he enjoyed this type of pretend play. And she said that they made frequent trips to the library. Perhaps this support and the richness of literacy experiences provided by his teacher were sufficient for this development to occur. It also is very important to note the interest that Ray demonstrated in books and any book-reading event. No matter what he was engaged with in school, he immediately abandoned it to join a book-reading event. The opportunities to engage in book reading and Ray's intrinsic desire to be a part of these episodes were most likely mutually responsible for his development. Ray fully participated in all book-reading sessions in his classroom and even when children next to him poked him, he ignored this behavior so that he could listen to a story.

Ray's behavior in preschool and at home was troublesome. He would cry and kick if another child touched a toy he was playing with, for example. Like Curtis, he seemed to have some difficulty controlling behavior in school settings. According to Melva, Ray's behavior was so out of control that she was expected to help the teacher in school. Importantly, Ray's teacher noted that his behavior was improving or as she said it, "He is settling."

Ray's Literacy at Age 5

Ray in Kindergarten

Ray attended a neighborhood kindergarten. The school day was 2½ hours long and there were 21 children in his class. All of these children were African American. His teacher, Ms. Parker, was a second-year teacher but this was her first year teaching kindergarten. She was new to this school and had taught at a middle-class school during the previous year. Ms. Parker was Caucasian and from a middle-class background. She was concerned about the children she was teaching this year, worrying that her students would not be ready for first grade by the end of the year. She noted that many of her students seemed to "have never seen a book before."

Ms. Parker's literacy curriculum was a combination of holistic and traditional practices. She used the letter of the week as an organizing strategy. The children worked on a letter all week both in whole-group exercises and in center work. She conducted shared-book experiences (Holdaway, 1979) with the children and used these books to provide instruction on the highlighted letter. The children completed worksheets in centers and had opportunities to write in journals. There was a library center in the room that was quite attractive and inviting, with many stuffed animals to which the children chose to read to during sustained silent reading. In one corner, there was a computer. Each day some children were able to go to the computer and practice letter-sound drills. Beyond this curriculum, the children watched *Sesame Street* each day.

As would be expected, Ray enjoyed the shared-book reading experiences. He always found a way to nudge up to the front of the group. He responded to the teacher's questions even when he was not called on. Often it appeared that he and the teacher were having a private conversation about the book. If the teacher asked if a child could find the letter *c* on a page, he scanned the whole page until he found each and every *c*. He was able to find letters in any location in a word, not just when they were in the place of initial consonant. Ray seemed happy completing his letter worksheets as well. He never sat at a center, but always stood as he worked. He often sang rap songs as he completed these sheets.

Ray was very interesting to watch as he worked in a center. He easily completed the task demands of a worksheet. He sang, said the name of a picture, and identified the initial consonant all at the same time. He often stopped his work to help another child who was having difficulty. He was able to keep track of what each child was doing at the center and he corrected a child if he or she made a mistake on a worksheet.

When worksheets were completed, the children could go to the library for free-choice reading. Ray loved visiting the library. He pulled many stuffed animals around him and pretended that they were his babies as he read. Once as he prepared to read he said, "Let me read to my little babies. Give me a book so I can read to you. I'll read two stories. I am going to read about Care Bears to you."

Ms. Parker was pleased with Ray and his progress during the year. In October, she made the following comment:

> Ray loves to read. He knows all of the Big Books that we have read. He can make all the letters. He is really smart. He is better at following directions and behaving. He likes center time best because he can move around.

Her comments were similar to those of his preschool teacher. They both noticed his behavior at first but they also acknowledged his ability to control himself in the classroom. They both recognized his intelligence, especially with respect to literacy.

During this year, Ray's comprehension and writing abilities developed. One spring day, Ms. Parker read a Winnie-the-Pooh story (Milne, 1957) to the class. Ray immediately moved to the front of the group to be able to get a closer look at the illustrations. Ray giggled when the book was completed, and Ms. Parker and Ray then entered into a discussion about the book as the other children listened in.

Ray:	That was fun.
Ms. Parker:	Tell me something that happened in the story.
Ray:	Pooh got fat from eating too much honey. He popped out. Then he ate more honey.
Ms. Parker:	How did Pooh feel at the end?
Ray:	Happy.

This conversation demonstrated Ray's abilities to summarize a story and his understanding of a character's feelings. I found it interesting that Ms. Parker interacted only with Ray in talking about the story. She did not solicit comments from the other children in the class.

Besides loving stories, Ray enjoyed writing in his journal. In November, he wrote, "I want to be a plsmn [policeman]." In a later entry he wrote, "I lov Miss Prkr." This writing demonstrated that he could express his ideas in words that could be read by others. He clearly was able to represent initial and final consonants and was experimenting with vowels. As he engaged in the process of writing, it was possible to hear him sound out each letter as he wrote it.

As the year was ending, Miss Parker told me that "Ray is doing a super job. He loves stories. He is mesmerized by them. He is reading out of the first- and second-grade basals already."

Understandings of Ray's Literacy at Age 5

At the end of Ray's kindergarten year, he had developed into a beginning reader and writer. He now was able to

- write his first and last name;
- recognize the full organization of a book;
- match speech and text (he had full concept of word in print);
- read a book independently in a word-by-word fashion (these books were often at a first- or second-grade level);
- represent words using the first and last consonant and a vowel;
- communicate ideas through writing; and
- enjoy involvement with book reading.

Throughout this year, Melva always found excuses to keep me from visiting Ray at home. Each time we set an appointment, she called to cancel. Finally she told me that it was best if I saw him only at school. She had enrolled Ray in summer school and she informed the teacher that I would be observing. As a result of her reluctance to let me visit, all my observations were made in his school settings.

Ray's classroom curriculum supported and nurtured his literacy growth. In this room, any inappropriate behavior quickly disappeared. He enjoyed listening to stories and he responded well to the freedom of working in centers, where he developed as a leader because he was always supportive and willing to work with other children. He was also quick to help them correct any mistakes they might have made. Ray moved from the emergent-reader-and-writer category to that of a beginning reader and writer. This development is notable for a child still in kindergarten. Perhaps it is surprising as his home situation is one that has been documented frequently as not being supportive of a child's literacy development (Allington & Walmsley, 1995; Graves, van den Broek, & Taylor, 1996; Hiebert, 1991).

Ray's Literacy at Age 6

Ray in First Grade

Ray was enrolled in a middle-class school for first grade that was quite a distance from his home. There were 30 children in this class with 2 teachers, Mrs. Green and Mrs. Garcia. The children sat in desks that were organized into rows. As might be expected by this configuration, the children were expected to be quiet when they worked independently.

The teachers organized their literacy curriculum around basal texts. They had current basal texts and linguistic readers from the 1970s that they used daily. The children were grouped by ability and they met with one of the teachers daily. Following this lesson, the children returned to their desks to reread a basal story or practice a story from the linguistic reader. After they concluded this reading, they completed worksheets that were most often phonics based. Although there were three identified ability levels in this room, the children all completed the same worksheets at their desk. In addition, there were other books available to the children which they could read during sustained silent reading.

The children began their day with an oral-language lesson. This lesson involved the children in responding to questions, most often focused on vocabulary, asked by the teacher. Then the teachers wrote two sentences on the board that needed correction. The children copied the sentences and corrected any grammar, spelling, or punctuation errors. After about 20 minutes, the teachers and children corrected these papers together. Once this activity was completed, the children began their reading group rotations.

During my first visit to the class, Mrs. Garcia talked to me about Ray. She told me that he thought I was his "counselor." She was frustrated because Melva was "not helping him with homework. Nothing comes back to school. She is impossible to get on the phone." As she continued to talk about Ray, she commented that he was "very bright and he is a good student. I think that lack of help at home may hinder him." This teacher was sharing a slightly different view of Ray than the views shared by his previous teachers. Later in the year, Mrs. Green conveyed a similar message to me:

> [Ray] is in the top reading group. I am amazed at how well he does because he does not have any support at home. On some days, he has a hard time sitting still. I think on those days, he hasn't slept much or been fed breakfast. I want him out of this foster home and into one that is more supportive. With home support, he could go to college. You know, he is getting an A in all subjects.

Ray was a pleasure to watch through this year. He loved to read, even in the linguistic readers (books that have text based on rhyming word families; an example of such a text might be *Nan can fan. Dan can fan*). He often asked his teachers if he could stay in from recess so that he could finish a story or an informational book. During this year, he fell in love with books about animals. He often chose to read books about snakes, dinosaurs, or spiders.

On one visit, I asked him how he had become such a good reader. He giggled at my question and then replied, "from reading." Following up on this question, I asked, "What book is your favorite?" He answered, "Every book is my favorite. I like books about animals." I then asked him if he would write for me. His writing on this occasion

152

is shared in Figure 23. When he had completed this writing, I asked him to spell the words from the developmental list. From his writing, it was possible to see that he was easily able to convey ideas. He had moved from representing words with just initial and final consonants and a single letter to represent a vowel. He was now including markers to indicate long vowels as is seen in his spelling of *drive* as *DIVE* and *float* as *FLOTE*.

As Ray was developing as a reader and writer, his teachers' concerns about his home situation were escalating. They had contacted the principal and were seeking outside help with a home investigation for neglect. Simultaneously, they realized that Ray might be bored with the classroom curriculum. Mrs. Garcia said, "Ray is often

Figure 23
Ray's Writing and Spelling

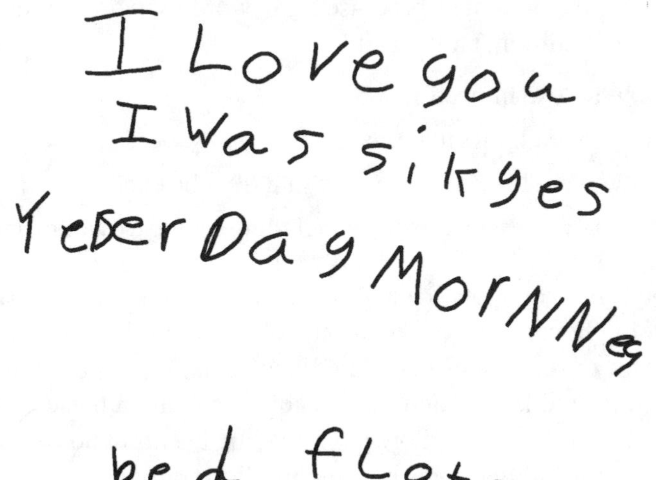

153

bored with the teaching in our room because he can already do what is being taught. He just needs to learn to hang in there."

After listening to the teachers' worries about home and their observations about the inappropriateness of the curriculum, I was surprised that they tried to improve only Ray's home life and had no plans to adapt their curriculum to his needs. I guessed that the home situation was seen as most critical to Ray's everyday existence, and I think most people would agree with their assessment. However, although they did what they could to change this situation, it was a difficult one to remedy and they neglected the school situation that would seem to be more easily adjusted to his needs. With Ray's love of books, providing more interesting text would have helped him develop as a reader and writer. By letting him experience a more exciting world in books, his school day would have been enriched.

Understandings of Ray's Literacy at Age 6

During Ray's first-grade experience, he became a fluent reader and writer. He no longer processed text word by word but in a fluent manner. In addition, he learned

- how to lose himself in a book;
- how to read informational text;
- how to read fluently even the first time he encountered text; and
- how to represent words by including a long-vowel marker.

Ray's literacy growth was dramatic during this year. He continued to develop beyond the expectations of a child in the first grade. It is important to remember that Ray, like Curtis, was in a middle-class school during this year and he was able to maintain these gains even when other children had more book-reading events at home. His reading in school and his teachers' support allowed him to build from the literacy strengths that he brought to first grade. The librarian often let him visit the library so that he could read outside the classroom as well.

The behavior that had caused other teachers concern displayed itself infrequently during this year. Ray's teachers said that he was only "moody" when he had not had enough sleep or any breakfast to eat. Their solution to these days was to let him go to a corner of the room and read. By recess time, he was able to join the class without any problems.

The major concern during this year was his home situation. These teachers, more than his kindergarten teacher, were worried about him. They began the year with the usual attempts of trying to talk to his mother to gain her support in helping him with schoolwork. They were never able to reach his mother by phone. And his mother never visited school. By the end of the year, they were frantic with worry. They talked to the principal and secured the help of the Nevada State Welfare Department to investigate this home. Perhaps unfortunately, Ray stayed with Melva and it appeared that no change would be forthcoming even at the end of the school year.

Ray's Literacy at Age 7

Ray in Second Grade

Ray remained at the same school during second grade. He entered a second-grade class with 14 children and one teacher, Ms. Hughes. I assumed that Ms. Hughes had a reading program because I saw basals on her reading table at the front of the class, but I never saw her teach reading, writing, or any subject in all of my observations. At the beginning of the year, I always called Ms. Hughes to set up an appointment to visit. As with the other teachers, I asked when it would be best to come and watch instruction in reading or writing. Ms. Hughes always gave me a time to come visit, but she was never teaching either of these subjects when I arrived. Later in the year, I visited spontaneously and I still did not see any instruction in these areas or other areas of the curriculum.

Each time I visited, I watched Ms. Hughes work with the students at the calendar. The children came to the back of the room, sat on carpet squares, and were to talk about the day of the week or the weather. Unfortunately, the children were never in control and she quickly began to send them to their seats for time out. Generally after 10 minutes, the majority of the children were in time out. Her expectation for time out was that children would sit at their desks with their heads down. When the children arrived at their seats, they often surreptitiously slid books from their desks and read. As I glanced at these books, I realized that they were old basal readers. If a child was caught reading, they were again punished, only this time they lost recess.

Following the calendar activity that often took up to an hour to complete, the children returned to their seats. Then Ms. Hughes started a sticker routine. She had a master chart for good behavior and the children all had individual charts. She checked her chart and then moved to each child and gave him or her stickers to place on his or her own chart. Ms. Hughes had a clipboard that she always had with her and she jotted down the names of children who behaved well. These notations were transferred to her master chart, and from here she distributed stickers. This routine generally took a half hour to an hour to complete.

I found it interesting that no matter when I observed this is the instruction that I saw. Beyond these routines, Ms. Hughes's sister, who also taught at this school, came into her class to help with management. It should be noted that the principal was aware of this situation and Ms. Hughes was fired at the end of the year. Unfortunately for Ray, he spent all of second grade with this teacher.

When I talked to Ms. Hughes, she said, "Ray knows the answers to all of my questions." That was about all that she said about him throughout the year. I learned more about him from the principal and assistant principal.

On several of my visits, I noticed that Ray complained of a stomachache. His teacher sent him to the office when he whined about this. On most occasions the principal found something for him to eat. When she was not there, however, he was sent back to class hungry. On these days he spent most of his time with his head down until after lunch.

Early in the year the principal called me into her office. She asked many questions about my study. She requested copies of my field notes. She was upset with me when I refused to give her these notes but she understood my ethical dilemma. She was very concerned about Ray's home situation and was trying to gather data to have him removed from this home. She told me that "Ray often comes to school hungry. He doesn't want to go home after school. He just wants to stay here." She went on to discuss the strategies that she was using to gather sufficient documentation so that he would be moved out of his home.

The principal and assistant principal became Ray's advocates during this year. They recommended that he be tested for the gifted pro-

Figure 24
Ray's Story About *The Simpsons*

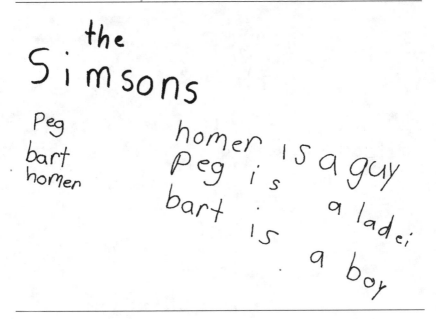

gram, for which he qualified. They gave him books to take home to read, although they had to keep this a secret from the classroom teacher. She refused to let him take books home because he sometimes lost them. They also visited his classroom each day, and always took him for a walk. This walk allowed him some time to talk to an adult who cared for him.

On many of my visits I took Ray outside for a walk. We chatted and then he wrote, read, and drew for me. He told me that he "is handsome and good at writing." He conversed a lot about his teacher. On one visit he told me, "I don't like my teacher. She won't let me take books home." He shared his plans for the summer. He was enrolled in a summer program that would take him on field trips each day. He wanted to go to "the library, swimming, and to Mount Charleston (a local mountain)."

On one occasion when I asked him to write and spell the words from the developmental list, he first wrote about the television show *The Simpsons*. As I had never seen the show before, he described the characters for me (see Figure 24). Scanning the developmental word list, shown in Fig-

Figure 25
Ray's Spelling

bed

drive

ship

when

well

~~boy~~

bomp

beaches

chase

flo.te

poping

catol

ure 25, I noted his ability to represent words. He was still experimenting with long-vowel patterns, but he was starting to represent some of
these patterns conventionally as seen in his spelling of *drive* and *chase*.

Understandings of Ray's Literacy at Age 7

This year was the most difficult for Ray. Although he remained in
this home, the school suspected that there was no real support there
physically, emotionally, or academically for Ray. To add to this situation, his classroom was chaotic at best. His teacher spent the whole

year reviewing the calendar and working on behavior charts. By any standards, this was not a classroom where children could learn. Despite these circumstances, Ray continued in his development. He learned

- how to find advocates to support his literacy outside of his classroom;
- how to enjoy chapter books independently; and
- how to refine his knowledge of long-vowel patterns.

Ray's teacher was so focused on controlling the behavior of 14 children that she never had time to teach. The classroom was not a place where children could thrive and develop as learners. Ray was more fortunate than many of the other children in his class because he built connections with others. The principal and assistant principal developed a special relationship with him. Their concern for Ray let them intervene in his classroom situation. They tried to connect with him each day and remove him from his classroom environment. They also made sure that he had books to read at home. Ray was able to develop as a reader and writer during this year because of their support. In the next chapter, you will see another child, Laquisha, who also learned to connect with teachers and others in her schools to provide similar support.

Concluding Thoughts

Ray, perhaps more so than the other children in this study, demonstrated resilience. Despite his home and school situations, he was motivated to do well in school. With the support of his preschool and kindergarten teachers, he learned to behave in school, and his strategy of curling up with a book instead of getting into an argument with a fellow classmate supported his in-school learning. All of his teachers recognized his intelligence, and most allowed him to spend considerable time reading.

Ray's home situation proved to be worrisome throughout the whole study. The teachers and principal were not successful in getting Ray to another foster home. Welfare was not able to document that this home was problematic, and they stated that the home was always clean and the children appeared to be well cared for. Because Melva kept me away from her home, I had no evidence to document the quality of this home either. I visited Ray at home the least of all the children in the study. During the 4 years, I was allowed to visit only twice. The first time was at the inception of the study and the second time was when he was in first grade. I think my second visit was a surprise for Melva. I had scheduled the appointment and she either forgot to call me and cancel or she forgot and did not leave her home prior to my arrival. During this second visit, Ray and I spent the entire time reading and writing. Melva quickly moved to another room and ignored us. I asked Ray to show me his books while I was there and he was unable to locate any. I doubt that Ray had many or any books at home until he was in second grade when his principal made sure that he did.

I also worried about Ray's placement in this home. I kept questioning why Melva found it difficult to allow me to visit and why she kept at a distance from school. This behavior left all of us puzzled about exactly what was happening. Yet even with this potentially harmful situation, Ray did well in school. His persistence in learning to read and write was inspiring to watch.

CHAPTER 9

Laquisha: How Did She Learn to Read and Write?

(written with Becky Schneider)

> Unpacking even just the few things in her brown suitcase, always seemed a waste of time to Gilly. She never knew if she'd be in a place long enough to make it worth the bother.
>
> (Paterson, K. [1978]. *The Great Gilly Hopkins* [p. 9]. New York: Harper-Collins)

Laquisha moved from numerous home and school settings by the time I came to know her when she was a fifth grader. By the beginning of fifth grade, Laquisha had been in 13 schools, a direct result of changes in her home situation. Sometimes she lived with her mother, other times with an aunt or a grandmother, and on three occasions she was placed in a Nevada State Welfare group home. Laquisha's self-portrait appears in Figure 26 on page 162.

My meeting Laquisha was serendipitous. In my work with schools, I spent considerable time with Becky Schneider, a teacher of a third-, fourth-, and fifth-grade multiage classroom. At the beginning of each year, she would identify a puzzling aspect of her classroom or a student in the classroom who was particularly interesting. Building from this initial identification, we would begin a year-long collaborative investigation of the child or an interesting curricular issue. Our first inquiry centered on Becky's first year with this classroom and how she used cross-aged tutoring to help her students become independent and responsible learners (Schneider & Barone, 1996). During the second

Figure 26
Laquisha's Self-Portrait

year, we followed the learning of a gifted student in her class (Barone & Schneider, 1996). He provided an interesting focus because her school had been designated at-risk by the school district because of the high-poverty background of the students.

During the third year of our collaborative work, Becky identified Laquisha as a student on whom we should focus. In Becky's class, the students stayed with her for 3 years. She typically added only new third-grade students to her class as the other students moved up in grade level. Because of this organization, her class could be described as having a family atmosphere. The teacher, students, and parents knew the culture of the classroom and felt comfortable with the learning and behavioral expectations. Laquisha moved into the class as a fifth grader, which was unusual but would not, by itself, provide the impetus for our study. Becky's first-week descriptions of Laquisha provide the rationale for our extended study:

> My first impression of Laquisha was of a shy, timid child. I was wrong. By lunchtime of the first day, I was wondering to myself, "How will I make it through the year?" By the end of the first week I had seen too many tantrums to count over very petty things. She crawled under the table during one of them because I asked her to find a novel to read. She told me, "I can't read them fat books!" Even after I went and picked three out for her to choose, she refused to read anything but a basal.

As the first week progressed, Becky added to the list of concerns about Laquisha. During a class meeting where students were brainstorming how to problem solve, Laquisha volunteered that she "would beat them up if they bother me." The students then talked about why physical violence does not solve a conflict, but Laquisha was firm in her idea that the best way to solve a problem was to beat up a student. She got into a fight because a child picked up her pencil by mistake, and both Laquisha and the other student were sent to the principal's office.

Laquisha's initial behavior changed markedly by the second week of school. Becky said that by the second week, "she had become my best friend. I'm not sure what changed her behavior, but I am very consistent in everything I do and she came into a trusting and reliable environment each day." Her behavior did not necessarily change in her interactions with other teachers however. She had difficulties with some teachers throughout the whole academic year. Becky theorized that "once she felt that you cared and she could talk to you, she behaved differently. Occasionally, she threw a fit, but it was short-lived and always was followed by a hug and an apology."

Laquisha's behavior led us to a year-long investigation to learn more about her. We talked to her current caregiver, other teachers, and Laquisha to find out about her as an individual and how she developed in literacy. Becky kept a reflective log focused on Laquisha. In addition to the interviews and log, we had access to her journals, book logs, portfolio, both formal and informal assessments, letters to university penpals, and all additional classroom work. Although Laquisha's initial behavior led us to want to learn more about her,

her fourth-grade reading ability level really intrigued us. We found it difficult to understand how a child who had moved among 13 schools and in and out of many home environments could be such a proficient reader, although a year below her current grade level. In fact, most research discusses the issues of poverty and minority status and how these children's learning needs are met infrequently in schools (Allington & Walmsley, 1995; Au, 1993; Baumann & Thomas, 1997; Delpit, 1995; Rossi, 1994). Au (1993) wrote that a disproportionate number of students coming from diverse backgrounds end up in the bottom reading group.

In addition to Laquisha's behavior and close-to-grade-level reading ability, we discovered early in our investigation that she had been prenatally exposed to crack or cocaine and perhaps other drugs as well. This knowledge was important because it allowed for the discovery of the literacy development of a child prenatally exposed to crack/cocaine who did not grow up in the stable environment common to the other children in the longitudinal study. By learning more about Laquisha, we have been able to open the window a bit further and consider how a child prenatally exposed to crack/cocaine and *not* living in a stable environment develops in literacy. Her story extends our knowledge of the quality of resilience.

Getting to Know Laquisha

> She began to cry softly into her pillow, not knowing why or for whom. Maybe for all the craziness she had tried so hard to manage and was never quite able to. (Paterson, 1978, p. 127)

Laquisha was always eager to talk about herself, her family, friends, and the books she was reading. Amazingly, she was very open about herself and many of the incidents she experienced. The best way to meet Laquisha is through a letter she wrote to a college penpal (see Figure 27). This was the first letter she wrote telling about herself as a way for them to get acquainted. She begins by asking how her penpal is. From this traditional beginning, she moves to a discussion of her life which includes a beating by her mother and an altercation between her sister and her aunt. Laquisha describes crying about the incidents, but there is a story-like quality to her rendition and it is impossible to

164

detect exactly how much these events have hurt her. Beyond these details, she talks about her love of the Babysitters' Club books and her acknowledgment that Anna's handwriting is very nice. This letter demonstrates Laquisha's ability to communicate through writing.

In one of Laquisha's interviews, I asked her to describe her childhood. Laquisha focused on serious incidents when she talked about

Figure 27
Laquisha's Pen-Pal Letter

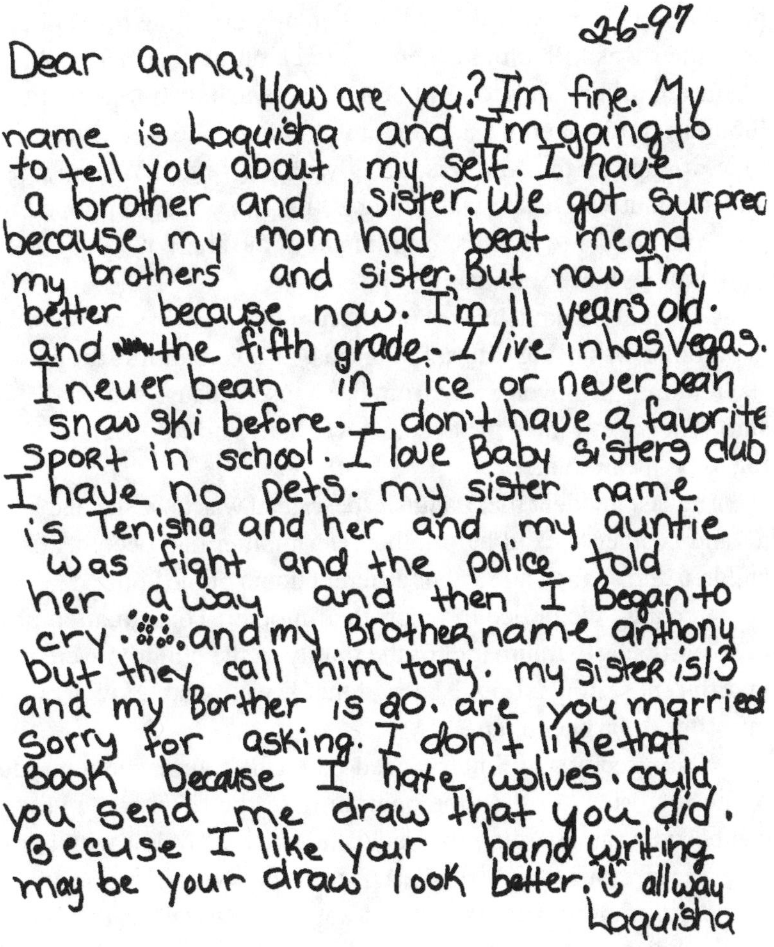

26-97

Dear Anna,
How are you? I'm fine. My name is Laquisha and I'm going to to tell you about my self. I have a brother and 1 sister. We got surpred because my mom had beat me and my brothers and sister. But now I'm better because now. I'm 11 years old. and the fifth grade. I live in has Vegas. I never bean in ice or never bean snow ski before. I don't have a favorite Sport in school. I love Baby sisters club I have no pets. my sister name is Tenisha and her and my auntie was fight and the police told her a way and then I began to cry. and my Brother name anthony but they call him tory. my sister is 13 and my Borther is 20. are you married Sorry for asking. I don't like that Book because I hate wolves. could you send me draw that you did. Becuse I like your hand writing may be your draw look better. allway
Laquisha

165

her young life. The first incident that she always mentioned was when she was burned on her leg; she talked about crawling in the kitchen and bumping the stove. She must have been burned from this encounter because she then recalled how her mother put grease on the burn. After talking about this incident, Laquisha showed me the scar on her leg. As her segue from this incident she talked about "always getting into trouble." I asked whether she was talking about trouble at home or school. She replied, "Home trouble. Because I was small and I didn't know what to do, I was getting hit very hard with a stick or cord." I asked her to tell me about the reasons for getting hit, but Laquisha always responded, "for nothing." Laquisha then described her seventh birthday, which was particularly upsetting for her because her father was killed in a stabbing attack on or near her birthday. A welfare worker came to tell her and she was taken to a shelter. Although Laquisha could not remember where she was living at this time, it appears that she was living with her father. When Laquisha talked about where she was living at this time, she mentioned moving from "dad's to mom's to granny's to the shelter," and back and forth among these settings.

Originally, Laquisha was taken from her mother's house because her mother was using drugs. Laquisha was aware of this drug use and she told me, "I moved away from her house because she do that drug stuff. Then she wanted me to come over but I said 'no' because she going to be mean to me."

The last incident that Laquisha described was how she and her sister and brother tricked her mother. Her mother had been beating the children and so they all ran out different doors of the house. Her brother then called the police to report their mother. This situation proved to be particularly traumatic for the family as the children were placed in different settings. Laquisha said that it was "bad. Now I can't see my sister or brother again."

When Becky and I interviewed Laquisha's aunt, she repeated all of these stories to us. At the beginning of the fifth-grade year, she had become the guardian for Laquisha who was living with her full-time. Before this, Laquisha had been living with her grandmother, but her grandmother became ill and was unable to take care of her (she required dialysis several times a week).

Laquisha's aunt filled in some of the puzzling details from Laquisha's childhood. She also said that she was unaware of much that went on because she did not realize how bad it was for her sister's children. She said that when Laquisha was born her sister "brought her home and she dropped her off to me and my mom and kept on going on her way. We raised her until she was about 2 and then my mom gave her back to [her mother to] give her another chance." When I probed about what Laquisha was like as a baby, she said that she really did not know but she "guessed that she was okay." She then told about the burning incident that Laquisha had recalled. Because Laquisha's mom rarely provided dinner, the children were cooking. Her 5-year-old brother turned on the stove and was heating water. When Laquisha bumped into the stove, the pan fell on her. After this incident, the children went back to living with their grandmother and aunt.

Laquisha never talked about other childhood experiences. In her journal two particularly noteworthy incidents were reported, however. The first involved her mother. Laquisha frequently wrote about her mother and how her mother wanted Laquisha to visit. Toward the end of the year, Laquisha started to visit her mother and the relationship seemed to be stable. Just as this relationship was being rekindled, Laquisha's mother was stabbed. For several days the doctors were not sure if she would live. Laquisha wrote about this incident:

> Dear Mrs. S.,
>
> How are you? I'm fine. Today is a happy day because I have not been getting in trouble. My auntie is still mean. My mom had came home yesterday but she's going back today because she got pain. She has a bag on her side. She got stabbed 2 times. She almost died but the doctor helped her. She been in the hospital for 7 days and she is already going back. She don't feel good. She has a temperature was 101. That's what she said.

The second incident revolved around her aunt. Laquisha's aunt and Laquisha had problems around the time that Laquisha was building a relationship with her mother. She wrote in her journal about her aunt hitting her. Becky had to report the incident and she told Laquisha about it and how difficult it was to break the confidence of the journal. Laquisha talked to the principal about the situation and told her that she would not go to the welfare shelter again: "I will run away if they come." As could be predicted when the representative from state welfare appeared at school, Laquisha ran. The principal tried to catch her but was unsuccessful. Laquisha was looking for Becky. She wanted to share how upset she was about the incident and how upset she was with Becky for telling.

Although this day was especially difficult for Laquisha, it also was hard on Becky who described it as her "worst day ever." To follow up, the principal talked to Laquisha about her teacher's and the school's responsibility to help children. She told Laquisha that if she wrote about being hurt her teacher had to tell. She said it was up to Laquisha to decide when she needed help and her writing about such incidents in her journal would signal that need. For several days after this, Laquisha's journal entries were folded over. She wrote about her anger but she did not want anyone, including her teacher, to read these entries. Laquisha never wrote about any difficulty at home after this.

Friends, Teachers, and Family

> I'm quite aware of Gilly's needs. I've been her caseworker for nearly five years. (Paterson, 1978, p. 94)

As Becky and I began to comb through Laquisha's journal entries we noted that she often wrote about friends, her teachers, and her family. In the 172 responses that she wrote, 37 were focused on her friends and the classroom, 30 were about her teachers with 19 of those about Becky, and 25 were about her family.

When Laquisha wrote about her friends, she recounted times when they slept over, watched movies, and had pizza. For example, she wrote the following:

> My weekend was fun because I met Adrian at her house and she took me swimming. I went under water and my big brother came over and went swimming too. He threw Adrian under water.

Although we were never able to document whether these parties ever happened, Laquisha wrote about them on several occasions. Her choice of friends in the classroom centered on the most popular students. She wanted to be Monic's best friend because "she is nice and pretty." Although Monic worked with her in the classroom, she did not reciprocate in wanting Laquisha to be her best friend. Laquisha's feelings often centered on how her relationships with her friends were going. She would write about having "a stupid day" because someone had not treated her in the way she expected. She would have "a great day" when her friends included her. When Laquisha was upset, especially at the behavior of her friends, it would be obvious in the classroom. She would pout, put her head down, and refuse to do anything. She made sure that her classmates, including the teacher, knew that she was upset. If she was angry about something that happened before school, this behavior could permeate the day. Becky often wrote about this behavior in her journal: "Came in grumpy and said her stomach hurt. She cried and would not work or go to the office. She was mad at Alycia for using her chair. She decided not to work at first. She saw the fun the kids were having and she joined in." Laquisha also wrote in her journal about these feelings, for example, "I'm telling my auntie to move me from this school because Kelsey and Heather are mean." On the other hand, when she and her friends were getting along, she would write and talk about "how great my week was." Clearly, friends were important to Laquisha.

In addition to finding friends, Laquisha made personal relationships with her teachers. When I talked to her about school, she hardly remembered any details about a class or school but she did remember the important adults. She talked about a kindergarten teacher who brought her a birthday cake. "I went to kindergarten every morning and on my birthday, since my mommy didn't buy me no cake, the teacher bought me a little cake and we had a party." Another teacher she recalled, told her to "get a lot of books and we just read them. If I didn't know the words she would go over them." She also remembered a school counselor who let her meet with him at school. After several talks about school, she clearly did not remember any of the details of her classroom, but she did recall these three important people.

Throughout the school year, she wrote notes to Becky about how much she liked her as a teacher. Her notes were attempts at building personal connections. In August she wrote, "Thank you for being my teacher. The teacher I had at my other school was mean." Often in Laquisha's journal she would ask to be a helper to Becky. If she did not think she was helping enough, she would use this communication as a way to complain. For example, she wrote, "Tomorrow could

I help you?" On another day she wrote, "How come I never get to do nothing and I always asking you first. Today is not a good day." As their relationship grew, Becky worried about how Laquisha would handle Becky's imminent maternity leave from the classroom. The students had been prepared for her departure after winter break and had helped select the substitute, but Laquisha and several other children were worrisome because of their vulnerability and close relationship with Becky. In January, when the students returned to the room after vacation, Laquisha wrote the following:

> Dear Mrs. Schneider,
>
> How are you? I'm fine. Soon as you left, I started to cry because I know that it was time for you to go. Maybe one day, I will stay the night at your house when your baby is a little older because as soon as you left I felt sad because you liked me. I take back all the mean things what I said.

Soon after this letter, Laquisha started writing to the substitute. She talked to her about the class and about how the new teacher dressed. She wrote to her each day about how nice she was. Interestingly, although many of the students had a very difficult time with the substitute (many found themselves in the principal's office), Laquisha maintained her good behavior while Becky was on maternity leave. However, her work suffered and often was not complete or legible. She called Becky at home at least once a week to report on the status of the class. She was always the first one to notice when Becky visited, and she was the first student to hold the new baby.

In addition to the classroom teachers, Laquisha established close relationships with the school secretary and the special-education teacher who worked in the classroom. The secretary provided a safe place for Laquisha to think when she was having a particularly difficult day. The special-education teacher formed an in-school and out-of-school relationship with Laquisha: When she came into the room, she always found time to briefly chat with Laquisha. She also included Laquisha in trips to the movies with her own children. When Becky returned to the room full time, she often heard Laquisha talk about these out-of-school excursions. Laquisha and Becky then made out-of-school plans too. On a few weekends, Laquisha visited her house and helped with the baby and then enjoyed a lunch outing. Her out-of-school relationships with the special-education teacher and Becky

Figure 28
Laquisha's Journal Writing About Her Family

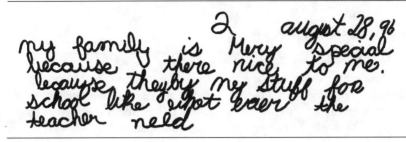

my family is a [Mercy] special august 28, 96 because there nice to me. because theyby my stuff for school like ript ever the teacher neld

continued throughout the summer. Currently, she calls Becky to tell her about middle school. She says that so far she likes it.

Although it is clear that Laquisha's home life has not been stable, she values her family (see Figure 28). In this writing, she shows how appreciative she is of the things they bought for her so that she would be ready for school. On another day, she wrote about her brother:

> He's nice and he is 16 years old and gots big feet and wears big shoes and has a lot of friends. He's nice and he likes school. He likes wearing baggy clothes. He loves me very much. He lives with his grandpa. Next time when he has time, he's going to come over. He is going to his uncle's house on his dad side. He's staying the night over there. But he likes to visit me.

Unfortunately, not all of Laquisha's writing about her family was positive. On some occasions she wrote about worrying about visiting her mother because of her recurrent use of drugs. At other times, she wrote about her aunt and troublesome events that occurred in this home:

> Dear Mrs. Schneider,
>
> Whatever you do don't tell nobody my aunt hit me last night. I got wallops on my legs. My legs hurt. She hit me with a hanger. Don't tell anyone please. Because if my aunt finds out I will be in trouble.
>
> Sometimes when I come to school mad is because I be getting in trouble at home. I have a lot of true friends.

On another day she continued her discussion about her family, writing the following:

Well I guess I was mad because I got in trouble for nothing. I saw my mom. She got nicer. She don't do drugs any more. When I grow up I'm going to be a teacher.

On a later occasion, she wrote,

Dear Mrs. S.

How are you? I'm not fine. This morning my auntie had hit me in the arm for nothing. That I did was just woke up and went to the bathroom. Then on my way to my room she just powed me. I don't like to live there. That why I like to go places with the teachers.

These letters demonstrated that home was not an emotionally consistent place for Laquisha. It is possible that Laquisha built relationships with her teachers to provide what she felt was missing from her home. She was skillful at developing and sustaining these relationships.

Laquisha's aunt did come in for numerous conferences throughout the year. Becky called her in August and her aunt said that she had heard from Laquisha's teachers in the past and that she thought Becky was "the first teacher to really like Laquisha." Laquisha's aunt felt that "she needed a lot of attention." When Becky and I talked to her aunt in December, she provided more information about Laquisha's childhood and how she was supporting her learning at home now. She remembered that Laquisha's teachers would send notes home but her "sister would throw them away. Sometimes I would catch them. If I caught them I would go to school but basically the teacher thought she wanted attention." One teacher had her tested for special education but she did not qualify. Her aunt said, "It was a behavior problem. She wouldn't do her work. Her mom didn't care if she did it, so she got all Fs." Our conversation then involved much discussion of events that happened in Laquisha's early life. Her aunt commented that she "didn't know how bad it really was." She talked about how sweet her sister is when she is not using drugs. She said that now that she knows how bad it was, she is going to raise Laquisha until she is 18. She talked about how she helped Laquisha with her homework, took her to the library each week, and let her watch only educational shows. With tears in her eyes, she recalled how Laquisha told her that "she likes me so much and she doesn't want to go to her mom's anymore. I had to leave the room cause I started bawling."

In the middle of this conversation, Laquisha's aunt shared what she thought was important for Laquisha. She said,

> I am trying to teach trust. Because at the beginning I was trying to check every single thing. And then in the middle she started bringing home reports that said she forgot something. And then I have to start back checking everything even for my daughter. I tell them over and over that I try to trust them but I have to go back to the old ways. They know that if I am not going to check on them they write down any old thing.

Laquisha's aunt is hinting at how she is trying to develop responsibility in both her own daughter and Laquisha. Although she trusted them at first to be honest about completing homework, she now checks their work each day. Becky commented that Laquisha always did her homework and she was proud when she turned it in. At the end of our chat, I asked her aunt to describe Laquisha. Her description began with "caring, smart, very demanding of the teacher, bossy a bit, and stubborn." She concluded by saying, "She's very stubborn."

After listening to Laquisha and her aunt, the conflicted nature of her home environment became evident. Her aunt, a single parent, was responsible for raising three children. She lived in public housing and she worked every day. Her life could not be considered easy. Laquisha loved her aunt and the other members of her family, but they did not treat her consistently and perhaps she was not consistent in the way she interacted with them. These relationships led her to develop friendships with teachers and other students. Again although the students varied in the way they responded to Laquisha, her teachers were more consistent. Laquisha developed relationships with her teachers both inside and outside of school. She overtly realized the need for the stability of these friendships.

School Reports About Laquisha

> The principal was studying records that must have been sent over from Gilly's former school, Hollywood Gardens Elementary. He coughed several times. "Well," he said, "I think this young lady needs to be in a class that will challenge her." (Paterson, 1978, p. 20)

Becky and I scanned the formal file kept on Laquisha to get a sense of what schools she had attended and to review any comments made by teachers. We hoped these data might fill in some of the parts of schooling that Laquisha had forgotten. After reading the files, it was obvious that no child could have remembered so many details about her elementary schooling.

During Laquisha's kindergarten year, she was enrolled at five schools. During first and second grade, she attended four schools. Third grade saw her back at the school she had gone to at the beginning of kindergarten. In fourth grade, she attended three schools. Each change in school meant a change in her home as well.

Her school reports described her at each grade level. In kindergarten, she knew letters and sounds and she was working at grade level. Her teacher noted that "she needed more self control." In first grade, her teacher wrote that "she needed to improve." She could read independently and listen attentively, but her spelling grade was an F. One of her second-grade teachers wrote, "Laquisha's management skills are a great asset. She has a great amount of positive energy, and she is learning to channel it. She can accomplish great endeavors." For her year grades, she received a C in reading, an N for needs improvement in spelling, and a D in math. Her third-grade teacher provided no comments about Laquisha. She gave her a B in each academic area. Fourth grade appeared to be more difficult for Laquisha. One of her three teachers noted, "She can read well but only when she wants to. Her behavior has improved for the most part, but she can still exhibit rude behavior." Her academic grades showed a D and C in reading and a satisfactory in spelling.

Besides the reports from her teachers, there were test results in her file. Early in fourth grade, she took a national standardized test. Her reading/vocabulary score was at the 24th percentile, comprehension 21st percentile, spelling 16th percentile, total reading 23rd percentile, and language 34th percentile. These reports also noted that she had a visual problem in one eye that was most likely a result of beatings. No other mention was made about this problem. In fourth grade one teacher referred her for special-education testing. This testing was completed in fifth grade, but Laquisha did not qualify for additional academic support.

What is particularly interesting from these fragments of information about Laquisha's early schooling is that she did so well. Several of her teachers noted her ability to read at grade level. After reading these reports and synthesizing the information shared by Laquisha and her aunt, our question became even more of a conundrum: How did Laquisha learn to read and write? Laquisha is a child who has not had a safe, consistent home environment. She has moved through numerous schools with varying teacher expectations. And in addition, she is a poor, minority child. We were puzzled at how she learned to read and write.

Laquisha as a Reader and Writer

She was a good reader because she had set her mind to be one. The minute that damn first-grade teacher had told Mrs. Dixon that she was afraid Gilly might be "slow," Gilly had determined to make the old parrot choke on her crackers. And she had. By Christmastime she was reading circles around the whole snotty class. Not that it made any difference. The teacher, Mrs. Gorman, had explained very carefully to Mrs. Dixon that she had twenty-five other children to look out for and that there was no way to set up a private reading time for one individual. Gilly would just have to learn some patience and cooperation. That was all. (Paterson, 1978, p. 39)

During the first weeks of fifth grade, Becky gathered informal assessments on each child. This assessment included Informal Reading Inventories (IRIs), spelling samples, and writing samples. As documented by the IRI, Laquisha was able to independently read narrative material at the fourth-grade level in August of her fifth-grade year. Her spelling showed that she was able to spell most single-syllable words, but she was having difficulty adding suffixes to words. In her spelling sample shown in Figure 29 on page 176, she began to have difficulty spelling the words *preparing* (#12), *popping* (#13), and *cattle* (#14). She had no trouble spelling the previous words that included short and long vowels, digraphs, and blends. Although she was not at grade level in reading, she was a competent reader and had no major difficulties with spelling or expressing herself in writing. Although Becky and I were pleasantly surprised at her literacy development, we had questions about how she became this proficient, particularly with her school and home history.

Figure 29
Laquisha's Spelling

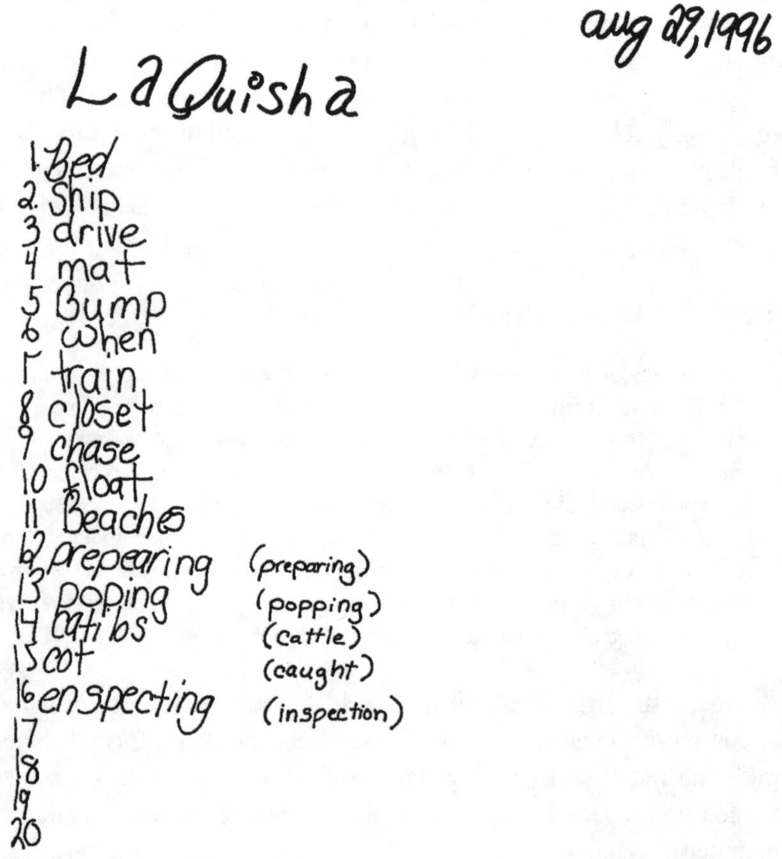

aug 27, 1996

LaQuisha

1. Bed
2. Ship
3. drive
4. mat
5. Bump
6. When
7. train
8. closet
9. chase
10. float
11. Beaches
12. prepearing (preparing)
13. poping (popping)
14. catibs (cattle)
15. cot (caught)
16. enspecting (inspection)
17.
18.
19.
20.

On several occasions, I asked Laquisha how she learned to read and write. For the most part she would reply, "I don't know." With persistence, Laquisha remembered a few episodes at school or at home that she felt helped her to learn to read and write. She recalled that her kindergarten teacher gave her easy books to read. "He was nice and he would say, 'try.' He would write stories on the board too and we read them." Another teacher (she was not sure of grade level or even if she was her classroom teacher) let her come into the classroom before school each day. Laquisha said, "She told me to grab a book or listen to a tape with a book. She taught me some words." I asked if she also read books at home. She said that she used to read to her mom. "If I didn't know the words I would get beaten," she said. She recalled reading *Amelia Bedelia* (Parish, 1963) and short chapter books to her mother. After numerous conversations, in which Laquisha would just giggle when I asked this question about learning to read, I never learned anything additional about how she learned to read or write. Perhaps just a few teachers at key times provided the scaffolding that Laquisha needed to develop her reading ability. Although her mother used inappropriate methods to support Laquisha's growing abilities with reading, her aunt, dad, and grandmother may have been more willing to support her as she struggled with getting the words right. And although Laquisha never mentioned it directly, maybe she was intrinsically motivated to learn to read.

Laquisha's Literacy in Fifth Grade

Reading

In Laquisha's class, students read on many occasions throughout the day. They might be reading a novel for a literature discussion group, a free-choice book, for a theme unit, or picture books in preparation for their tutoring of kindergartners, first graders, or second graders. Although there were many extension activities tied to reading, the students also wrote routinely in response notebooks about the books that they were reading in literature groups. At the beginning of the year, Laquisha refused to read anything but a basal. When she was given an easy novel to read, she stomped and pouted and said that she "couldn't read them fat books." Becky found a basal on a shelf that Laquisha felt comfortable reading. She read through this and then, with support, was willing to join a literature group that was reading novels and to choose novels during independent reading. Some of the books that Laquisha read throughout this year included *Chocolate Fever* (Smith, 1972), Encyclopedia Brown series (Sobol), Babysitters' Club series (Martin), *Ralph S. Mouse* (Cleary, 1965), all of the Wayside School series (Sacher), Ramona series (Cleary), *Matilda* (Dahl, 1988), and *Maniac Magee* (Spinelli, 1991). In the letters that she wrote her university penpal and me, she always talked about the Babysitters' Club books that she was reading. She was very pleased that her aunt had purchased several of them for her. In Figure 30, which includes a letter written to me, Laquisha describes the plot in Book 11 of this series. In her writing, it was evident that she was able to read these books and comprehend the plot.

Figure 30
Laquisha's Letter

12-12-96

Dear Dr. Barone, how are you doing? I'm fine. How did you get the words on that colorful. That is pretty. I read a alot of books of the Baby sitter. I had read Super special 11 $13 and eleven it about when they went to hawilli and they had stayed there and they left a Baby sitter club member beause she broke her leg and and she wrote Kristy wrote

Dear Kristy I don't meen to fall out the tree. I was only so I'll never do it agan the babby sitters what I said ok maybe they coon't be mad again

At the end of the year, I listened in on a literature group of which Laquisha was a member. This group was just beginning to read *Maniac Magee*. The members, guided by Becky, began their discussion by talking about the cover.

Laquisha: It looks like a mystery because he is running away.

Nathan: It won an award. It's a Newbery—best children's book.

Jered: He ran away or something.

Heather: I think he didn't have friends so he ran away.

Amanda: I think he is going to run away because of things that happened.

Matt: He is like Matilda and his parents are mean to him.

Laquisha: Like his parents are always ripping up his book.

Cody: Parents call him names and it makes him mad.

Becky then read the introduction to the students and their conversation continued.

Heather: His parents put him in a dumpster.

Laquisha: Maybe the girl made fun of him.

Cody: I think he is like a myth. He's like a bull.

Becky: What's a myth?

Cody: Like something that is true and it happened a long time ago.

The conversation demonstrates how these students were able to look closely at the cover and predict, often based on the events from their lives or other books, what might happen. After the introduction was read, they seemed perplexed at figuring out the character called Maniac Magee. Slightly confused, they left to read the first chapter independently and to write in their response notebooks. Although many of the students wrote about personal connections in many of their responses throughout this book, Laquisha usually chose to write about the literal plot. This pattern held up as she read *Maniac Magee*. In one of her responses, for example, she wrote the following:

Maniac had went to a game. He was watching the game until somebody said, "Get the ball, get my hat." Magee run into the field and got it. The man had hit the ball over the fence. More people cheered.

As a result of so much reading both in home and school throughout this school year, Laquisha's end of the year IRI indicated that she could read narrative material independently at the sixth-grade level. She grew, by this measure alone, two full grade levels in 1 year of school.

Writing and Spelling

The students in Becky's class engaged in a writing workshop each day for at least an hour. They knew about writing to their own ideas, revision and editing, and sharing their work with the class. Laquisha moved into writing with less tension than was demonstrated in reading. She seemed to be comfortable expressing her thoughts in writing and blank paper was not as troublesome as "fat books." She was one of the only students to complain that 20 minutes was not enough time for journal writing.

The majority of the stories and poems that Laquisha wrote, as might be expected, were centered on family, friends, and teachers. Her first story of the year that went through the whole writing process, from generating ideas to a final draft enriched by peer and teacher response, was about her family. She wrote the following:

Me and My Family

I have my mom, cousin, my aunt, and the baby. Everyone in my house is nice, special. My aunt and my mom, they gave me snack money everyday. My aunt, she has long hair and she has braids. I love the baby but sometimes when he's mine, he fight and kick. But I still love him. When he is in the room, he'll crawl over into the living room. I love my family. The people in my house names are Britney, Mellie, Laquisha, Brianna, Betty, and Tadrey.

Laquisha also drew a picture of her family that accompanied this story (see Figure 31). It shows most of her family members with Tadrey in the center with a big smile.

Her next story was only about her aunt. Several of the ideas shared in the story about her family recurred in this story. She began

Figure 31
Laquisha's Family Portrait

with, "My aunt is nice and she has three kids." Her story then moved to her young cousin and how she thought that he "was mean." The remainder of this story related to the daily routine that her aunt expected of family members. For the most part this routine centered on homework, snacks after school, and playing with friends.

Her other stories were very similar throughout the year. They always focused on people who were important to Laquisha. In her only exploration of poetry, Laquisha wrote a poem about the special-education teacher with whom she had formed a close friendship:

Maryanne
Happy, tired
Teaching, helping, talking
Sad, happy, shy, love
Mrs. Maloney

For the final writing experience of the year, Becky asked each student to write a fairy tale. As a class, the students explored many fairy tales and examined their structures. They also brainstormed possible themes for their own fairy tale. Although Laquisha's fairy tale was never fully completed, she included her teacher and several of the students in the class as the main characters.

Becky informally assessed her students' development as writers. She periodically structured the class so that all students were writing for a 10-minute period. Through this timed writing, she determined if students could select a topic and write about it within a short time-frame. She noted the structure of the writing such as paragraphing, sentence formation, subject-verb agreement, and spelling. These assessments let students and parents see their growth in writing throughout the year. Because some students created only one long piece of writing in a semester, these assessments allowed for a more sequenced assessment of student writing. Figure 32 is a 10-minute freewrite completed by Laquisha in April. In this first draft it is clear that Laquisha can select a topic, in this case her friend Jackie, and write about it. She also addresses an audience and sets a focus as seen in her introductory sentence, *Hi, my name is Laquisha and I'm going to tell you [about] Jackee*. Although there are interesting errors throughout this writing, Laquisha is able to produce a considerable amount of text about a topic written in a short period. She knows about paragraphs, punctuation, and capital letters, and spells most of the words she attempts correctly. She has forgotten some words and used an interesting spelling for role model (*roadmodle*). These errors are not major and certainly could be corrected if she felt this writing was worth revision and editing. By scanning this first-draft writing, it is obvious that Laquisha can effectively express herself through writing.

To facilitate writing and reading, the students in this class explored words through word study. There were several groups of students who explored particular word concepts. For example, students who just started to represent short vowels in words studied short-vowel patterns. Students who started to represent the long-vowel sounds with a marker (for example, *bake* spelled as *baek* or *float* spelled as *flote*) examined long-vowel patterns. Laquisha spent most of the year exploring prefixes and suffixes. This instruction was based on her knowledge of words shown when she was asked to spell a developmental list of words. In Figure 28 on page 171, her representations of these words in the beginning of the year were shown. At the

Figure 32
Laquisha's 10-Minute Writing

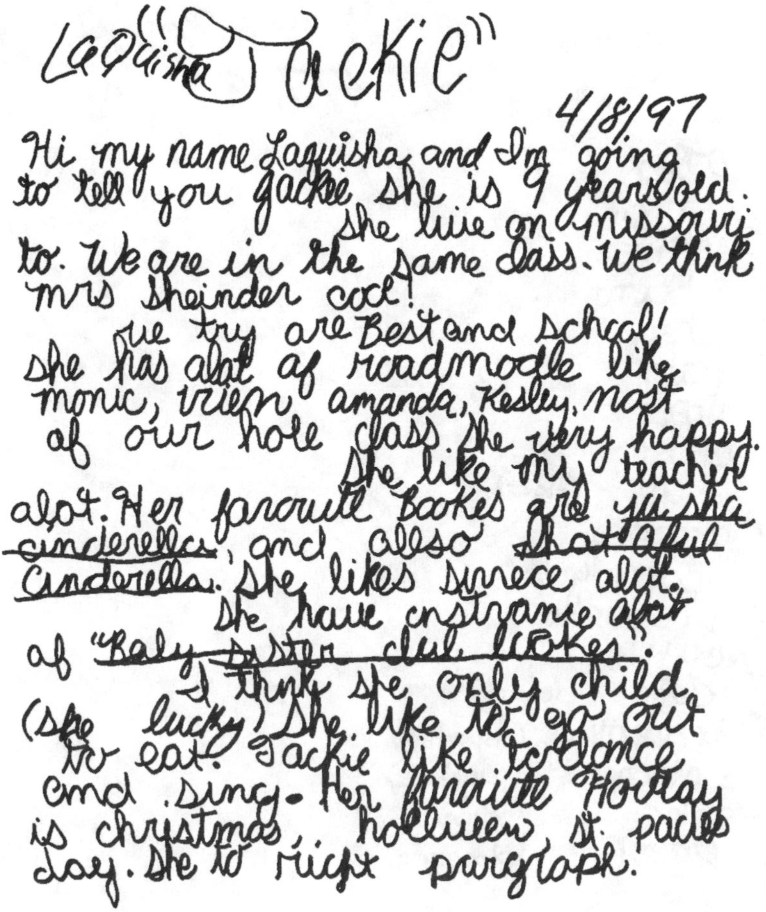

Laquisha "Jackie"

4/8/97

Hi my name Laquisha and I'm going to tell you Jackee she is 9 years old. she live on missouri to. We are in the same class. We think mrs sheinder cool!

we try are Best and school! she has alot of roadmodle like monic, trien amanda, Kesley, most of our hole class she very happy. She like my teacher alot. Her favoute bookes are yu sha cinderella, and also that aful Cinderella. She likes surece alot. She have enstranje abot of "Baly tister dul bookes". I think she only child. (she lucky) She like to go out to eat. Jackie like to dance and sing. Her faraite Holay is christmas, holiween st. packs Day. She to right purgraph.

end of the year, Laquisha once again was asked to spell these words (see Figure 33 on page 184). Although Laquisha surprisingly had difficulty with *float* this time, she had internalized the patterns for adding a suffix to a word. This skill is demonstrated in her correct spelling of *popping*, *preparing*, and *cattle*.

Figure 33
Laquisha's Spelling

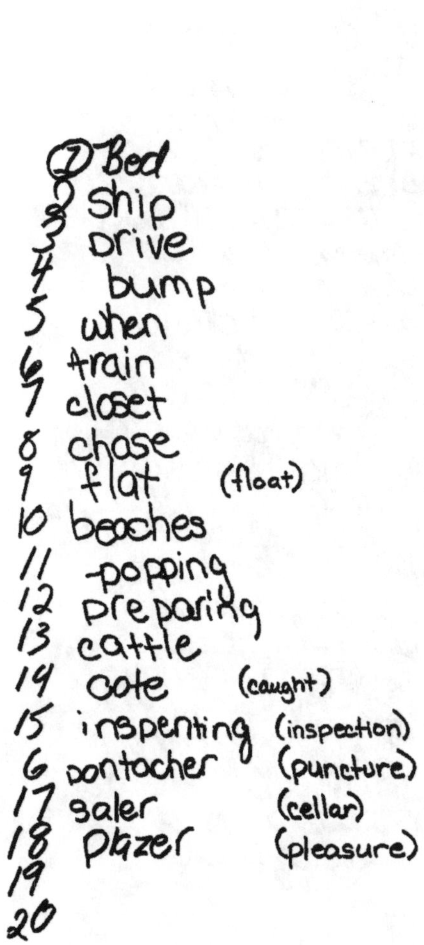

Laquisha
4/7/97

1. Bed
2. ship
3. Drive
4. bump
5. when
6. train
7. closet
8. chase
9. flat   (float)
10. beaches
11. popping
12. preparing
13. cattle
14. oote   (caught)
15. inspenting (inspection)
16. pontocher   (puncture)
17. saler   (cellar)
18. plizer   (pleasure)
19.
20.

What Laquisha Teaches Us

Although Becky and I ended the year still not sure how Laquisha became such a proficient reader and writer, we did learn how a child, despite an unstable home situation, could be successful as a learner. When considering the literature on the difficulty that poor minority children have being successful in school (Allington & Walmsley, 1995; Bartoli, 1995; Cuban, 1989; Hidalgo, Siu, Bright, Swap, & Epstein, 1995), her story is especially powerful. The difficulties she experienced were profound. They included

- prenatal drug exposure to crack/cocaine;
- coming home as a newborn to a mother who still was a drug user;
- being poor and a minority child;
- moving among several homes and child welfare protective services;
- being beaten by her mother and perhaps her aunt;
- living with physical danger as demonstrated in her beatings, the death of her father, and the stabbing of her mother; and
- moving among 14 schools during elementary school. (These moves include her fifth-grade placement.)

To counteract some of these difficulties and to provide a fragmentary explanation of her success, it is necessary to look at the support offered to her and sought out by her:

- Laquisha valued her family, despite their limitations;
- Laquisha found friends to provide support;
- Laquisha was able to build close relationships with teachers inside and outside of school;
- Laquisha's family supported her literacy by listening to her read, taking her to the library, and purchasing books for her; and
- Laquisha's teachers found ways to engage her in reading beyond the regular classroom time. One teacher opened her door to her before school. Becky gave her books to read at home.

Although the difficulties outnumber the supports, perhaps only a few essential supports need to be in place at critical times to allow a child to become successful as a learner. And while we admire her success, it is also important to remember that Laquisha places demands on teachers. When she is upset, she wants the teacher to be aware of her distress. She requires her teachers' patience to understand her. But when given this understanding and appropriate discipline when necessary, Laquisha flourishes in her school setting.

At the end of her fifth-grade year, Becky was worried at how Laquisha would adjust to middle school. In the fall, she would be in a school where she would move among many teachers. Becky talked to Laquisha and met with her several times over the summer. On each occasion, Laquisha seemed ready to move to middle school. On their last visit before school, she showed Becky her new clothes. In their talking, Becky asked her if she was going to climb under a desk as she had on her first day in fifth grade. Laquisha laughed at that memory and said that she had to behave like an adult now. She did not plan on going under any desks in middle school. As the fall semester progressed, Laquisha called Becky about every other week to check in. Initially she thought middle school was fine. (Laquisha is not the only student calling Becky. Most of the previous year's fifth graders call once or twice a month to tell her about middle school.)

At the end of a full year of study, Laquisha is still a puzzle in many ways. We are still wondering about her success at becoming an above-grade-level reader and writer. Perhaps our attempts to be specific about how Laquisha learned to read and write were futile. This result could be looked at as an unsuccessful research endeavor. However, the fact that Laquisha has been able to develop so successfully is a positive outcome. Just the fact that we are able to describe her demonstrates that children like her can also be successful as literacy learners. Her case defies the myths that exist about children prenatally exposed to crack/cocaine, especially children who have not had stable home experiences. Laquisha's story demonstrates that caring teachers who provide numerous opportunities for reading, writing, and reflection are the critical element in a child's success, or at least a very important element (Ladson-Billings, 1994).

CHAPTER 10

Why These Children's Stories Are Important

Children
Children are like
Precious flowers
That break if you
Don't treat them right.
They were angels
In another world
And hope to become
Human in this world
And also grow like flowers.
That's why nobody should
Be left out.
(Janice Aldaro, Grade 6. From Lyne, S. [Ed.]. [1996]. *Ten-Second Rain-showers: Poems by Young People* [p. 30]. New York: Simon & Schuster.)

The beginning and end of this poem make me think directly about the children who were the focus of my study and this book. Each of them should be considered precious. That each one survived to birth is amazing. And once they were born, the need for safe environments with loving adults was critical to their development (Novick, 1998). The poem ends with the idea that no one should be left out. For me, this final line illustrates why these children's stories are so important.

In the early 1990s many adults, teachers among them, believed that children who were prenatally exposed to crack/cocaine were not worth the effort. Unfortunately, this attitude still exists today. Teachers and administrators are convinced that these children are not able to maintain control in a classroom, despite the teachers' efforts, and that they will develop into sociopaths (Odom-Winn & Dunagan, 1991; Waller, 1993). The children who were highlighted in this book and the other children in the study provide evidence that children who suffered prenatal drug exposure *are* worth the effort and should not "be left out."

As I considered the articles and books that I read, the observations and interviews conducted during the study, and the multitude of conversations that I have had about these children with parents, children, and colleagues, I discovered that the best way to think about the importance of the children's stories was to focus on the children, their parents, and their schooling. This chapter is organized around these three topics. Although each topic will be presented in a separate section they are not meant to be thought of as existing in isolation. Clearly, the children, their parents, and the schools and classrooms they attended all were connected and important to each child's emotional, physical, and intellectual development.

The Children

Initial Assumptions

I am assuming that when you read this book you will think, just as I assumed when I began the study, that the crack/cocaine prenatal exposure would always be the primary focus of my research. I was convinced that this one event would be the most important to these children. In believing the reports about prenatal drug exposure, my common sense disappeared and I believed that a single event would influence the development of a child. I ignored the realization that a child is a complex being and that a single event could not determine who an individual would be. I was not alone in this type of thinking; Henkin (1998) discussed the issue of complexity in her book on equity and social justice. She wrote, "Even though we *say* we embrace complexity, we still yearn for simple solutions" (p. 19). It could be said accurately that at the beginning of this study I was yearning "for simple solutions."

However, as I came to know each child individually, my biases vanished. By the second year of the study, I stopped consciously thinking about the label that originally identified the children, realizing that this label did not define who they were. I understood the value of discovering children as individuals rather than simply considering them as a group, organized under a label. I listened to Dyson (1995) as she urged the literacy community to see the value of looking at cases, rather than being more satisfied with large, quantitative studies:

> What *can* be done with thousands of children but count them? In mass, children—and the challenges they present—are faceless, nameless, and overwhelming. But these massive numbers of children are not isolated individuals; they're social participants included, or so we hope, in particular classrooms and schools, in particular institutions and communities. (p. 51)

I am hoping that as you read these children's stories and thought about each of the children as an individual you too were astounded at who they are. I also hope that you set their prenatal drug exposure aside and celebrated their growth as readers and writers. The section that follows is a recap of the children's stories, each of which provides a unique window into the resilience of children who experience multiple risk factors.

The Stories

Sean, one of the youngest children in the study, gives us a view of precociousness. Although I first visited him when he was 1 year old, he loved books. The story that I always remember when thinking about him is his reading in his bed at night when he was supposed to be sleeping. He was very resourceful at hiding books so that he would have a supply even after his mother put several away.

Billy's story lets us witness a different way of becoming literate. His religious preschool prepared children for public school in a way that would not be recommended by experts in literacy. He learned about letters and sounds by rote memorization. He had no experiences with books or authentic writing experiences during this time, but he saw himself as a successful learner and he learned to read and write. His story again allows us to see the importance of teachers and parents, rather than a specific literacy program (Ladson-Billings, 1994). Although one may argue that he might have been even more sophisticated in his literacy learning with a more developmentally appropriate preschool experience, for Billy and his family the preschool he attended provided the most appropriate curriculum.

Melina's story allows us to see the importance of friends in learning to read and write. Melina was most successful in school when she had her best friend next to her. Her story also lets us witness the importance of gender. Melina chose to surround herself with girls, and she vehemently told boys to move to other parts of the room when they tried to join in. Being near girlfriends appeared to give her confidence in her learning endeavors. Melina always formed a girls' club in her classroom. She loved to learn surrounded by friends, especially girlfriends. Her story reminds me of those shared by Dyson (1995). Melinda's social community provided the foundation for her literacy learning.

Curtis's story shows us how determined to learn a child can be. Curtis was an independent learner from the first moment I met him. The only time he had difficulty controlling himself in school was when someone interfered with his learning process, and his expectation for himself as a learner was that his work would always be perfect. Curtis would rather give up momentum in his reading and writing to maintain accuracy. His written work was often more like an artistic rendering than the mere completion of a routine worksheet.

Ray's story provides us with an opportunity to see reading as a means of escape. Reading allowed Ray to leave the immediate environment of home or school. Ray also lets us learn about a child who was vulnerable to risk factors such as a poverty, a less-than-ideal home situation, loss of his physical family, classrooms that were not always supportive, a dangerous neighborhood environment, and prenatal drug exposure, but who was successful as a literacy learner. Ray's story forces us to see beyond the negative statistics that often are presented for children considered to be at risk.

And the final story, Laquisha's story, may be the most powerful of all. I still do not fully understand how Laquisha developed her literacy skills. Certainly, she allows us to know the importance of significant people in one's life. The teacher who allowed her to come to her room to read, the counselor who found time to listen to her, and her teachers who made the effort to share time with her inside and outside of school all were critical to her both personally and intellectually. Laquisha still finds ways to connect with people to help her: Recently, she was taken from her mother who had beaten her and was placed in state care. While in a protective facility, she became close to one of the teachers, who found ways to facilitate a meeting with Becky Schneider, her fifth-grade teacher. Although it was a long process to get permission to visit Laquisha in this setting, this teacher expedited Laquisha's privileges to allow her to call Becky and set aside the rules so that her teacher could visit her and bring her books and a journal. Laquisha still communicates with Becky even though she is living with her mother again. More than any child in the study, Laquisha demonstrates resilience (Allen et al., 1993; O'Connor, 1997). Despite her repeatedly negative home situations, she is still trying to make her home better and to do well in school. This is no easy task for such a young child.

For each child, prenatal history, early home situations, and entry and continuation in school all overlap. Their individual experiences share some events and vary in others. These individual experiences can be combined into one larger story that demonstrates the power of these individual narratives. If only one child who had experienced prenatal drug exposure, poverty, and the other variables such as gender or race, were successful, many questions still would remain as to whether this one child was an anomaly. But the strength of the larger story is that it is made up of many stories. Some have been shared in this book, others are a part of the study, and there are innumerable stories that have yet to be told.

Parents and Home Support

This story cannot close without a consideration of the children's homes. Most of the homes were stable and supportive; in a few instances, the home was stable only in the sense that the child was expected to stay in this home. Research and common wisdom support the idea that the children in homes that were both stable *and* supportive were more successful as learners. Although Ray and Laquisha were successful as learners without exceptional support from home, they might have been more successful given this support. It also is important to note that they were both competent at finding supportive adults outside the home to help them with emotional and intellectual pursuits. Their success at finding such persons underscores the importance of having these adults in their lives.

Most of the children found themselves in homes that, although they were poor, had a mother who did not work outside the home. This situation is not common for most children today, so these children were very fortunate to receive this support. Many of the foster parents also belonged to a very proactive group that looked for any and all services that might benefit their children. They secured support from state welfare to bring in speakers who helped them understand the children they cared for. For example, on one occasion the parents brought in an expert in prenatal alcohol exposure so that they would better know how to care for their children. They also provided support for one another: When a foster mother needed a few days without her foster children, another foster mother cared for them. These brief times away from high-risk foster children allowed them to return to their children renewed and ready to again accept the responsibility for their care.

The Parents' Backgrounds

The background of these parents is critical in understanding the success of their children. As was said earlier in this book, children who are poor, of minority status, prenatally exposed to drugs, and still living with their natural parents would most likely not be as resilient or successful.

When considering the parents of the children who were highlighted in this book, each one had unique contributions to offer to their child. Some saw their role as mainly mother, although others expanded this role to tutor as well.

Sean's mother saw her role as parent, religious leader, and teacher. She provided a book-filled environment for Sean and often used religious texts to combine reading and religious instruction. To enrich her more informal sharing of books with Sean, she purchased a commercial phonics program when she decided that she would be his teacher as well as his mother. As our time together ended, she was saving to provide him with a computer as well. Sean's mother was very involved with his academic growth in literacy.

Billy's grandmother saw a different role for herself than did Sean's mother. Although she valued Billy's religious upbringing, she allowed a preschool to provide this instruction. She was convinced that this was the best setting for Billy's early development, and she valued the close connections between instruction in preschool and the expectations for participation in religious services. Later, when Billy was in public school, she became proactive and had him changed from one school to another when she was disturbed with the classroom environment.

Melina's grandmother supported her literacy at home by letting her participate in book clubs. Although she did not have much time to read to Melina, she recognized the value of having books in her home. Melina's family informally supported education by their expectation that their children and grandchildren would go to college. When Melina's uncle was getting ready to go to college, the whole family participated in getting him ready to go. This preparation allowed the children to see the importance attached to such an event.

Curtis's mother was involved with both her own children's and her community's school endeavors. She devoted each evening to working with her children on school assignments. She also built a neighborhood store to better protect her children from unsafe neighborhood events. Finally, she petitioned the school district to change the arrangement of schools in her neighborhood. She was responsible for bringing back elementary schools to her neighborhood and for the creation of a new elementary school with an Afrocentric curriculum.

Ray's family support is more difficult to detail. His mother did say that she took him to the library and she did get him to school most days. He was always clean, although not always fed. Her home environment might not be considered rich, but it was consistent. This consistency would not have been present for Ray if he had been allowed to stay with his natural mother.

Finally there is Laquisha. Of all the children I came to know, her home situations were the most problematic. Her mother, who was still a drug user, periodically kept her, but she vacillated between being kind to Laquisha and abusing her. Her grandmother took her in, but she became ill and could not care for Laquisha. One of Laquisha's aunts took her in but decided that she was too much to handle in combination with her own children. She was living in a housing project and having Laquisha proved too burdensome. There was suspicion that she beat Laquisha. Laquisha's other home was a protective, temporary facility run by state welfare. The only obvious literacy support provided in any of these locations was that on some occasions

Laquisha was taken to the library and that her aunt bought her Babysitters' Club books for her very own.

The parents' stories might surprise some readers. Often, parents of children in poverty are not described as providing literacy experiences for their children (Auerbach, 1989; Delgado-Gaitan, 1992; Elish-Piper, 1996/1997; Taylor, 1993, 1994). These parents did provide experiences that varied from a visit to the library to frequent reading with their child. All the parents saw value in reading to children, however, not all of the parents consistently found time to do so.

Teachers and School Support

The variety of school experiences covered in this study is evident. Some teachers might be classified as exemplary because of their success with students, although they would not all teach reading and writing in the same way. Although I had read about this in "The Cooperative Research Program in First-Grade Reading Instruction" (Bond & Dykstra, 1967/1997), in Heath's work (1983), in Delpit's work (1995), and in Ladson-Billings's work (1994), it took 4 years of observation to convince me: The teachers were the critical element in children's success in learning in school. Many of the teachers I observed were directly responsible for the success that the children in the study experienced in school. Other teachers whom I observed were unable to establish a learning environment in their classrooms; as a result no children learned.

Looking at Schools

The schools in the study were complex and it was difficult to evaluate their support of diverse children. On the one hand it would have been easy to classify the schools by their physical appearance. At the beginning of the study, the schools would have fallen into discrete categories. Those filled with middle-class children were attractive as you walked into them. There were grass, trees, and flowers surrounding the entrance and inside were filled with art and student work. The schools that served predominantly poor children were not particularly attractive as you entered. They were in need of repair, there was minimal landscaping, they were framed with fences, and there was no art or student work in evidence. However, the physical appearance was often deceptive in terms of predicting the quality of instruction. For example, in several of the middle-class schools, I found that the teachers viewed all learners in their class as having the same levels of literacy knowledge. All children were expected to read the same stories from a basal and complete workbook pages independently. If children found this expectation difficult, it was up to them to remedy the situation. This situation was particularly problematic when children of color were bused to this school from high-poverty situations. Many of these children had few, if any, book-reading episodes at home or in kindergarten and they were expected to have the same knowledge about books and print as did the middle-class students whose classes they entered. This unrealistic expectation on the part of the teachers set up these children for failure, and many of these children were referred for special-education support by the end of first grade. The teachers often talked about these students' lack of preparation and blamed the parents for this. They did not see it as their responsibility to spend any additional time with these students or to provide accommodations for them as learners so that they would be successful.

Similarly, many of the schools with a significant representation of high-poverty children also blamed the children for what they did not bring to school. Many of these teachers also felt it was up to the individual child to be successful in school. Like the teachers in the middle-class schools, they taught all children the same curriculum on the same day. If a child did not learn, it was the child's fault, not theirs. Additionally, in these schools the teachers often had lower expectations for their students. Even those students who were seen as high achievers would be considered low-level achievers in a middle-class school. Unfortunately, lower expectations for high-poverty children are not uncommon (Nieto, 1998; Wang & Gordon, 1994).

Thankfully, not all the schools that I visited shared these beliefs. Several of the schools serving high-poverty youngsters had a posted philosophy that all students were expected to learn. The teachers worked hard to fulfill this philosophy. In Curtis's school, which his mother helped to establish, all teachers and community members worked on a shared philosophy. Once the philosophy was created, they found ways to achieve it. Community members came to school to work with students who were having difficulty. The school hired a literacy consultant who collaborated with teachers in improving classroom instruction or in problem solving about a particular child. During the school's first year of operation, they focused solely on literacy learning and instruction. All meetings and teachers' professional development were focused on literacy. Although not all children might be considered at grade level at the end of the first year of this school's operation, all children had grown in literacy knowledge and the majority of children viewed themselves as successful learners.

What was remarkable about this school was its energy; visitors could feel it upon entering. Teachers talked to one another about strategies they were trying, and they consulted with one another about how best to support a struggling child's learning. These discussions were very different in substance from those shared by teachers who saw only the child as the problem.

Looking at Teachers

The same sorts of characteristics proved to be important in determining teachers who made a difference in the academic lives of the students they taught. This close inspection of teachers who made a difference and those who did not is also complex to describe. For instance, teachers like Mrs. Tabner did not use many of the strategies recommended for literacy teachers. She centered her instruction on the basal text, but she balanced this narrow focus with a belief that all children could be successful learners in her class. This belief and her nurturing of her students resulted in the majority of these students reading at grade level at the end of the year and testing at 50% or above on standardized tests of reading achievement.

Although these teachers varied in their approach to teaching reading and writing, there were several common elements in many of the classrooms that would be considered exemplary in literacy instruction and learning. These teachers were able to maximize the learning of all the students in their classrooms and were especially successful with children of color and children from high-poverty backgrounds. I returned to the list of characteristics of literacy-rich classrooms that I shared in Figure 1 on page 12 in Chapter 1 to identify the elements these teachers used:

- They had in-class libraries for their students (Bear & Barone, 1998; Morrow, 1992);

- They read to their students on a daily basis and engaged students in discussion about these books (McGee & Richgels, 1996; Morrow, 1995; Teale, 1982);
- They provided their students with opportunities for writing (Temple, Nathan, Burris, & Temple, 1993); and
- Children were encouraged to talk during formal sharing times and informally as they completed independent work (Bear & Barone, 1998; McMahon & Raphael, 1997).

In addition, these teachers modeled

- an integration of skills and comprehension instruction (Freppon & Dahl, 1998); and
- writing and conventions of writing by using their students' words to compose texts (Allen, 1976; Stauffer, 1980).

When thinking about the teachers who were represented in the case studies, the best teachers used all of these elements in addition to other strategies. Perhaps what was the most important to the success of their students is that these elements were modeled and available on a daily basis.

Bias to Children of Color

The teachers who were exemplary were always a pleasure to observe. I always learned about the fine craft of teaching by watching them as they interacted with their students. Unfortunately, some otherwise capable teachers were biased against children of color. Sometimes the bias was explicit and at other times the bias was implicit and became overt only with extended observation. I found it difficult to mask my feelings when a teacher shared his or her opinions of children of color, and was embarrassed that the teacher felt it was acceptable to share such beliefs openly. For example, one teacher said, "All these children [of color] will ever be able to do is low-level work. Look, they have no clue about reading and their parents can't read either. If they don't try in my class, I put them in the back so that they don't bother my other kids." I am not sure how this teacher expected me to react. My guess is that she wanted me to support her segregation of students in her class. When I found myself involved in such conversations, I chose to leave and visit another room, which as a researcher, was a very difficult ethical dilemma. As a teacher educator, I wanted to work with the teacher to reorganize his or her room and to work on his or her attitudes about children of color. As a researcher, I had chosen not to change the classroom environments in which my participants found themselves. Therefore, I did not intervene when such opinions were shared. This was not a comfortable resolution, but I felt it necessary.

In other classrooms, the bias was much more subtle. I witnessed teachers who always put children of color in their lowest ability reading groups. This decision was made even when the children were quite proficient readers. I also found that the children of color who attended middle-class schools were more often referred for special-education services than the Caucasian children in their school and that their teachers often pondered retention (Nieto, 1998; Stockard & Mayberry, 1992). Allen et al. (1993) talked about such bias and discrimination demonstrated by teachers, but I was still saddened when I witnessed it.

Implications for Practice

Qualities of Exemplary Teachers

Although all of the teachers in this study influenced their students, I will focus on those teachers who had a special bond with their students. These are the teachers who believed that their students could be successful literacy learners (Thomas & Barksdale-Ladd, 1995) and then saw the results of their beliefs. These are the teachers that I hope are remembered for their quality work with all children.

These teachers demonstrated the important qualities necessary to develop students' literacy understandings. None of them approached the task in the same way, yet they all imparted to their students the expectation that they were successful learners (Bisplinghoff & Allen, 1998). This expectation, coupled with their relationship with their students, provided the necessary emotional comfort that allowed for learning to take place.

In one of the concluding chapters in *The Dreamkeepers: Successful Teachers of African American Children* (1994), Ladson-Billings identified characteristics that the successful teachers in her study demonstrated:

1. When students are treated as competent they are likely to demonstrate competence.
2. When teachers provide instructional scaffolding, students can move from what they know to what they need to know.
3. The focus of the classroom must be instructional.
4. Real education is about extending students' thinking and abilities.
5. Effective teaching involves in-depth knowledge of both the students and the subject matter. (pp. 123–135)

Although I was not focused on teachers in this study, I realized during the second year of my research that I could not adequately describe the children's learning without including the teachers. I did not set out to document the characteristics that were demonstrated by exemplary teachers. However, after reading Ladson-Billings's book, I realized that these characteristics were also those that I observed in several of the teachers participating in my study. In this section, I will highlight the characteristics described by Ladson-Billings and how the teachers in this study exemplified them. Additionally, I will make reference to how these characteristics can be applied in all classroom situations by all teachers for all students.

WHEN STUDENTS ARE TREATED AS COMPETENT THEY ARE LIKELY TO DEMONSTRATE COMPETENCE. The first teacher whom I consider immediately when thinking about this characteristic is Billy's kindergarten teacher, Mrs. Campbell. As I watched her teach throughout a year, I was impressed by the number of compliments she gave to her students. When they came into the room, she might say, "I can tell that you are ready to learn today. Look at how beautiful you are. You took time to get ready for today." She might tell another child after a brief lesson that she "saw that he was trying and that was important for learning." Mrs. Campbell knew that these children did not come to school with the same preparation as other children. She commented that "many had been exposed to drugs and they were low-language functioning and lacked language." Although she knew these things about her students, she did not let them lower her expectations as is often the case of teachers of such children (Spear-Swerling & Sternberg, 1996; Wang & Gordon, 1994). Each day she welcomed her students to learning and she expected their participation and success. She enlisted the support of the parents of her students, and she had remarkable success at gaining their support.

Mrs. Campbell, in her tenacity, is a model for all teachers. Many teachers welcome students similar to those greeted by her to their classrooms. They have a choice as to how to value these children. They can focus on what they have not experienced or on the perceived limitations and problems they have brought to the school situation *or* they can focus on what these students already know and build on these strengths. In making the second choice, the teacher is in charge, and he or she can move beyond complaints about what did or did not happen for these children, creating a high-expectancy learning environment.

WHEN TEACHERS PROVIDE INSTRUCTIONAL SCAFFOLDING, STUDENTS CAN MOVE FROM WHAT THEY KNOW TO WHAT THEY NEED TO KNOW. Many of the teachers in this study understood and practiced helping children move from what they knew to what they were considering. I think this ability was most noticeable for students who had literacy knowledge beyond the grade-level expectations at the beginning of the year, especially Curtis. In kindergarten, in which teachers often teach the same curriculum to all students on the same day, Curtis's Chapter 1 teacher varied from this routine. She built on the literacy knowledge that Curtis brought to school. Instead of having him focus on initial consonant sounds as is often the practice in kindergarten, she supported his exploration of short-vowel patterns. Although the majority of children spent time looking for items that began with a particular consonant, Curtis explored CVC words from his reading. His teacher also built his social competence by expecting him to work with students who did not have as much literacy knowledge as he did. Curtis spent time reading books to children who had had few such experiences before coming to kindergarten. Curtis enjoyed these experiences as did the students who benefited from his reading and talking about stories.

As I work with teachers, I find that one of their major concerns is finding the time both in class and in planning to work with students who have differing literacy knowledge. They are aware that not all students in their classrooms are at the same developmental level (Adams, 1990; Bear & Barone, 1998; Chall, 1983; Templeton, 1995), but they are not confident about how to provide varying instruction to them. They worry about the demands of teaching small groups and managing the students with whom they are not in direct contact, those students left to work independently. These are important concerns, certainly, but teachers like Curtis's Chapter 1 teacher demonstrate that this individualization need not be burdensome. This teacher simply had Curtis work on short-vowel words while others worked on initial consonants. All the children had blank paper for this activity, and the only change required was that Curtis collected words while other children collected pictures of items that began with a specific consonant. Her only other modification was that she encouraged Curtis to read to other students in the class. For other teachers, the modifications for this individualization might be more extensive, but if simple solutions are found first then later more complex routines will not be seen as so unrealistic.

THE FOCUS OF THE CLASSROOM MUST BE INSTRUCTIONAL.   This was one characteristic that I witnessed each time that I observed, although Becky Schneider was one of the best teachers in maintaining this focus. She had a large class, about 35 students, and they quickly were brought into the culture of the class that focused on learning. When a student acted inappropriately, which did happen, especially at the beginning of the year, Becky had a private conversation with the student. I often overheard her talk about "choices." In a quiet voice, she and the student talked about the choice that was made and alternative choices that might have been made. By the end of August, her students talked independently to one another about choices. They were aware that they, not the teacher, were responsible for their personal behavior. She also allowed students to get in control of themselves before she had these conversations. This often showed in her work with Laquisha, whom she allowed to put her head down and sometimes cry at her table, giving her the time and space to gain emotional control. The students in this classroom modeled this behavior and treated one another with similar respect.

Becky's class knew they were there to learn, and they all valued this learning environment. During class meetings, students often commented on what they had observed in terms of the learning of another student in the room. For example, Brittany complimented Heather when she finished reading a book because she knew that this was a big achievement for Heather. Students valued these compliments from fellow students and the teacher.

Other teachers did not find this focus on curriculum as easy to achieve. An unfortunate example of this was in Ray's second-grade class. Ms. Hughes was able to focus only on classroom management. Her narrow focus left the students without any content instruction. This limited focus has been documented in other studies of teachers, particularly teachers of poor children (Stockard & Mayberry, 1992). The dilemma associated with this focus is that children might evidence fewer management issues if they were engrossed in exciting learning.

The issue for teachers is to balance the need for an orderly classroom with a focus on learning. Ms. Hughes never achieved this reality. The students in her class rarely experienced learning of reading or writing because they were always learning to behave. This situation is particularly unfortunate because her students really needed their teacher to provide this academic learning. They came from homes that had few literacy materials available to them and they needed Ms. Hughes to provide these experiences. She demonstrated that it is important for teachers to develop an orderly class as they simultaneously teach children a meaningful curriculum. Her singular focus on management was not sufficient for the development of these children.

REAL EDUCATION IS ABOUT EXTENDING STUDENT'S THINKING AND ABILITIES. The model for this characteristic from this study is Curtis's second-grade teacher, Mrs. Cambell. I remember walking into her classroom and seeing books everywhere—in bookcases, in bins, on the ledges under the chalkboards, and on children's desks. When she read to students, they always put on their visors so that they could engage "extra-special thinking powers." As she read and engaged her students in conversation about what she was reading, she built from literal questions, such as Who is in this story? What happened? and How did it end? to inferential questions, such as What other story does this remind you of? Why do you think he behaved that way? and What did you learn from this story? She challenged her students to move beyond the literal.

She began this focus on thinking the minute a student entered her room. She might tell a child, "I can tell that you are thinking. I saw you look at that book. Are you planning on reading it today and telling us about it?" For another child, she might ask, "Did you find out any more information about frogs last night? I know you were interested and I thought you might have talked to your parents about them." Her students knew that in her classroom you were expected to think and you were expected to take this thinking from school to home and back again.

This expectation of thought is not difficult for all teachers to achieve. For Mrs. Cambell it was easy as she modeled her constant questioning to students. She wanted to learn about everything. She had many of her own questions that she shared with students. In achieving this expectation, it was important to model this search for knowledge on a daily basis. Teachers who have not yet established this environment might begin by initiating a discussion centered on read alouds with the whole class. *The Book Club Connection: Literacy Learning and Classroom Talk* (McMahon & Raphael, 1997) can provide a resource for these kinds of discussions.

EFFECTIVE TEACHING INVOLVES IN-DEPTH KNOWLEDGE OF BOTH THE STUDENTS AND THE SUBJECT MATTER. Few teachers in my study knew both subject-matter knowledge and the children that they taught, but Ray's first-grade teachers, Mrs. Green and Mrs. Garcia, worked at mastering both. Their teaching of reading and writing was grounded in their basal guides and their explicit instruction grew from the recommendations in these manuals. However, they also had a rich library of other children's books that they encouraged them to read. In addition, these teachers attempted to meet all the parents of their students and to understand the home background of their students. They spent a considerable amount of time trying to communicate with Ray's foster mother. They were the first teachers to suspect that his home was less than desirable for a young boy, and they made contact with the school principal and the school counselor to try to get help for Ray and to attempt to get him removed from this home.

This type of involvement may be troublesome for teachers. Although they value having parents support academic and behavioral concerns at home, they are less comfortable with intervening in a child's life or letting the concerns from the home enter school. However, having parents significantly involved in schools affects the motivation of teachers and students and the achievement of students (Stockard & Mayberry, 1992). Additionally, students feel valued when their home culture and perhaps language is valued in class (Cole, 1995). There is a continuum of involvement that can be demonstrated by a teacher by simply bringing a significant event in a child's life into the classroom through an activity like Daily News in which the teacher writes about a memorable event in the life of a student. Or a teacher might solicit the help of parents with daily instruction; for example, a parent might read with children individually during class time. Another simple way for teachers to become familiar with the home situations of the students they teach is to drive into the neighborhoods where they live. Teachers who do not find this drive useful might schedule home visits with each family. In this way they gain a real understanding of the home circumstances of the children they teach and make an important personal connection to the families that will serve to improve the social and academic lives of their students.

What Can We Conclude From the Observed Teachers?

I was impressed with the way the teachers I observed developed students' competencies and beliefs that they were capable and expected to be successful in learning. I was surprised at how quickly they established that the classroom was a place to learn, and that inappropriate behavior would not be tolerated. For these teachers, behavior management was evident but not overt. It was a seamless part of their curriculum; classroom management was in place, but it was combined with instructional expectations. And perhaps most importantly, these teachers understood their students. They knew their parents, they knew the neighborhoods in which their students lived, and they allowed each student's home culture to be seen as valuable.

I saw positive and negative perspectives of literacy teaching and learning, but unfortunately, the negative images are often remembered more easily. When you read about Ray's second-grade teacher, Ms. Hughes, you probably made audible gasps at many of the ways she engaged students. The same reaction most likely occurred when reading about Billy's initial first-grade teacher. Fortunately, there were few teachers that I observed who were as inept as these teachers at providing instruction for students.

The vast majority of the teachers in this study provided models of the type of instruction one would wish for all students. What I quickly discovered was that the teachers who were most successful with their students treated them with dignity (Hynds, 1997). They were pleased to see their students and they enjoyed hearing about their lives both inside and outside of school. The children in these class-rooms participated in learning events as successful students. They understood the responsibilities associated with such environments and they did not disrespect the learning process. This was true for students regardless of their racial or socioeconomic backgrounds.

These teachers perceived themselves as responsible for the learning of students in their classrooms (Rossi, 1994). They brought in support through parent and community involvement; however, they assumed the responsibility for their students' academic learning. They used the materials that were supplied by the district, and they found ways to embellish these materials: They visited the district curriculum lab and borrowed materials for their room; they inspected catalogs and request-ed materials from their principals; and they visited stores and personal-ly bought materials for students. In addition, they constantly informal-ly assessed their students' literacy knowledge, so that they could plan lessons that built on their students' current knowledge. This assess-ment meant that they frequently changed group configurations. For ex-ample, students who were working on literal comprehension might be grouped together for an explicit lesson on comprehension. Later, an-other configuration of students would be grouped for a lesson on word patterns. These teachers used multiple grouping arrangements through-out the school day to best facilitate their students' learning.

Finally, these teachers had reasonable yet high expectations for their students (Labov, 1995). They kept in mind the grade-level ex-pectations of the school district as they taught their students, and they believed that the majority of their students could achieve these grade-level expectations. Unlike many of their colleagues, they believed that it was unacceptable for students to be at least one grade level below their peers in literacy achievement because the students were of col-or or from high-poverty backgrounds. These teachers constantly prod-ded their students to do more while at the same time supported them in the new knowledge they had just attained. These teachers were ac-celerating the learning that is typically expected in the course of one academic year for most of their students. If a student came to them 6 months behind, they worked to have that student grow by at least a year and a half during 1 year. To accomplish this task, they encouraged parents to help, providing them with specific tasks that they could do at home to help their child. They also were reluctant to recommend a child for special-education support or retention. These recommendations came only after all other venues were explored, and typically only for a single child.

It is not difficult to learn from these teachers and bring what was successful for them to other classroom situations. Basically, they respected students and their families even if they came from backgrounds other than traditional middle-class backgrounds. They held themselves responsible for their students' learning and did not lay the blame for a struggling student on the parents. They had high expectations for all of their students, which represented the expectations for all students in all schools within their school district.

Final Thoughts

Every time I think about these children I am amazed at what I discovered about them. Most importantly, I learned how supportive parents and teachers were to these children and to the others in their care. The parents were concerned about their child's progress in school and valued reading and writing knowledge. They trusted schools to be responsible for teaching their child and were willing, even after a full day of work, to help their child at home with school tasks. Perhaps, more importantly, they enjoyed reading to their child.

I found new respect for teachers of children in high-poverty schools. Despite the many recent newspaper articles, these teachers were successful with the teaching and learning of all the children who filled their classrooms. They found ways to set aside expectations and labels and to focus on teaching and learning. They let their students know in formal and informal ways that they held beliefs and expectations that all students in their class could learn and expected them to learn. They used the families of these children to support them in their work in school.

Finally, the children made the labels attached to them meaningless. They were always inquisitive about learning and consistently demonstrated that they were at grade level or above in literacy development. This development is critical for young children: Children who are behind grade level in the primary grades tend to stay there as they move through school (Clay, 1979; Juel, 1988; Lundberg, 1984; Smith, 1997). Additionally, the children in this study were able to accommodate the expectations for behavior and learning shared by their teachers. They were resilient (Novick, 1998).

Looking at the title of this book, a reader might have expected stories with sad endings. I anticipate that readers were pleasantly surprised to discover that these children's stories are positive. It would be naive to believe, however, that there are no areas for concern. These children continue to live in poverty and, as a result, their home and school situations are not always ideal (Applebee, 1991; Hiebert, 1996; Shannon, 1998). One may wonder at how the accumulation of such experiences over time will wear on these children. Will they continue to be successful or will their success wither? For the most part, beyond their conditions of poverty, many of these children are African American and the success stories for African American children are not as frequent as for those of other racial or cultural backgrounds (Washington, 1989). Will these children eventually become part of these negative statistics? Finally, there is little known about children who live in foster care situations for their entire childhood. Will having a temporary set of parents be harmful to these children? These are all important questions and there are many others that need to be considered when pondering the long-term academic and emotional potential of these children. But for today, as most of these children come to the end of their elementary school experiences, they are successful. Despite their prenatal drug exposure, despite their cultural backgrounds, despite their poverty levels, despite the danger in their neighborhoods, despite having teachers who are not always exemplary, despite living in foster care—they are successful! This is the power of their stories.

APPENDIX

Summaries of Literacy Development
Year 1 Through Year 4 (organized by entry ages of children)

Name and age of child at beginning of study	Year of study	Drawing	Name	Concepts of book/print	Concept of word	Storytelling–reading (see key on page 220)	Orthographic knowledge
Chantilly, 1	1	scribbles	no	none	no	listens to stories	refusal
	2	scribbles	no	none	no	(1) no story	prephonemic
	3	not in study					
Twilea, 2	1	scribbles	no	none	no	listens to stories	prephonemic
						(1) no story	
	2	scribbles	no	none	no	(2) forms story	prephonemic
	3	scribbles/ difference between drawing and writing	yes	front of book	no	(2) forms story	prephonemic
	4	same as Year 3	yes	aware of book organization	no	(5) read predictable text	semiphonemic

(continued)

Becky, 2	1	scribbles/difference between drawing and writing	no	none	no	(2) forms story (3) storytelling and reading	prephonemic
	2	same as Year 1	initial letter	front of book turns pages top/bottom beginning/end	no	(3) storytelling and reading	prephonemic
	3	self-portrait	initial letter	aware of book organization	no	(4) book language (5) read predictable text	prephonemic
	4	self-portrait	yes	same as Year 3	no	(5) read predictable text	semiphonemic
Sean, 2	1	not in study					
	2	scribbles/differences between drawing and writing	initial letter	front of book turns pages top/bottom beginning/end	no	(3) storytelling and reading	prephonemic
	3	self-portrait	initial letter	aware of book organization	no	(4) book language	prephonemic
	4	self-portrait	yes	full understanding	almost	(5) read predictable text	semiphonemic

(continued)

Summaries of Literacy Development (continued)

Name and age of child at beginning of study	Year of study	Drawing	Name	Concepts of book/print	Concept of word	Storytelling–reading	Orthographic knowledge
Anna, 3	1	self-portrait	no	none	no	(2) forms story	prephonemic
	2	self-portrait	yes	aware of book organization	no	(3) storytelling and reading	prephonemic
	3	self-portrait	+ last name	full understanding	almost	(3) storytelling and reading (4) book language	semiphonemic
	4	self-portrait	+ last name	full understanding	almost	(5) read predictable text	semiphonemic
Billy, 3	1	scribbles/ difference between drawing and writing	yes	front of book turns pages top/bottom	no	(3) storytelling and reading (4) book language	semiphonemic
	2	self-portrait	Same as Year 1	aware of book organization	almost	(5) refusal (5) read predictable text	semiphonemic
	3	self-portrait	+ last name	full understanding	yes	(6) independent reader word-by-word	letter name
	4	self-portrait	+ last name	full understanding	yes	Same as Year 3	letter name

(continued)

Summaries of Literacy Development (continued)

	4	self-portrait	+ last name	full understanding	almost	(5) read predictable text	semiphonemic
Jamal, 3	1	scribbles/differences between drawing and writing	no	front of book	no	listens to story (1) no story	prephonemic
	2	Same as Year 1	initial letter	aware of book organization	no	(2) forms story	prephonemic
	3	self-portrait	yes	Same as Year 2	no	(2) forms story (3) storytelling and reading	prephonemic
	4	self-portrait	+ last name	Same as Year 2	no	(3) storytelling and reading	prephonemic
Jose, 3	1	scribbles/differences between drawing and writing	no	front of book	no	(2) forms story	prephonemic
	2	Same as Year 1	no	aware of book organization	no	(3) storytelling and reading	prephonemic
	3	self-portrait	yes	Same as Year 2	no	(3) storytelling and reading	prephonemic
	4	self-portrait	+ last name	Same as Year 2	no	(5) reads predictable text	prephonemic

(continued)

Summaries of Literacy Development (continued)

Name and age of child at beginning of study	Year of study	Drawing	Name	Concepts of book/print	Concept of word	Storytelling–reading	Orthographic knowledge
Anna, 3	1	self-portrait	no	none	no	(2) forms story	prephonemic
	2	self-portrait	yes	aware of book organization	no	(3) storytelling and reading	prephonemic
	3	self-portrait	+ last name	full understanding	almost	(3) storytelling and reading (4) book language	semiphonemic
	4	self-portrait	+ last name	full understanding	almost	(5) read predictable text	semiphonemic
Billy, 3	1	scribbles/difference between drawing and writing	yes	front of book turns pages top/bottom	no	(3) storytelling and reading (4) book language	semiphonemic
	2	self-portrait	Same as Year 1	aware of book organization	almost	(5) refusal (5) read predictable text	semiphonemic
	3	self-portrait	+ last name	full understanding	yes	(6) independent reader word-by-word	letter name
	4	self-portrait	+ last name	full understanding	yes	Same as Year 3	letter name

(continued)

Summaries of Literacy Development (continued)

Jennifer, 3	1	self-portrait	initial letter	front of book / turns pages / top/bottom	no	(3) storytelling and reading / (4) book language / (5) refusal	semiphonemic
	2	self-portrait	yes	aware of book organization	almost	(4) book language / (5) refusal	semiphonemic
	3	self-portrait	+ last name	full understanding	yes	(6) independent reader word-by-word	letter name
	4	self-portrait	+ last name	full understanding	yes	(7) independent reader fluent	within-word pattern
Mark, 3	1	scribbles/difference between drawing and writing	no	front of book / turns pages	no	(3) storytelling and reading / (4) book language	prephonemic
	2	self-portrait	yes	aware of book organization	almost	(5) refusal / (5) reads predictable text	semiphonemic
	3	self-portrait	+ last name	full understanding	almost	Same as Year 2	semiphonemic
	4	self-portrait	+ last name	full understanding	yes	(6) independent reader word-by-word	letter name
Dante, 4	1	self-portrait	initial letter	front of book / turns pages	no	(3) storytelling and reading / (4) book language / (5) refusal	prephonemic
	2	not in study					

(continued)

Summaries of Literacy Development (continued)

Name and age of child at beginning of study	Year of study	Drawing	Name	Concepts of book/print	Concept of word	Storytelling– reading	Orthographic knowledge
Christopher, 4	1	not in study					
Charles, 4	1	scribbles/ difference between drawing and writing	initial letter	front of book turns pages	no	(3) storytelling and reading (4) book language	prephonemic
	2	not in study					
Mario, 4	1	self-portrait	initial letter	front of book turns pages	no	(4) book language (5) refusal	prephonemic
	2	self-portrait	yes + last name	aware of book organization	no	Same as Year 1	semiphonemic
	3	self-portrait	yes + last name	full understanding	yes	(6) independent reader word-by-word	letter name
	4	self-portrait	yes + last name	full understanding	yes	(7) independent reader fluent	within-word pattern

(continued)

Summaries of Literacy Development (continued)

Ray, 4	1	self-portrait	yes	aware of book organization	no	(3) storytelling and reading (4) book language (5) refusal	prephonemic
	2	self-portrait	+ last name	full understanding	yes	(6) independent reader word-by-word	letter name
	3	self-portrait	+ last name	full understanding	yes	(7) independent reader fluent	within-word pattern
	4	self-portrait	+ last name	full understanding	yes	(7) independent reader fluent	within-word pattern
Curtis, 4	1	self-portrait	yes	front of book turns pages	almost	(3) storytelling and reading (4) book language	semiphonemic
	2	self-portrait	+ last name	full understanding	yes	(6) independent reader word-by-word	letter name
	3	self-portrait	+ last name	full understanding	yes	(7) independent reader fluent	within-word pattern
	4	self-portrait	+ last name	full understanding	yes	(7) independent reader fluent	within-word pattern
Donette, 4	1	self-portrait	yes	aware of book organization	no	(4) book language	semiphonemic
	2	self-portrait	+ last name	aware of book organization	no	Same as Year 1	semiphonemic
	3	self-portrait	+ last name	full understanding	almost	(5) refusal (5) read predictable text	semiphonemic

(continued)

Summaries of Literacy Development (continued)

Name and age of child at beginning of study	Year of study	Drawing	Name	Concepts of book/print	Concept of word	Storytelling–reading	Orthographic knowledge
	4	self-portrait	+ last name	full understanding	yes	(6) independent reader word-by-word	letter name
Melisha, 4	1	self-portrait	initial letter	front of book	no	(2) forms story	prephonemic
	2	self-portrait	initial letter	top/bottom beginning/end	no	(3) storytelling and reading	semiphonemic
	3	self-portrait	yes	aware of book organization	no	(3) storytelling and reading	semiphonemic
	4	not in study					
Josh, 4	1	self-portrait	yes	aware of book organization	almost	(4) book language	semiphonemic
	2	self-portrait	+ last name	full understanding	yes	(6) independent reader word-by-word	letter name
	3	self-portrait	+ last name	full understanding	yes	Same as Year 2	letter name
	4	self-portrait	+ last name	full understanding	yes	(7) independent reader fluent	syllable juncture

(continued)

Summaries of Literacy Development (continued)

Melina, 4	1	self-portrait	yes	front of book turns pages top/bottom	no	(3) storytelling and reading	semiphonemic
	2	self-portrait	+ last name	aware of book organization	almost	(4) book language (5) refusal	semiphonemic
	3	self-portrait	+ last name	full understanding	yes	(4) book language (5) refusal (5) reads predictable text (6) independent reader word-by-word	letter name
	4	self-portrait	+ last name	full understanding	yes	(7) independent reader fluent	within-word pattern
Lakisha, 5	1	self-portrait	yes + last name	aware of book organization	no	(1) no story	prephonemic
	2	self-portrait	+ last name	full understanding	almost	(5) read predictable text	semiphonemic
	3	self-portrait	+ last name	full understanding	yes	(6) independent reader word-by-word	letter name
	4	self-portrait	+ last name	full understanding	yes	(6) independent reader word-by-word	letter name

(continued)

Summaries of Literacy Development (continued)

Name and age of child at beginning of study	Year of study	Drawing	Name	Concepts of book/print	Concept of word	Storytelling–reading	Orthographic knowledge
Danny, 5	1	self-portrait	yes + last name	full understanding	yes	(3) storytelling and reading (4) book language (5) reads predictable text	semiphonemic
	2	self-portrait	+ last name	full understanding	yes	(6) independent reader word-by-word	letter name
	3	self-portrait	+ last name	full understanding	yes	(6) independent reader word-by-word	letter name
	4	self-portrait	+ last name	full understanding	yes	(7) independent reader fluent	within-word pattern
Dontay, 5	1	self-portrait	yes + last name	full understanding	yes	(3) storytelling and reading (4) book language (5) reads predictable text	semiphonemic
	2	self-portrait	+ last name	full understanding	yes	(6) independent reader word-by-word	letter name
	3	self-portrait	+ last name	full understanding	yes	(6) independent reader word-by-word	letter name

(continued)

Summaries of Literacy Development (continued)

4	self-portrait	+ last name	full understanding	yes	(7) independent reader fluent	within-word pattern
Kevin, 5						
1	self-portrait	yes + last name	full understanding	yes	(3) storytelling and reading (4) book language (5) reads predictable text	letter name
2	self-portrait	+ last name	full understanding	yes	(6) independent reader word-by-word	letter name
3	self-portrait	+ last name	full understanding	yes	(7) independent reader fluent	within-word pattern
4	self-portrait	+ last name	full understanding	yes	(7) independent reader fluent	syllable juncture
Loren, 7						
1	self-portrait	yes + last name	full understanding	yes	(6) independent reader word-by-word	within-word pattern
2	self-portrait	+ last name	full understanding	yes	independent reader	syllable juncture
3	self-portrait	+ last name	full understanding	yes	(7) independent reader fluent	syllable juncture
4	self-portrait	+ last name	full understanding	yes	(7) independent reader fluent	syllable juncture

(continued)

Key

Storytelling and reading

(1) no story—child retells story illustration by illustration; no story is formed
(2) forms story—child retells story illustration by illustration; a story is formed
(3) retelling and reading—child retells story using oral tradition and book language
(4) book language—child retells story using book language
(5) read predictable text—child reads a memorized predictable text
(5) refusal—child refuses to read
(6) independent reader/word-by-word—child reads text independently at a slow pace
(7) independent reader/fluent—child reads text fluently, in phrases rather than by word

Orthographic knowledge

(1) prephonemic—no relationship between writing and sounds/letters in word represented
(2) semiphonemic—initial and perhaps final consonants are represented, no vowels
(3) letter name—most phonemes are represented, vowels included but often confused (example—*BAD* for *bed*, *DRIV* for *drive*)
(4) within-word pattern—long-vowel patterns are represented in single syllable words but often confused (example—*DRIEV* for *drive*)
(5) syllable juncture—single syllable words are generally spelled correctly, child is confused about the addition of affixes (example—*POPING* for *popping*)

References

Adams, M. (1990). *Beginning to read: Thinking and learning about print.* Cambridge, MA: Massachusetts Institute of Technology Press.

Allen, J., Michalove, B., & Shockley, B. (1993). *Engaging children: Community and chaos in the lives of young literacy learners.* Portsmouth, NH: Heinemann.

Allen, R. (1976). *Language experience in communication.* Boston, MA: Houghton Mifflin.

Allington, R.L. (1983). The reading instruction provided readers of different reading abilities. *The Elementary School Journal, 83,* 549–559.

Allington, R.L., & Walmsley, S.A. (Eds.). (1995). *No quick fix: Rethinking literacy programs in America's elementary schools.* New York: Teachers College Press; Newark, DE: International Reading Association.

Anderson, A., & Stokes, S. (1984). Social and institutional influences on the development of literacy. In H. Goelman, A. Oberg, & F. Smith (Eds.), *Awakening to literacy* (pp. 24–37). Portsmouth, NH: Heinemann.

Angelou, M. (1993). *Life doesn't frighten me.* New York: Stewart, Tabori & Chang.

Applebee, A. (1991). Literature: Whose heritage? In E. Hiebert (Ed.), *Literacy for a diverse society: Perspectives, practices, and policies* (pp. 228–236). New York: Teachers College Press.

Au, K. (1993). *Literacy instruction in multicultural settings.* Orlando, FL: Harcourt Brace Jovanovich.

Auerbach, E. (1989). Toward a social-contextual approach to family literacy. *Harvard Educational Review, 59,* 165–181.

Aylward, G. (1990). Environmental influences on the developmental outcomes of children at risk. *Infants and Young Children, 2,* 1–9.

Bandstra, E., & Burkett, G. (1991). Maternal-fetal and neonatal effects of in utero cocaine exposure. *Seminars in Perinatology, 15,* 288–301.

Barone, D. (1993a). Dispelling the myths: Focusing on the literacy development of children prenatally exposed to crack/cocaine. In D. Leu & C. Kinzer (Eds.), *Examining central issues in literacy research, theory, and practice: Forty-second yearbook of the National Reading Conference* (pp. 197–206). Chicago, IL: National Reading Conference.

221

Barone, D. (1993b). Wednesday's child: Literacy development of children prenatally exposed to crack or cocaine. *Research in the Teaching of English*, *27*(1), 7–45.

Barone, D. (1994). The importance of classroom context: Literacy development of children prenatally exposed to crack/cocaine—Year two. *Research in the Teaching of English*, *28*(3), 286–312.

Barone, D., & Schneider, R. (1996, December). *Turning the looking glass inside out: A gifted student in an at-risk setting*. Paper presented at the National Reading Conference, Charleston, SC.

Bartoli, J. (Ed.). (1995). *Unequal opportunity: Learning to read in the U.S.A.* New York: Teachers College Press.

Bartolome, L., & Macedo, P. (1997). Dancing with bigotry: The poisoning of racial and ethnic identities. *Harvard Educational Review*, *67*, 222–246.

Bateman, D., Ng, S., Hansen, C., & Heagarty, M. (1993). The effects of intrauterine cocaine exposure in newborns. *American Journal of Public Health*, *83*, 190–193.

Baumann, J., & Thomas, D. (1997). "If you can pass Momma's tests, then she knows you're getting your education": A case study of support for literacy learning within an African American family. *The Reading Teacher*, *51*, 108–120.

Bear, D., & Barone, D. (1989). Using children's spellings to group for word study and directed reading in the primary classroom. *Reading Psychology: An International Quarterly*, *10*, 275–292.

Bear, D., & Barone, D. (1998). *Developing literacy: An integrated approach to assessment and instruction*. Boston, MA: Houghton Mifflin.

Bear, D., Invernizzi, M., Templeton, S., & Johnston, F. (1996). *Words their way: Word study for phonics, vocabulary, and spelling instruction*. Englewood Cliffs, NJ: Merrill.

Beeghly, M., & Tronick, E. (1994). Effects of prenatal exposure to cocaine in early infancy: Toxic effects on the process of mutual regulation. *Infant Mental Health Journal*, *15*, 158–175.

Bennett, F. (1992). Recent advances in developmental intervention for biologically vulnerable infants. *Infants and Young Children*, *3*, 33–40.

Berlin, C. (1991). Effects of drugs on the fetus. *Pediatrics in Review*, *12*(9), 282–287.

Bisplinghoff, B., & Allen, J. (1998). *Engaging teachers: Creating teaching and researching relationships*. Portsmouth, NH: Heinemann.

Bond, G., & Dykstra, R. (1967/1997). The cooperative research program in first-grade reading instruction. *Reading Research Quarterly*, *32*, 9–86.

Brodkin, A., & Zuckerman, B. (1992). Are crack babies doomed to school failure? *Instructor*, *101*(7), 16–17.

Burgess, D., & Striessguth, A. (1990). Educating students with fetal alcohol syndrome or fetal alcohol effects. *Pennsylvania Reporter*, *22*(1), 1–3.

Bussis, A., Chittenden, E., Amarel, M., & Klausner, E. (1985). *Inquiry into meaning: An investigation of learning to read.* Hillsdale, NJ: Erlbaum.

Calkins, L. (1986). *The art of teaching writing.* Portsmouth, NH: Heinemann.

Carver, R. (1992). *Reading rate: A review of research and theory.* New York: Academic Press.

Chall, J. (1983). *Stages of reading development.* New York: McGraw-Hill.

Chall, J., & Snow, C. (1982). *Families and literacy: The contributions of out-of-school experiences to children's acquisition of literacy. Final Report.* Washington, DC: National Institute of Education. (ERIC Document Reproduction Service No. ED 234 345)

Chasnoff, I. (1988a). Cocaine: Effects on pregnancy and the neonate. In I. Chasnoff (Ed.), *Drugs, alcohol, pregnancy and parenting* (pp. 1–16). Boston, MA: Kluwer.

Chasnoff, I. (1988b). Drug use in pregnancy: Parameters of risk. *The Pediatric Clinics of North America, 35,* 1403—1412.

Chasnoff, I. (1991). Drugs, alcohol, pregnancy, and the neonate. *The Journal of the American Medical Association, 266*(11), 1567–1568.

Chasnoff, I. (1992). President's message. *Perinatal Addiction Research and Education Update,* 2–3.

Chasnoff, I., Landress, H., & Barrett, M. (1990). The prevalence of illicit-drug and alcohol use during pregnancy and discrepancies in mandatory reporting in Pinellas County, Florida. *New England Journal of Medicine: Special Article, 322,* 1202–1206.

Chasnoff, I., Lewis, D., & Squires, L. (1987). Cocaine intoxication in a breast-fed infant. *Pediatrics, 80*(6), 836–838.

Clarke, L. (1988). Invented versus traditional spelling in first graders' writings: Effects on learning to spell and read. *Research in the Teaching of English, 22,* 281–309.

Clay, M. (1979). *Reading: The pattern of complex behavior.* Auckland, New Zealand: Heinemann.

Clay, M. (1985). *The early detection of reading difficulties* (3rd ed.). Portsmouth, NH: Heinemann.

Clay, M. (1991). *Becoming literate: The construction of inner control.* Portsmouth, NH: Heinemann.

Cohen, S., & Taharally, C. (1992). Getting ready for young children with prenatal drug exposure. *Childhood Education, 69*(1), 5–9.

Cole, R. (Ed.). (1995). *Educating everybody's children: Diverse teaching strategies for diverse learners.* Alexandria, VA: Association for Supervision and Curriculum Development.

Coles, C., Platzman, K., Smith, I., James, M., & Falek, A. (1992). Effects of cocaine and alcohol use in pregnancy on neonatal growth and neurobehavioral status. *Neurotoxicology and Teratology, 14*(1), 23–33.

Commeyras, M. (1990). Analyzing a critical-thinking reading lesson. *Teaching and Teacher Education, 6,* 201–214.

Cuban, L. (1989). The "at risk" label and the problem of urban school reform. *Phi Delta Kappan, 70,* 780–801.

David, P. (Producer), & Duke, B. (Director). (1992). *Deep Cover* [Film]. (Available from New Line Home Video, 116 N. Robertson Blvd., #200, Los Angeles, CA)

Delgado-Gaitan, C. (1987). Mexican adult literacy: New directions for immigrants. In S.R. Goldman & K. Trueba (Eds.), *Becoming literate in English as a second language* (pp. 9–32). Norwood, NJ: Ablex.

Delgado-Gaitan, C. (1992). School matters in the Mexican-American home: Socializing children to education. *American Educational Research Journal, 29,* 495–513.

Delpit, L. (1988). The silenced dialogue: Power and pedagogy in educating other people's children. *Harvard Educational Review, 58,* 280–298.

Delpit, L. (1995). *Other people's children: Cultural conflict in the classroom.* New York: New Press.

DeSylvia, D., & Klug, C. (1992). Drugs and children: Taking care of the victims. *Journal of the American Optometric Association, 63*(1), 59–62.

Dyson, A. (1993). *Social worlds of children learning to write in an urban primary school.* New York: Teachers College Press.

Dyson, A. (1995). Children out of bounds: The power of case studies in expanding visions of literacy development. In K. Hinchman, D. Leu, & C. Kinzer (Eds.), *Perspectives on literacy research and practice: Forty-fourth yearbook of the National Reading Conference* (pp. 39–53). Chicago, IL: National Reading Conference.

Eisenhart, M., & Howe, K. (1992). Validity in educational research. In M. LeCompte, W. Millroy, & J. Preissle (Eds.), *The handbook of qualitative research in education* (pp. 643–726). San Diego, CA: Academic Press.

Elish-Piper, L. (1996/1997). Literacy and their lives: Four low-income families enrolled in a summer family literacy program. *Journal of Adolescent & Adult Literacy, 40,* 256–268.

Eyler, F., & Behnke, M. (1995). Prenatal cocaine exposure: Consequences for child and family. *Journal of the Florida Medical Association, 82,* 603–606.

Frank, D., & Zuckerman, B. (1993). Children exposed to cocaine prenatally: Pieces of the puzzle. *Neurotoxicology and Teratology, 15,* 298–300.

Freier, M., Griffith, D., & Chasnoff, I. (1991). In utero drug exposure: Developmental follow-up and maternal-infant interaction. *Seminars in Perinatology, 15,* 310–316.

Freppon, P., & Dahl, K. (1998). Theory and research into practice: Balanced instruction: Insights and considerations. *Reading Research Quarterly, 33,* 240–251.

Gittler, J., & McPherson, M. (1990). Prenatal substance abuse: An overview of the problem. *Children Today, 19*(4), 3–7.

Goldenberg, C. (1984, October). *Low-income parents' contributions to reading achievement of their first-grade children*. Paper presented at the meeting of the Evaluation Network/Evaluation Research Society, San Francisco, CA.

Gonzalez, N., & Campbell, M. (1994). Cocaine babies: Does prenatal exposure to cocaine affect development? *Journal of the American Academy of Child and Adolescent Psychiatry, 33*, 16–19.

Goodman, E. (1992, January 22). "Crack babies" another premature panic. *Las Vegas Review-Journal*, p. 12B.

Graves, M.F., van den Broek, P., & Taylor, B.M. (Eds.). (1996). *The first R: Every child's right to read*. New York: Teachers College Press; Newark, DE: International Reading Association.

Greenfield, E., & Little, L. (1979). *Childtimes*. New York: Crowell.

Gregorchik, L. (1992). The cocaine-exposed children are here. *Phi Delta Kappan, 73*, 709–711.

Greider, K. (1995). Crackpot ideas. *Mother Jones, 20*, 52–56.

Griffith, D. (1992). Prenatal exposure to cocaine and other drugs: Developmental and educational prognoses. *Phi Delta Kappan, 74*, 30–34.

Griffith, D. (1995). Prenatal exposure to cocaine and other drugs: Developmental and educational prognoses. *Juvenile and Family Court Journal, 46*, 83–92.

Harste, J., Woodward, V., & Burke, C. (1984). *Language stories and literacy lessons*. Portsmouth, NH: Heinemann.

Heath, S. (1983). *Ways with words: Language, life, and work in communities and classrooms*. Cambridge, UK: Cambridge University Press.

Heath, S.B. (1991). The sense of being literate: Historical and cross-cultural features. In R. Barr, M. Kamil, P. Mosenthal, & P.D. Pearson (Eds.), *Handbook of Reading Research: Volume II* (pp. 3–25). White Plains, NY: Longman.

Henderson, E. (1990). *Teaching spelling* (2nd ed.). Boston, MA: Houghton Mifflin.

Henkin, R. (1998). *Who's invited to share? Using literacy to teach for equity and social justice*. Portsmouth, NH: Heinemann.

Hidalgo, N.M., Siu, S., Bright, J.A., Swap, S., & Epstein, J.L. (1995). Research on families, schools, and communities: A multicultural perspective. In J.A. Banks & C.A.M. Banks (Eds.), *Handbook of research on multicultural education* (pp. 498–524). New York: Macmillan.

Hiebert, E. (Ed.). (1991). *Literacy for a diverse society: Perspectives, practices, and policies*. New York: Teachers College Press.

Hiebert, E. (1996). Creating and sustaining a love of literature...And the ability to read it. In M.F. Graves, P. van den Broek, & B.M. Taylor (Eds.), *The first R: Every child's right to read* (pp. 15–36). New York: Teachers College Press; Newark, DE: International Reading Association.

Hiebert, E., & Raphael, T. (1998). *Early literacy instruction*. Fort Worth, TX: Harcourt Brace.

Hiebert, E., & Taylor, B. (Eds.). (1994). *Getting reading right from the start.* Boston, MA: Allyn & Bacon.

Holdaway, D. (1979). *The foundations of literacy.* Sydney, Australia: Ashton Scholastic.

Howard, B., & O'Donnell, K. (1995). What is important about a study of within-group differences of "cocaine babies"? *Archives of Pediatric and Adolescent Medicine, 149,* 663–664.

Hutchings, D. (1993). Response to commentaries. *Neurotoxicology and Teratology, 15,* 311–312.

Hynds, S. (1997). *On the brink: Negotiating literature and life with adolescents.* New York: Teachers College Press; Newark, DE: International Reading Association.

International Reading Association. (1985). *Literacy development and pre-first grade.* Newark, DE: Author.

Jackson, S. (1990). "Crack babies" are here! Can you help them learn? *California Teachers Association Action,* 11–13.

Johnson, H. (1993). Prenatal exposure to drugs and early development. *Early Child Development and Care, 84,* 81–89.

Jones, K. (1988). *Smith's recognizable patterns of human malformation* (4th ed.). Philadelphia, PA: W.B. Saunders.

Jorgensen, D. (1989). *Participant observation: A methodology for human studies.* Newbury Park, CA: Sage.

Juel, C. (1988). Learning to read and write: A longitudinal study of 54 children from first through fourth grade. *Journal of Educational Psychology, 80,* 437–447.

Labov, W. (1995). Can reading failure be reversed: A linguistic approach to the question. In E. Hiebert (Ed.), *Literacy for a diverse society: Perspectives, practices, and policies* (pp. 39–68). Cresskill, NJ: Hampton Press.

Ladson-Billings, G. (1994). *The dreamkeepers: Successful teachers of African American children.* San Francisco, CA: Jossey-Bass.

Lester, B., & Tronick, E. (1994). The effects of prenatal cocaine exposure and child outcome. Special issue: Prenatal drug exposure and child outcome. *Infant Mental Health Journal, 15,* 107–120.

Lewis, K. (1991). Pathophysiology of prenatal drug-exposure: In utero, in the newborn, in childhood, and in agencies. *Journal of Pediatric Nursing, 6*(3), 185–190.

Lundberg, I. (1984, August). Learning to read. *School Research Newsletter.* Stockholm, Sweden: National Board of Education.

Manzo, A. (1969). The ReQuest procedure. *Journal of Reading, 12,* 123–126.

Mayes, L. (1992). Prenatal cocaine exposure and young children's development. *The Annals of the American Academy of Political and Social Science, 521,* 11–27.

Mayes, L., Granger, R., Bornstein, M., & Zuckerman, B. (1992). The problem of prenatal cocaine exposure. *The Journal of the American Medical Association, 267* (3), 406–408.

McGee, L., & Richgels, D. (1996). *Literacy's beginnings: Supporting young readers and writers.* Boston, MA: Allyn & Bacon.

McMahon, S., & Raphael, T. (Eds.). (1997). *The book club connection: Literacy learning and classroom talk.* New York: Teachers College Press; Newark, DE: International Reading Association.

Merriam, S. (1998). *Case study research in education: A qualitative approach.* San Francisco, CA: Jossey-Bass.

Miles, M., & Huberman, A. (1994). *Qualitative data analysis* (2nd ed.). Thousand Oaks, CA: Sage.

Miller, G. (1989). Addicted infants and their mothers. *Zero to Three Bulletin of the National Center for Clinical Infant Program, 9*(5), 20–23.

Millroy, C. (1989, September 17). A time bomb in cocaine infants. *Washington Post*, B3.

Morris, D. (1983). Concept of word and phoneme awareness in the beginning reader. *Research in the Teaching of English, 17*, 359–373.

Morrow, L.M. (1983). Home and school correlates of early interest in literature. *Journal of Educational Research, 75*, 339–344.

Morrow, L.M. (1992). *Literacy development in the early years* (2nd ed.). Boston, MA: Allyn & Bacon.

Morrow, L.M. (1995). *Literacy development in the early years* (3rd ed.). Boston, MA: Allyn & Bacon.

Nachan, J. (Ed.). (1990, May 8–11). Children of the damned (Special report). *New York Post.*

National Association for the Education of Young Children. (1988). NAEYC position statement on standardized testing of young children 3 through 8 years of age. *Young Children, 43*, 42–47.

Nespor, J. (1997). *Tangled up in school: Politics, space, bodies, and signs in the educational process.* Mahwah, NJ: Erlbaum.

Nieto, S. (1998). Fact and fiction: Stories of Puerto Ricans in U.S. schools. *Harvard Educational Review, 68*, 133–163.

Novick, R. (1998). The comfort corner: Fostering resiliency and emotional intelligence. *Childhood Education, 74*, 200–204.

O'Connor, C. (1997). Dispositions toward (collective) struggle and educational resilience in the inner city: A case analysis of six African American high school students. *American Educational Research Journal, 34*, 593–629.

Odom-Winn, D., & Dunagan, D. (1991). *"Crack kids" in school: What to do—How to do it.* Freeport, NY: Educational Activities.

Osterloh, J., & Lee, B. (1989). Urine drug screening in mothers and newborns. *American Journal of Diseases of Children, 143*, 791–793.

Paley, V. (1981). *Walley's stories: Conversations in kindergarten.* Cambridge, MA: Harvard University Press.

Pelligrini, A., Perlmutter, J., Galda, L., & Brophy, G. (1990). Joint bookreading between black Head Start children and their mothers. *Child Development, 61*, 443–453.

Phillips, L., Norris, S., & Mason, J. (1996). Longitudinal effects of early literacy concepts on reading achievement: A kindergarten intervention and five-year follow-up. *Journal of Literacy Research, 28*, 173–195.

Purcell-Gates, V. (1996). Stories, coupons, and the TV Guide: Relationships between home literacy experiences and emergent literacy knowledge. *Reading Research Quarterly, 31*, 406–428.

Richardson, G., & Day, N. (1994). Detrimental effects of prenatal cocaine exposure: Illusion or reality? *Journal of American Academy of Child and Adolescent Psychiatry, 33*, 28–34.

Richardson, G., Day, N., & McGaughey, P. (1993). The impact of prenatal marijuana and cocaine use on the infant and child. *Clinical Obstetrics and Gynecology, 36*, 302–318.

Rist, M. (1990). The shadow children: Preparing for the arrival of crack babies in school. *Phi Delta Kappan* (Research Bulletin), *9*, 1–6.

Rodning, C., Beckwith, L., & Howard, J. (1989). Characteristics of attachment organization and play organization in prenatally drug-exposed toddlers. *Development and Psychopathology, 1*, 277–289.

Rossi, R. (Ed.). (1994). *Schools and students at risk: Context and framework for positive change.* New York: Teachers College Press.

Sautter, R. (1992). Crack: Healing the children. *Phi Delta Kappan, 74*, K1–K12.

Schneider, J., & Chasnoff, I. (1987). Cocaine abuse during pregnancy: Its effects on infant motor development—A clinical perspective. *Topics in Acute Care and Trauma Rehabilitation, 2*(1), 59–69.

Schneider, R., & Barone, D. (1996). Cross-age tutoring. *Childhood Education, 73*, 136–143.

Schutter, L., & Brinker, R. (1992). Conjuring a new category of disability from prenatal cocaine exposure: Are the infants unique biological or caretaking casualties? *Topics in Early Childhood Special Education, 11*(4), 84–111.

Shannon, P. (1998). *Reading poverty.* Portsmouth, NH: Heinemann.

Smith, S. (1997). A longitudinal study: The literacy development of 57 children. In C. Kinzer, K. Hinchman, & D. Leu (Eds.), *Inquiries in literacy theory and practice: Forty-sixth yearbook of the National Reading Conference* (pp. 250–264). Chicago, IL: National Reading Conference.

Spear-Swerling, L., & Sternberg, R. (1996). *Off track: When poor readers become "learning disabled."* Boulder, CO: Westview Press.

Stauffer, R. (1980). *The language-experience approach to the teaching of reading* (2nd ed.). New York: Harper & Row.

Stockard, J., & Mayberry, M. (1992). *Effective educational environments.* Newbury Park, CA: Corwin Press.

Sulzby, E. (1985). Children's emergent reading of favorite storybooks: A developmental study. *Reading Research Quarterly, 21*, 360–406.

Taylor, D. (1983). *Family literacy*. Exeter, NH: Heinemann.

Taylor, D. (1993, May). *Family literacy: Special contexts within the community for children learning to read and write*. Paper presented at the 38th Annual Convention of the International Reading Association, San Antonio, TX.

Taylor, D. (1994, May). *The idealogies and ethics of family literacy pedagogies: A postformal perspective*. Paper presented at the 39th Annual Convention of the International Reading Association, Toronto, ON.

Taylor, D., & Dorsey-Gaines, C. (1988). *Growing up literate: Learning from inner-city families*. Portsmouth, NH: Heinemann.

Teale, W. (1982). Toward a theory of how children learn to read and write naturally. *Language Arts*, *59*, 555–570.

Teale, W. (1984). Reading to young children: Its significance for literacy development. In H. Goelman, A. Oberg, & F. Smith (Eds.), *Awakening to literacy*. Exeter, NH: Heinemann.

Temple, C., Nathan, R., Burris, N., & Temple, F. (1993). *The beginnings of writing* (3rd ed.). Boston, MA: Allyn & Bacon.

Templeton, S. (1995). *Children's literacy: Contexts for meaningful learning*. Boston, MA: Houghton Mifflin.

Thomas, K., & Barksdale-Ladd, M. (1995). Effective literacy classrooms: Teachers and students exploring literacy together. In K. Hinchman, D. Leu, & C. Kinzer (Eds.), *Perspectives on literacy research and practice: Forty-fourth yearbook of the National Reading Conference* (pp. 169–179). Chicago, IL: National Reading Conference.

Tyler, R. (1992). Prenatal drug exposure: An overview of associated problems and intervention strategies. *Phi Delta Kappan*, *73*, 705–711.

Urzua, C. (1986). A children's story. In P. Rigg & D.S. Enright (Eds.), *Children and ESL: Integrating perspectives* (pp. 93–112). Washington, DC: Teachers of English to Speakers of Other Languages.

Villarreal, S.F., McKinney, L.E., & Quackenbush, M. (1991). *Handle with care: Helping children prenatally exposed to drugs and alcohol*. Santa Cruz, CA: ETR Associates.

Waller, M. (1993). Helping crack-affected children succeed. *Educational Leadership*, *50*, 57–60.

Wang, M., & Gordon, E. (1994). *Educational resilience in inner-city America: Challenges and prospects*. Hillsdale, NJ: Erlbaum.

Washington, V. (1989). Reducing the risks to young black learners: An examination of race and educational policy. In J. Allen & J. Mason (Eds.), *Risk makers, risk takers, risk breakers: Reducing the risks of young literacy learners* (pp. 281–294). Portsmouth, NH: Heinemann.

Weaver, C. (1988). *Reading process and practice*. Portsmouth, NH: Heinemann.

Weiss, R., & Mirin, S. (1987). *Cocaine: The human danger—the social costs—the treatment alternatives*. New York: Ballantine.

Werner, E. (1992). *Overcoming the odds: High risk children from birth to adulthood*. Ithaca, NY: Cornell University Press.

Williams, B., & Howard, V. (1993). Children exposed to cocaine: Characteristics and impications for research and intervention. *Journal of Early Intervention, 17*, 61–72.

Wolcott, H. (1994). *Transforming qualitative data.* Thousand Oaks, CA: Sage

Wolin, A., & Wolin, S. (1993). *The resilient self: How survivors of troubled families rise above adversity.* New York: Random House.

Yin, K. (1994). *Case study research: Design and methods* (2nd ed.). Thousand Oaks, CA: Sage.

Yolton, K., & Bolig, R. (1995). Psychosocial, behavioral, and developmental characteristics of toddlers prenatally exposed to cocaine. *Child Study Journal, 24*, 49–67.

Zuckerman, B., & Bresnahan, K. (1991). Developmental and behavioral consequences of prenatal drug and alcohol exposure. *Pediatric Clinics of North America, 38*, 1387–1406.

Children's Literature References

Allard, H. (1977). *Miss Nelson is missing.* Boston, MA: Houghton Mifflin.

Brown, M. (1947). *Stone soup.* New York: Scribner.

Carle, E. (1971). *The grouchy ladybug.* New York: Crowell.

Carle, E. (1981). *The very hungry caterpillar.* New York: Putnam.

Cleary, B. (1965). *Ralph S. Mouse.* New York: Morrow.

Cleary, B. Ramona series. New York: Morrow.

Cleary, B. (1969). *Ramona the pest.* New York: Dell.

Cleary, B. (1984). *The Ramona Quimby diary.* New York: Morrow.

Cleveland, D. (1978). *The April rabbits.* New York: Scholastic.

Dahl, R. (1988). *Matilda.* New York: Puffin Books.

Fox, M. (1986). *Hattie and the fox.* New York: Bantam Doubleday Dell.

Greenfield, E. (1988). *Nathaniel talking.* New York: Black Butterfly Children's Books.

Hale, S. (1990). *Mary had a little lamb.* New York: Scholastic.

Lobel, A. Frog and toad series. New York: HarperCollins.

Lyne, S. (Ed.). (1996). *Ten-second rainshowers: Poems by young people.* New York: Simon & Schuster.

Martin, A. Babysitters' club series. New York: Scholastic.

Martin, B. (1967). *Brown bear, brown bear, what do you see?* New York: Holt, Rinehart & Winston.

Martin, B., & Archaumbault, J. (1989). *Chicka, chicka, boom, boom.* New York: Simon & Schuster.

Melser, J. (1982). *Fizz and splutter.* New Zealand: Shortland Publications.

Milne, A.A. (1957). *Winnie-the-pooh.* New York: Dutton.

Parish, P. (1963). *Amelia Bedelia.* New York: Harper & Row.

Paterson, K. (1978). *The great Gilly Hopkins.* New York: HarperCollins.

Rylant, C. (1992). *Missing May.* New York: Dell.

Sacher, L. Wayside school series. New York: Avon Camelot Books.

Smith, R. (1972). *Chocolate fever*. New York: Coward, McCann, & Geoghegan.

Sobol, D. Encyclopedia Brown series. New York: Scholastic.

Spinelli, J. (1991). *Maniac Magee*. Boston, MA: Little, Brown.

Wood, A. (1984). *The napping house*. New York: Harcourt Brace Jovanovich.

Author Index

Note: Page reference followed by *f* indicates figure.

∫ubject Index

Note: Page references followed by *a* and *f* indicate appendix and figures, respectively.

A

ADOPTIVE AND FOSTER CARE. *See also* case studies; home environments: and children prenatally exposed to crack/cocaine, 30; as contributors to resiliency, 50; and support of children's literacy, 16–17, 72–73, 191–194
ASSESSMENTS, of literacy, 4, 60–61, 175, 180

B

BARONE, DIANE: professional background of, 35; role as a researcher, 35–38
BAYLEY ASSESSMENT TEST, 61
BILLY, case study of, 74–98
BOARDER BABIES, 54

C

CASE STUDIES. *See also* children prenatally exposed to crack/cocaine; home environments: Billy, 74–98; characteristics of children studied, 4–5, 6–10, 39–43; children and their environments in, 52–57, 74–78, 99–103, 123–127, 141–144, 161–173; conclusions from observing teachers in, 204–206; conclusions of, 206–207; and credibility of the study, 34–35; and criteria for selecting the children for study, 4–5; Curtis, 123–140; data analysis of the study, 43–45; final thoughts about, 72–73, 97–98, 121–122, 139–140, 158–160; finding and identifying children to observe for, 3–4, 5–6; focus of, 10; formal testing in, 60–61; and implications for practice, 198–206; importance of stories of, 187–207; Laquisha, 161–186; literacy at age 2, 57–60; literacy at age 3, 61–67, 78–84; literacy at age 4, 67–72, 84–89, 103–108, 127–130, 144–148; literacy at age 5, 89–93, 108–111, 130–133, 148–151; literacy at age 6, 93–96, 111–117, 133–136, 151–155; literacy at age 7, 117–121, 136–139,

155–158; literacy development results of, 45–49, 51, 208a–220a; literacy in fifth grade, 177–183; Melina, 99–122; observation schedule of, 38–39; organization of, 33–35; Ray, 141–160; reasons for, 1–2; religious beliefs in, 55, 56, 78, 98; and the researcher (D. Barone), 35–38; and resiliency of children studied, 50, 98, 158–159, 191; school reports about children in, 173–175; Sean, 52–73; summaries of, 208a–220a; and teachers' awareness of children being studied, 39–40; and teachers of children studied, 39–40, 196–197; teachings of, 184–186

CHILDREN OF COLOR. *See* race; race discrimination

CHILDREN PRENATALLY EXPOSED TO CRACK/COCAINE. *See also* case studies; home environments; prenatal drug exposure: ability to succeed, 29–31; adoptive and foster care's role with, 16–17, 30, 50, 72–73, 191–194; characteristics of children studied, 4–5, 6–10, 39–43; classroom diversity and, 11–13; classroom requirements for, 28–29; conclusions of case studies, 206–207; credibility of the study, 34–35; criteria for selecting the children for study, 4–5; data analysis of the study, 43–45; developmental literacy concepts of, 40–43; discrimination issues, 14–16; expectations for, 30–21; finding and identifying children to observe, 3–4, 5–6; focus of study, 10; implications of the study for practice, 198–206; importance of stories of, 187–207; initial research on, 2–3; intervention required to support learning of, 26–28; literacy development difficulties of, 48–49; literacy development results of study, 45–49, 51, 208a–220a; literacy development success of, 51; myths about, 23–29, 186; need for stimuli-reduced classrooms, 28–29; observation schedule of study, 38–39; organization of the study, 33–35; parents' (adoptive and foster) support of, 16–17, 191–194; race and, 25–26; reasons for studying, 1–2; resiliency of, 50, 98, 158–159, 191; role of study researcher, 35–38; socioeconomic factors of, 25–26; special-education support and, 7–10, 49, 50, 170–171; summaries of case studies of, 208a–220a; teachers and school support of, 194–198; teachers' awareness of home environments, 10, 17–18; teachers of children studied, 39–40, 196–197; urine toxicology and, 4

CHILDREN STUDIED. *See also* case studies; children prenatally exposed to crack/cocaine: Billy, 74–98; Curtis, 123–140; Laquisha, 161–186; Melina, 99–122; Ray, 141–160; Sean, 52–73

CLASSROOM PRACTICES. *See also* case studies; school and classroom environments; teachers: literacy instruction, 10, 11, 12f; and race discrimination, 10; and socioeconomic factors, 10, 11–14, 98

CLASSROOM REQUIREMENTS, for children prenatally exposed to crack/cocaine, 28–29

COCAINE. *See also* children prenatally exposed to crack/cocaine: definition of, 1; general background about, 22–23